Redemption in Black Theology

Olin P. Moyd

Judson Press® Valley Forge

REDEMPTION IN BLACK THEOLOGY

Copyright © 1979
Judson Press, Valley Forge, PA 19481
Second Printing, 1979

Unless otherwise indicated, Bible quotations in this volume are in accordance with the Revised Standard Version of the Bible, copyrighted 1946, 1952, 1971, 1973 © by the Division of Christian Education of the National Council of the Churches of Christ in the United States of America, and are used by permission.

Other versions of the Bible quoted in this book are:
The Holy Bible, King James Version.
The New English Bible, Copyright © The Delegates of the Oxford University Press and The Syndics of the Cambridge University Press, 1961, 1970.

Library of Congress Cataloging in Publication Data
Moyd, Olin P.
    Redemption in Black theology.

    Includes index.
    1. Afro-Americans—Religion.   2.   Salvation.
3.   Black theology.   I.   Title.
BR563.N4M69   234′.3   78-23816
ISBN 0-8170-0806-3

The name JUDSON PRESS is registered as a trademark in the U.S. Patent Office.
Printed in the U.S.A. ⊕

*TO
THE BLACK PREACHERS
AND
THE BLACK FOLKS
OF
AMERICA*

Contents

Preface

Redemption is the root and core motif in Black theology. Redemption has the double meaning of liberation and confederation. In Black theology, liberation means deliverance from human-caused states and circumstances of oppression as well as salvation from sin and guilt. Confederation in this study means the formation of a group of people who live in a covenant relationship with one another and with their Redeemer.

Nowhere in the Old Testament is the word *padah* (one of the Hebrew words from which "redemption" is derived and which will be defined in chapter 2) used to mean redemption from sin alone. It always means deliverance from some visible and tangible menace which might or might not be regarded as a consequence of the sin of the people. And in the Exodus story, which is central in Black religious thought and Black liberation theology, the liberation from Egyptian bondage is always inextricably intertwined with the Canaan hope. The Exodus from Egypt was only the first step in the divine plan of bringing the Israelites into Canaan—a community of the redeemed.

Most Euro-American theologians and theologies have rejected or ignored the religious thoughts of Black Americans. Therefore

Euro-American theology does not reflect the significance of God-talk in the Black community. This is particularly true of Euro-American theology in the treatment of the concept of redemption.

Neither the Black theologians nor the Euro-American and Latin American "liberation" theologians have used redemption as a point of departure. While liberation is one dimension of redemption, it is limited in that it points primarily to the Exodus out of Egypt or out of Black oppression and neglects the other important dimension of redemption which has to do with coming into Canaan or the forming of a community among the people of God. The major catastrophe which immediately afflicted the four million Blacks when the Emancipation Proclamation became effective on January 1, 1863, arose out of the fact that only one aspect of redemption became operative. While they were liberated out of the hands of their oppressors, there were no adequate provisions for their going into or forming their own communities.

Redemption, both liberation and confederation, is the central theme in Black religious thought. And since its significance has been ignored by Euro-American theologians and its extended meaning has been overlooked by the Blacks and other "liberation" theologians, there is a need for serious examination of the concept of redemption in Black religious thought. This is the task which I have assumed in this research.

As a pastor-scholar, I approach this investigation from the Black folk religious experience. While no Black person in this country has ever escaped some of the fallout of white oppression, most Blacks who have achieved the status of scholars have had some opportunities to achieve educational, social, and economic development somewhat apart from the masses of Black folks.

I was born in the backwoods—a kind of Nazareth—in South Carolina. I walked with the Black masses to inferior schools while white children were bused to better schools, shouting racial epithets as they were riding past. Upon attaining the age of eighteen, I moved to Baltimore—"way-up-South"—worked in various menial jobs and lived with the folks in the ghettos. On being drafted into the U.S. Army in 1953, I resumed my educational pursuit and later accepted the call into the preaching ministry and have been serving as a pastor for more than fourteen years. My participation and leadership in the civil rights and Black identity struggles have made me more aware of the content and value of Black folk religion.

It is out of this background that I embark upon this investigation. I feel somewhat unique as a person to examine the meaning of redemption in Black folk religious thought. During my academic sojourn, I have never been removed from the folk. I have suffered what they have suffered; I am presently where they are; and I have experienced both plantation and ghetto.

This research manuscript was first written as my dissertation in partial fulfillment for the Degree of Doctor of Philosophy in Theology for the Ecumenical Institute of Theology, St. Mary's Seminary and University, Baltimore, Maryland.

Many people have given valuable assistance and suggestions as I undertook this investigation. While I will not list each of them, the contributions of the following persons have been so significant that I must single them out at this point. Dr. J. Deotis Roberts, Sr., Howard University School of Religion, my adviser and first reader, has not only been a constructive critic, but he has also been a constant source of inspiration throughout this research. His reading and rereading of the drafts of my dissertation manuscript and his suggestions for revisions and clarification have been undergirded by his genuine interest and patience. Without reservations, it has been for me a signal honor to have had him as my adviser and first reader. Dr. Richard I. McKinney, Morgan State University, graciously accepted the invitation to be my second reader. His meticulous pruning of the manuscript and his hours of discussion with me were invaluable to the final development of the dissertation. Mrs. Lydia Brown has rendered a valuable service in reading the manuscript for spelling and typographical errors.

Thanks to Fr. C. Stephen Mann, Dean, and Fr. Robert Leavitt, Associate Dean, of the Ecumenical Institute of Theology, St. Mary's Seminary and University, for their constant concern, availability, and guidance throughout my academic career at the Ecumenical Institute of Theology. The administrators, faculty, and staff of both the Ecumenical Institute of Theology and St. Mary's Seminary and University have been a constant source of assistance and inspiration. Robert M. Matthews, Jr., and the library staff at St. Mary's have been most helpful as I used the works and facilities of the library. My reproduction person, Fred Adams, has been most cooperative in helping me to get the needed copies of the dissertation reproduced.

Mrs. Ophelia G. Bell (Fifi) deserves my deep appreciation for her invaluable services in typing the final draft of the dissertation. I must express my highest gratitude to my secretary, Mrs. Deloris Mack, who interpreted and unscrambled my writing, typing the original manuscript and the revision for this book. Thanks to the Reverend Dr. Milton Owens who encouraged me and assisted me in presenting this manuscript to Judson Press.

I owe much gratitude to the officers of the Mount Lebanon Baptist Church for their cooperative leadership and to the members for their support and inspiration during the period of our study, research, and writing of this book. Finally, my family has been the basic source of my strength. My wife has been most patient, understanding, and sympathetic. My five daughters have been very helpful by taking on so many of my little jobs and projects so that I could be free to pursue this program. They have also been willing to postpone family activities because of my involvement in this study and writing.

I am grateful to all of the persons who have contributed to the development of this research. But the responsibility for any demerits in content and/or construction of this book rests entirely with this writer.

Foreword

The contents of this study emerged out of Dr. Moyd's Ph.D. studies at St. Mary's Seminary and University, Baltimore, Maryland. As a member of his committee and first reader of the dissertation, it has been my privilege to witness the birth and development of this splendid study. Having taught Moyd in his first professional degree in divinity, I had every confidence in his ability. He not only took the research successfully to its conclusion, but also has now consummated the tedious task of revising and upgrading the original manuscript into book form. It is a distinct privilege to write the foreword to launch this important work.

In the early stages of the study, Moyd was tempted to stay close to the studies already in print by other Black theologians. One understands this temptation on the part of a beginning scholar. It became clear to me that Moyd should not limit himself in this manner, for he has a distinctive contribution to make. His perception, creativity, and maturity of experience as a churchman and scholar would have been curtailed if he had selected this course. Other Black theologians are mainly in the academy. Moyd, on the other hand, found himself in a pastorate in the heart of Baltimore's inner city. Furthermore, his interest in Black folk religious experience is profound. His challenge, then, was to bring theological reflection to bear upon Black religious experience as a pastor-scholar. This he has done with excitement, rigorous scholarship, and commitment. We rejoice that he has met this demand and has made a unique contribution to the general field of Black religious studies as well as to Black theology.

This study will speak for itself. There are, however, a few highlights which merit special attention. Here I would like to linger close to those aspects of the study which seem to be rather unique in the field. The only other work in Black theology with a similar coverage is Cecil Cone's *Identity Crisis in Black Theology* (Nashville: African Methodist Episcopal Church, 1975). Cecil's book presents celebration in Black religious experience and belief in an Almighty Sovereign God as the hallmarks of this tradition. Cecil's main discussion, however, is a critique of other Black theologians. In my judgment, Cecil does not develop adequately his own distinctive contribution. Moyd, on the other hand, has provided a programmatic statement of his thesis.

Now, we shall examine Moyd's work briefly on his cardinal points. First, he chooses the important doctrine of redemption as the pivot of his study. He defines *redemption* as *liberation* and *confederation*. Liberation is deliverance from human-caused states of oppression as well as salvation from sin. Confederation is the formation of a group of people who live in a covenant relationship with each other and with God. Second, Moyd has not only looked carefully at the biblical understanding of redemption, but also he has explored the broad Jewish contribution to a holistic understanding of this doctrine. Third, he lifts up the theme of redemption inherent in Black religious experience, using source materials from the Black folk tradition, e.g., spirituals, poems, folklore, and sermons. And, fourth, Moyd provides serious theological interpretation of several doctrines of the Christian creed, e.g., humankind, revelation, Jesus, church, and last things. This he does in a fresh and informative manner consistent with the redemption-theme.

Moyd's book is being released at a propitious moment. Forecasters of theological trends indicate that Black theology will be one of the significant programs within the eighties. The reason for this is that the theological initiative is coming from the South rather than from the North Atlantic community. Humanization calls for a theology of *praxis*. Theological reflection is shaped by involvement to overcome poverty, racism, and sexism. As a pastor-theologian, Moyd's work compares favorably with that of priest-theologians in Latin America. The context is different, but the mood is similar. This work also contributes to the African/Afro-American connection in an ongoing theological dialogue. It joins other third-world theologies from "the underside of history."

This volume on Black theology should have a wide readership by persons in all vocations and stations in life. It is a major breakthrough in the understanding of religious expression, history, and culture of Blacks. All who feel a need for such knowledge may now consult this source. It is a distinct privilege to share this release. I congratulate the author and the publisher for their joint effort in making this valuable work available to churches, educational institutions, and the general public.

J. Deotis Roberts
Professor of Systematic Theology
School of Religion
Howard University
Editor, *The Journal of Religious Thought*

1

Introduction

O Mary, don't you weep, don't you mourn
  O Mary, don't you weep, don't you mourn
Pharaoh's army got drownded.
  O Mary, don't you weep.[1]

Some day ah'm gonna lay down dis heavy load,
Gonna grab me a train,
Gonna clam aboh'd.

Gonna go up No'th,
Gonna ease mah pain,
Yessuh, Lord, gonna catch dat train.[2]

Afro-Americans will readily recognize that the above are Black folk expressions put into songs. The former are lines from a spiritual, and the latter are lines from a blues song. In the midst of circumstances which pointed to a certain dead end and annihilation, Afro-Americans created songs which were in direct contradiction to their apparent destiny. They looked forward to redemption from their state of oppression. So they could say to the collective Marys in bondage: Don't weep, don't mourn, because we know that the collective Pharaohs of history were drowned by the redeeming acts of

15

God who is now our Redeemer. Redemption from physical bondage is clearly summed up in those lines from the blues. Everyone would lay down the human-inflicted heavy load, grab a train, get aboard, and go North where Blacks expected the easing of the physical and spiritual pains of oppression.

Redemption was not understood to be limited to liberation from oppression; it also meant the divine process of being formed into a community where love and justice would prevail. Although the physical and social realization of that redemptive hope on the part of Blacks has been intentionally and systematically obstructed and deferred by white oppressors and their heirs in this land, redemption is the core motif in Black folks' aspirations and expressions. An examination of the historical understanding of redemption in Black thought, then, is the central focus of this book.

My aim is to join those Black scholars who have dared to isolate and describe Black theology in literary form. This research will not be limited to doing a critical analysis of what has been done in Black theology. Throughout this investigation there will be a critical engagement with the works of the two major Black theologians, namely James H. Cone and J. Deotis Roberts, Sr., and also with others. This book will extend beyond what has been done in Black theology in that it will use redemption as the core motif. Redemption has not been used as the core motif or point of departure in literary Black theology as far as this investigator knows. Liberation and reconciliation, which are only elements of redemption, have been the major central themes in Black theology to this point.

Here we assume the double task of critically engaging some of the works in Black theology and of testing the hypothesis that redemption is at the center of Black religious thought.

The Problem

The Black people in this country have lived largely in spatial and/or social isolation from their white counterparts. As a consequence, they have developed masses of distinctively Black churches and a number of gigantic, distinctively Black denominational bodies.

William L. Banks gives the following breakdown for Black national denominational bodies, based upon the U. S. Census for 1970: National Baptist Convention, U.S.A., Inc., 6,487,003; National Baptist Convention of America, 2,668,799; Progressive National

Baptist Convention, 521,692; African Methodist Episcopal (AME), 1,166,301; African Methodist Episcopal Zion (AMEZ), 850,389; and Christian Methodist Episcopal (CME), 466,718. These six distinctively Black denominations contained more than twelve million communicants.[3] Of course, each of these denominational bodies has grown considerably since 1970. There are also many Black Baptist churches of various varieties, particularly storefront, which do not hold membership in the major bodies.

There are 800,000 communicants in the fourteen all-Black Pentecostal denominations, and there are probably another 800,000 in the storefront churches of the ghettos, according to James S. Tinney.[4] Adding the 1,600,000 all-Black Pentecostals to the more than 12 million members of other Black religious bodies, one is made aware of the fact that well over half of the Black population in America in 1970 belonged to distinctively Black denominations. Banks estimates that about two million Blacks belonged to predominantly white denominations in 1970.[5] It is Black "folk theology," and not white creeds, which has been the major influencing factor on Black people's minds and souls, and this is evident in their world view, ethical principles, and moral behavior.

The Black churches of these Black denominations developed as the centers for all of Black life. The Black churches were the places for bathing the wounds of oppressions; they were the centers of soul refreshing and the releasing of emotions. Blacks met in church for the purpose of fellowship with one another and communion with the Eternal. The churches were also the centers where Black people met to organize their economical enterprises, to plan their political strategies, and to design their programs of protests against social injustices. Guiding their footsteps through these varied life experiences was the One who led Moses and the Israelites through the Exodus experience. Blacks preached, sang, prayed, testified, and talked about their God whose plan of salvation was continuously unfolding in their midst.

Over the years of the development of these distinctively Black churches and denominations, the revelation of God has been prevalent in the Black community. The opening lines in the letter to the Hebrews assert that "in many and various ways God spoke to our fathers by the prophets" (Hebrews 1:1). In the next verse the author asserts "but in these last days [God] has spoken to us by a Son. . . . " Because God has spoken by the Son in these last days, according to verse 2, this does not negate the fact of verse 1 which declares that God (spoke) speaks in various ways. The revelation of God has come to different people in different places at different times and in different ways.

In an article entitled "The Black Caucus and the Failure of Christian Theology," J. Deotis Roberts, Sr., suggested that "the other side of the Barthian 'God speaks, and man listens' is 'man cries, God hears.'"[6] This statement has great relevance for the Black religious community because unlike the majority group in America, who might have heard God speak and listened, the Black encounter with God has been, to a great degree, from a different stance. It was not so much God's speaking which caught the attention of our fore-parents. A more accurate description of the encounter would be "our fathers cried and God heard their cries." The revelation of God in the history of the Black people is akin to that of the Hebrews in Egyptian bondage. God said to Moses, " . . . I have seen the affliction . . . and have heard their cry . . . " (Exodus 3:7).

Charles V. Hamilton in his book, *The Black Preacher in America,* includes the following quote from a prayer offered by the Reverend Peter Williams, Jr., after a law went into effect prohibiting slave trade as of January 1, 1808.

> Oh God! we thank thee, that thou didst condescend to listen to the cries of Africa's wretched sons; and that thou didst interfere in their behalf. . . .
> May the time speedily commence, when Ethiopia shall stretch forth her hands; when the sun of liberty shall beam replendent [sic] on the whole African race; and its genial influences, promote the luxuriant growth of knowledge and virtue.[7]

Here, in the prayer of a Black preacher, God is the one who is self-revealing in response to the cries of the wretched sons of Africa. This is his testimony. This is the way he understands God's self-manifestation in this event.

The experiencing, responding, and witnessing to that revelation among Blacks have been different from that of the oppressors and those who have benefited from the oppression of Blacks.

It is true that some of the Black denominations adopt the creeds and rituals of white denominations. However, where these creeds and rituals have not been redesigned, they have been reinterpreted to meet the needs of an oppressed people.

For example, although Black Baptists accepted the eight

objectives of the International Council of Religious Education (I.C.R.E.), as early as 1886 when the "colored" Baptists met in St. Louis, even though they had not yet become engaged in the production of literature, they drafted and interpreted their own objectives. The first objective of the religious educational program of the Black Baptists was "The enrichment of the Negro's personality under the influence of the ideals of Jesus."[8] Note the contrast in points of departure. The I.C.R.E. starts with the call for a "God consciousness." The Black Baptists see the development of human dignity as the beginning point. So their first objective is "the enrichment of the Negro's personality."

The first dimension of the problem, then, is that of theologically examining and describing the body of expressions and ideas about the redemptive events and goal of God which have shaped the distinctive Black churches, denominations, and communities. James H. Cone and J. Deotis Roberts, Sr., are leading exponents of Black theology, but it will take years and a large cadre of researchers to do the task of Black theology. So my aim is to join those who have left the starting gate in doing Black theology.

The second dimension of the problem is that of working toward clarifying the meaning of Black theology. It seems that Black theology is kerygmatic, apologetic, and eristic, as these terms will be presently defined. Black theology seems to look in two directions at the same time. It looks back to the past historical experiences and traditions of the Black fathers and, at the same time, looks forward to those future hopes of the "not yet" and of the new possibilities of the further inbreaking of the kingdom which kept them alive in the middle of oppression. While examining the past and the "not yet," Black theology must not lose sight of its existential dimension. Black theologizing is a mammoth undertaking. A brief review of some of the classical definitions of kerygma, apologetics, and eristics might be helpful at this point.

Kerygma is a noun derived from the Greek verb meaning "to proclaim." It could refer to the content of the proclamation or the act of proclaiming itself. Kerygma is that eternal message—the "good news" of the fulfillment of the prophecy in Christ. It is a dynamic revelation of eternal truth which needs reinterpretation for every generation. It differs from dogmatics in that it is not the scientific exposition of supernatural truth.

The task of a dynamic theology is to clarify what the kerygma is saying in every generation. It must be done in the most intelligible concepts available. Not many people in America will deny the fact that Black Christians have experienced the kerygma—the breaking through of the eternal message. Having been brought to these shores in chains, introduced to a strange and unknown God without a place in which to worship and without the literacy to read the theology of their masters, Black people experienced the kerygma. The eternal message of God—the fulfillment of the Old Testament prophecies in Jesus Christ—broke through in the community of Black suffering servants. The kerygma brought new life to the Black community in its oppressed state.

Traditionally, in Christian theology apologetics denotes reasoned defense of the Christian religion against intellectual objections. It is an attempt to establish certain elements of that faith as true or, at least, not demonstrably untrue. The kerygma as experienced by the Black suffering servants must be reasonably defended against intellectual objections of all serious inquisitors. Roberts seems to be correct in his statement that Black theology must "be apologetic in the best meaning of this august tradition in theology." It must be an "answering theology" to the questions raised by the "'situation of racism' in the United States."[9] In this sense, Black theology must be apologetic. Black theology must express the kerygma as conceived by the oppressed just as it has been expressed as it was conceived by the oppressors. White theologians cannot write an apologetic Black theology. They have never been attached to the mainstream of the lives of the Black community of faith. The "inner-felt" must be combined with the "outer-known"; therefore, only those who have the "inner-felt" of the Black religious experience can combine it with the "outer-known" in intelligible and comprehensive terms. The theological task of Black theology is the codification and explanation of the eternal message inherent in the kerygma.

Emil Brunner prefers the word "eristics" rather than the word "apologetics," says Bernard Ramm. Eristic is derived from the Greek word *eristikos* meaning to strive, to dispute. Brunner "does not believe that there is a 'bar of reason' before which Christians can appeal." Christians, he contends, "are called upon to call [their] own generation into disputation. The word that expresses this disputational activity best is 'eristics.'"[10] This is precisely what James Cone, J. Deotis Roberts, Sr., and other Black theologians have done in recent years. While I have not found the term "eristics" in their writings, in fact, their activities have been that of calling their generation, particularly white theologians, who have made little response, into disputation. The dispute is centered in the fact that very few Euro-American theologians and theologies have taken into account the religious experience of Black people in this "one nation, divided."[11]

Black theology must be both apologetic and eristic. It must be apologetic in the sense that it responds to the questions raised by the "situation of racism" in America and eristic in the sense that it does not wait for the raising of the questions in literary theology: it takes the initiative in calling traditional Western theology into disputation.

Black theology is the emerging product of persistent and scholarly reflections of Black theologians, scholars, and lay persons. It seeks to explicate the Black community's understanding of God's promise and the goal toward which God is directing the world while the Black people in America were and are going through dehumanizing experiences. "Theology," says Bruce Vawter, "like gold, is where you find it."[12] The primary place where Black theology is found is in the folk expressions in Black (oral) history. The program of Black theology will have to be carried out by Blacks. We have this bit of wisdom from Ralph Waldo Emerson:

> There is a time in every man's education when he arrives at the conviction that envy is ignorance; that imitation is suicide; that he must take himself for better for worse as his portion; that though the wide universe is full of good, no kernel of nourishing corn can come to him but through his toil bestowed on that plot of ground which is given him to till.[13]

Black theology is Black people's idea about God and his relationship to humankind and to the universe. Any theological nourishment which will come to the Black community will come primarily as a result of toil of the Black theologians and scholars bestowed upon the ground which is theirs to till.

The problem in this work is one of theologically examining and describing the ideas of redemption in Black thought and working toward clarifying the meaning of Black theology.

Importance of This Study

The question which comes from people of all walks in life is, "Why a Black theology?" In the Christian world we have "dogmatic theology," "political theology," "theology of hope," and "theology of liberation." The more important question ought to be, "Why has it taken this long to develop a Black theology in literary form in America?" Most Black theologians recognize the need for Black theology. And, while Black theology does not need white endorsement in order to make it legitimate, we will note in passing that even a few eminent Euro-American theologians have come to realize the value of Black theology. Among them is Rosemary Ruether who affirms "black theology . . . is reconciling rather than alienating, catholic rather than racist, and . . . really restates the authentic message of the prophets within a black perspective."[14] Frederick Herzog believes that Black theology ought to arouse the awareness of white theologians, and it is a "relevant orientation point of theology."[15] The German theologian Jürgen Moltmann suggests that Black theology offers white theology a chance to rid itself of its blindness and to become Christian in life as well as in thought.[16]

While these Euro-American theologians have recognized the need and value of Black theology, they represent only a small number of white theologians who have achieved this sensitivity to the need for Black theology. So the question still persists: "Why a Black theology?" And anyone who writes on the subject of Black theology must respond to that question explicitly and implicitly.

There is an Indian folktale about six blind persons "seeing" an elephant with their hands. Each person touches a different part of the elephant and therefore imagines a different version of the elephant. His smooth side suggests that he is like a wall to one person; his round trunk suggests a snake to another, his tusk a sword, his tall leg a tree, his wide ear a fan, and his thick tail a rope. The six blind persons vigorously disagree on the portrait of the entire elephant. "He is a big animal," explains a wise man. "Each of you touched only one part. You must put all the parts together to find out what an elephant is like." Christian theology is a big "animal"; Euro-American theologians have touched various parts. Today, Black American Christians are touching yet other parts. There is likely to be further vigorous disagreement as to the true portrait of this "animal"—Christian theology. But one hopes that the day will come when theologians will listen to some wise person who explains: "Although each of you has touched an authentic part of theology, you must put all the parts together to find out what Christian theology is all about." However, this cannot happen until each indigenous group refines its own theology.

This study is important because it represents a serious attempt to participate in the program of examining and refining the indigenous, theological views of the Black people in this country which will enrich Christian theology in this country and in the world.

Definitions of Terms

Black—the proper name for people of African descent. It is used in the place where the word "Negro" and "Colored" have been used to refer to Afro-Americans and people of African descent. Therefore the first letter of the word is capitalized whether used as a noun or an adjective.

Black Theology—the Black community's attempt to reflect upon the historical relationship—events—between God and themselves. It is the Black community's attempt to describe those events in the clearest and most coherent language at its disposal. Black theology is the Black community's attempt to articulate its understanding of "what in the world God was doing" or "what God was doing in the world" while Blacks were undergoing slavery, Jim Crowism, second-class citizenship, the struggle for "integration," and the strides for Black Power, Black identity, and social justice. Black theology seeks to explicate the Black community's understanding of God's promise and the goal toward which he is directing the world while Black people in America are and were going through dehumanizing experiences.

Chosen People—these are the people through whom God is calling the nation to a life of right and righteousness. They are chosen people, not because of their situation of suffering but because they said "yes" to God in a way similar to that of Abraham, Isaac, and Isaiah. This "yes" is not merely an assent of the mind formulated into theological concepts; "yes" is expressed in the organization and reorganization of the lives of the individuals and the life of the community of the chosen in the light of what they understand to be the will of the Redeemer. This includes conducting themselves in relationship with other human beings in such a way as to affirm their humanity. (All Black people do not behave in accordance with the will of God; neither did all Hebrews, but this did not change the fact of their chosenness.)

Confederation—the forming of a community, local and universal, of the chosen people of God resulting from their understanding of the will of God, also the practice of a life-style which is consistent with the fulfillment of a covenant relationship with God.

Liberation—a state of being wherein the Black race will be totally autonomous—a state of salvation from human-caused and human-imposed disabilities and constraints all over this world. Liberation also means salvation from sin and guilt through the unmerited favor of God, the Liberator.

Liberation Theology—the theology being developed out of the situation of oppression in Latin America and the theology being developed under the heading "liberation theology" by white, Euro-American theologians. This is intended to be only a reference distinction between liberation theology and Black theology for convenience.

Nonbeing—the term "nonbeing" is used to express an attitude which some white folks hold in reference to Afro-Americans. This widespread, racist attitude does not in fact diminish the quality of being of Black folks.

Redemption—salvation from the states and circumstances which destroy the value of human existence or human existence itself. Redemption is salvation from sin and guilt and salvation from oppression. It is a term which describes what God has done, is doing, and will do in his historical relationship with humankind and the universe. Redemption in Black thought also means liberation and confederation.

White Theology—when the terms "white theology" or "Euro-American theology," and "white theologians" are used, they refer to the major element of white or Euro-American theology and to the majority of the white or Euro-American theologians. There are incidents of white or Euro-American theology and a number of white or Euro-American theologians whose works reflect a biblical application to the problem of oppression.

The Presuppositions

Several basic assumptions undergird my thinking and will influence my research and writing. The first basic assumption is that there is a Black experience, a Black tradition, and a Black culture. For convenience I have opted to refer to the Black experience, Black tradition, and Black culture collectively as Black history. And the elements of Black history, though largely submerged in the sea of an oral tradition, can be isolated, identified, and described.

The second basic assumption is that our Black history

constitutes a basic source for Black theological reflections and refinement. The third basic assumption is that African nonmaterial, cultural survivals influenced the shaping of Black history. Roberts points out that Blacks have "a different temperament from those rooted solely in the Euro-American milieu. He has what Carter G. Woodson [an eminent Black historian 1875-1950] describes as 'an oriental mind.'"[17] There have been, in this country, consistent efforts to eliminate all elements of African customs and practices from Black minds.

The thrust was of such magnitude that Black historian and sociologist E. Franklin Frazier said, " . . . because of the manner in which the Negroes were captured in Africa and enslaved, they were practically stripped of their social heritage." He points out that the work gangs lost the meaning of "cooperative undertaking with communal significance." There was a loss of social cohesiveness in the area of kinship, language, tribal life, marriages, and religious myths.[18] This is only partially true. These views have their origin and perpetuation in the white community which had both the reason and the means to promote such views.

Despite Frazier's position, the prevailing view among Black scholars, including W. E. B. Du Bois, holds that there are African survivals in Black culture in America. Melville Herskovits offers a convincing argument supporting the view of African survivals among Afro-Americans. In chapters 6, 7, and 8 of his book *The Myth of the Negro Past,* he provides evidence to support his belief about African survivals in three major areas of Afro-American life-style. The first is "Africanisms in Secular Life." Here he speaks of the retention of motor habits. These include walking, speaking, laughing, dancing, singing, and burden carrying. He believes that African survivals are expressed in polite behavior, community control by the elders, kinship groupings, attitude, mode, and behavior centering around children. He also makes a point about the extent of funerals. The Afro-American belief and practice which affirm that life must have a proper ending are directly connected with ancestor worship in Africa, he believes.

A second grouping of African survivals he lists under the heading "Africanisms in Religious Life." Here he supports his belief by pointing to the connection between African belief in supernatural-ism as a major focus or interest and Afro-American religious beliefs. He also points to emotional expressions, ritual expressions in songs and dance, rhythm, and congregational participation in worship as African cultural survivals. He believes that the ease with which Africans became Baptist is directly connected to the idea of the river cult in Africa. (And we do know that today there are more Black Baptists than Blacks in all other denominations combined in America.) There is a connection, he believes, between Blacks in Baptist congregations which have local autonomy and the local autonomy of the African tribes. Voodooism among Blacks is also an African survival, he declares.

Under the heading "Language and the Arts," he finds other African survivals. These are evidenced in Black music, songs, dance, folklore, grammar, syntax, inflections, sounds, and intonations.[19]

These are only samples of the exhibits Herskovits offers in support of his thesis concerning African survivals among Afro-Americans. He concluded that his research sustained his thesis.

Henry H. Mitchell, who in 1976 completed directing a Doctor of Ministry study program in Black Religious Experience, which took the study group to Africa, has this to say in his new book *Black Belief: Folk Beliefs of Blacks in America and West Africa:*

> I am now convinced that the slaveocracy failed to erase African culture, but slowly succeeded in getting Blacks to be ashamed of it. The result was that even though we Blacks continued to use and adapt our heritage, we eventually dropped many aspects of it.[20]

Mitchell is convinced that the evidence gathered in research supporting African survivals among Blacks in this country is so conclusive that one must wonder how we missed it for so long. The fact of the matter is that "we" have not "missed it for so long"; "we" knew it all along, but our limited access to the means for research and to the media of publication and distribution prevented us from getting the word around. Some of the African survivals which Mitchell mentions include "dress up" for worship and the worshipful significance which is attached to this mode of dress, and an "African temperament" having a remarkable resiliency. He also speaks of the survival of the African belief system which is characterized by a *positive view* of human experience, the spirit world, and the belief in the wise and powerful good God who created the whole business.[21] Mitchell believes that it was impossible to kill the African culture of the captives when they were brought to these shores.

To kill a culture you have to kill the bearers of that culture. That is to say, the life stance and world view of a people are deeply ingrained and not readily changed. To have life is to depend on these defenses and, as we have already said, pressure to destroy them often succeeds only in driving them underground. Much of a people's culture is therefore outside rational consciousness. It is transmitted from "unconscious" to "unconscious," as well as from rational conscious to rational conscious. To stamp out a culture and its world view would require total genocide. . . .[22]

From the evidence offered by those who support the African survivals' view, it seems reasonable to assume that this view is correct.

A fourth and final basic assumption is that theologizing is dynamic. James Cone is correct, one thinks, when he states that "theology is the community's continued attempt to define in every generation its reason for being in the world."[23] But although implicit in his works, Cone did not go far enough. He might have pointed out that not only must every generation do its own theology but also that every community which has experienced spatial and/or social isolation from any other community must do its own theology, even if the members of the various communities belong to the *same* generation.

In his new book *God of the Oppressed,* Cone does go a step further than he did in *A Black Theology of Liberation.* He draws upon H. Richard Niebuhr's observation that "theological opinions have their roots in the relationship of the religious life to the cultural and political conditions prevailing in any group of Christians."[24]

From this statement, Cone correctly concludes that "white theological perspectives which ignore color are nothing but white cultural projections."[25] In essence, he confirms my position that different theologies will emerge from members of the same generation if they are grouped in situations in which they find themselves experiencing different cultural and political conditions.

Cone again examines the definitions of theology advanced by both Harold DeWolf and Paul Tillich. DeWolf says: "'Systematic Theology is the critical discipline devoted to discovering, expounding and defending the more important truths implied in the experience of the Christian community.'" Tillich contends that "'theology, as a function of the Christian Church, must serve the needs of the Church. A theological system is supposed to satisfy two basic needs: the statement of the truth of the Christian message and the interpretation of this truth for every new generation.' Despite [his] affinity with the existential orientation of Tillich against DeWolf's rationalism," Cone points out the cultural similarity of both which is conspicuous in that "neither one defines theology as a discipline which speaks for and about the liberation of the oppressed from *political* bondage."[26] This supports my thesis that every class and caste group in every generation ought to do its own theological reflections.

C. Eric Lincoln was correct when he said to a group of white Presbyterian pastors in Pittsburgh, "To assume that theology has been written with any degree of finality is to cut off the possibility of God's continuing revelation to man."[27] As indigenous groups refine their own theologies, there ought to be opportunities for the coming together of theologians representing the individual groups for the purpose of determining the universals.

My four basic presuppositions are (1) there are a Black experience, a Black tradition, and a Black culture which together constitute Black history; (2) Black history, elements of which can be isolated and described, is the basic source for doing Black theology; (3) African nonmaterial, cultural survivals, influenced the shaping of Black history; and (4) theologizing is a dynamic process not limited to any special group or generation.

Hypothesis

Redemption in Black religious thought means liberation and confederation. The liberation dimension of redemption means salvation from oppression as well as salvation from sin and guilt. Redemption in Black religious thought also means a confederation, the formulation of a community among the people of God and with God in a covenant relationship. It is this understanding of redemption which gave rise to the ethical principles and moral behavior of Black people. Redemption in traditional white Christian theology is generally limited to salvation from sin and guilt while redemption in Black religious thought and expressions is consistent with the full meaning of the term by the Hebrews who brought it into religious usage. This redemption theme can be discovered through a theological examination of the expressions and notions which are imbedded in Black history, although Black religious history is largely oral. An examination of the sermons, prayers, songs, and testimonies of Black people will uncover this redemption motif.

Method, Sources, and Norm

The theo-historical approach seems to be adequate for this

research. The elements to be reflected upon must surface through historical examinations and analyses. The temporal process of history is the place in which Osmund Lewry sees God working out his purpose in the revelation of himself as the Alpha and the Omega. "History," he declares, "should be a preoccupation of the Christian theologian because of the characteristic relationship between Christianity and history."[28]

While the theo-historical approach is common to Western theology, the attempt to come to terms with Black American history theologically has been neglected. Historical methodology is defined by William L. Lucey as: " . . . a systematic body of rules and procedures for collecting all possible witnesses of a historical era or event, for evaluating the testimony of these witnesses, for ordering the proven facts in their causal connections, and finally, for presenting this ordered knowledge of events."[29]

Bernard Lonergan warned, however: "Method is not a set of rules to be followed meticulously by a dolt." It is rather a "framework for collaborative creativity." In contemporary theology he sees eight distinct tasks: "research, interpretation, history, dialectic, foundations, doctrines, systematics, and communications."[30]

Wolfhart Pannenberg quotes Hartmut Gese to the effect that the uniqueness of Israel's historical consciousness was found in "the fact that history moves from God's promise toward a goal, and that God's covenant is consequently not an archetypal, pre-temporal event but a 'historical process.'"[31]

The methodological suggestions from Lucey, Lonergan, and Pannenberg will provide an initial "framework for collaborative creativity" in the theo-historical approach in this work.

The historical events of the revelation of God in the Black experience had meanings which transcended the initial meaning of those events in a particular time and place. Those events were seen as steps in God's movement in history from promise to goal. These events amounted to progressions in redemption.

The sources of theology generally include experience, history, culture, Scripture, revelation, tradition, and reason. Sources are formative factors which determine the character of a given theology. Norm is the criterion to which the sources must be subjected. Sources are the data, and the norm determines how the data will be used. Norm also determines which specific source gets elevated. It is common knowledge that both Karl Barth and Paul Tillich used

Scripture and culture in their theological systems. It is also common knowledge that the emphasis for Barth was upon Scripture while the emphasis for Tillich was upon culture.

Since norm has to do with the hermeneutical principles—determining how the data will be used—it might be well to discuss my hermeneutical approach first and then say a word about my sources.

Hermeneutics is generally defined as the inquiry which is concerned with the "presuppositions and interpretations of some form of human expression. . . ."[32] Van A. Harvey goes on to point out that this hermeneutical interpretation usually applies to the written text, but it could apply to an artistic expression of some kind. It is in the broad sense of the interpretations and the reinterpretation of some form of human expression—the Black sermons, prayer, spirituals, the blues, songs, testimonies, and literature—that the hermeneutical method will be applied.

The term "hermeneutic" is descriptive of the intended use of the word in this research. George Kehm, translator of *Basic Questions in Theology,* offers an explanation as to why Pannenberg used "hermeneutic" instead of "hermeneutics." He puts it this way:

> "Hermeneutic," in the singular, was preferred to the plural, "hermeneutics," because it signifies a difference in the character of the modern form of the discipline called *"Hermeneutik"* as compared to the older form of this discipline. Whereas it had been conceived as dealing with the principles of textual exegesis, the newer conception regards it as a comprehensive theory of understanding, including analysis of the ontological conditions of understanding.[33]

Kehm contends that such a radical change in the character of a discipline gives rise to the need for a somewhat different name to identify its new form. This meaning of the term is apropos for this study.

The hermeneutical task is that of bridging the gap—to span the chasm—between the event and/or the foundation of the expression and the interpreter. The concern in this study will be that of bridging the gap between the initial and historical expressions of the Christian faith by Blacks, as they understood the revelation of God and the present interpreter. A "fusion of horizons" sums up, for us, the hermeneutical task. The norm for Black theology in this research is shaped by the Black people's situation of oppression and their views of redemption in the light of the revelation of God both in the Holy Scriptures and in the Black experience. The norm must arise out of the Black people's understanding of redemption in their experience.

I will draw from the expressions of the masses—the "folk"—primarily. The reason for this is that many of the Black elites, who have been processed through the white institutions and Black institutions with white orientations, speak a different language from that of the "folk." They express themselves in the language and forms of the master, and they, like the masters, have stereotyped the expressions of the "folk" as primitive.

But the expressions of the "folk" have great theological significance. Johannes Pedersen, a Danish scholar, in his book *Israel: Its Life and Culture,* tells us that the purpose of the book was "to describe the conception of the life in Israel as it was until the collapse of the nation" when it came in contact with Hellenistic culture.[34] Isolating the expressions used by the Israelites, Pedersen meticulously describes the culture of Israel. Words used by the Israelites were expressions of the essence of their souls. Pedersen declares: "Behind the word stands the whole of the soul which created it. If he who utters a word is a strong soul, then the word expresses more reality than a weak soul can put into it. . . . "[35]

Following that same line of thought is Gerhard Von Rad. According to Von Rad:

> The subject matter which concerns the theologian is, of course, not the spiritual and religious world of Israel and the conditions of her soul in general, nor is it her world of faith, all of which can only be reconstructed by means of conclusions drawn from the documents: instead, it is simply Israel's own explicit assertions about Yahweh. The theologian must above all deal directly with the evidence, that is with what Israel herself testified concerning Jahweh. . . .[36]

This is precisely the approach which will be used in constructing a theology from Black history. This will be an examination of what the masses of the members of the Black community themselves testified concerning Yahweh. While culture, tradition, Scripture, revelation, and reason will be included in this research, it is the stuff of the Black experience which constitutes Black history and serves as a basic source. The source is transmitted through Black folk expressions, some of which have been collected in Black literature.

Scope and Limitations of This Study

In this study I will use the valuable guidelines and insights from the works available to me. However, I will not be limited to or by these works. I bring my own experience and insights to the study. This means that the study will, of necessity, be subjective as well as objective. Kenneth B. Clark, a Black psychologist, attempts to solve the problem of objectivity versus subjectivity in his book *Dark Ghetto: Dilemmas of Social Power:*

> The question of the nature of objectivity in law, in science, in human relationships, is complex and cannot be resolved by attempts to make it synonymous with the exclusion of feeling and value. Objectivity that implies detachment or escape from psychological reality decreases understanding and can be used merely to avoid the problem. In the social sciences, the cult of objectivity seems often to be associated with "not taking sides." When carried to its extreme, this type of objectivity could be equated with ignorance.[37]

Clark contends that when the investigator's experience is a part of the evidence "the exclusion of feeling [is] neither sophisticated nor objective, but naive and violative of the scientific spirit at its best. Where human feelings are part of the evidence, they cannot be ignored." He acknowledges that "feeling may twist judgment, but the lack of feeling may twist it even more."[38] As I pursue this study, it will be subjective to the extent that personal experience and feelings constitute part of the evidence. As required in scientific research, I intend to be as objective as possible in order to guard against the distortion of facts.

It is difficult, almost impossible, to establish the origin and eventual formulation of Black theological thoughts which are still largely oral. But the primary historical period for the casting of Black Christian thought in this country was the half century from the Civil War to about 1914.

The past, the present, and the future all play an important role in Black religious thoughts. The past provides the historical source which is the basic element in this work. The existential present in the midst of all of the contingencies of Black existence must be considered. And Black hope for new possibilities which was always in the "not-yet"—the future—has been, and still is, a basic foundation upon which Black people stand theologically. Without that hope for the future, it seems that at times the past and the present would have lost their ontological values.

At this point in my own theological development and maturation process, I refuse to be forced into either camp. I find myself walking a tightrope from one camp to the other as I explore

Black theological expressions. At one juncture the emphasis is upon what God has done in the past; at another juncture the emphasis is upon the Jesus who walks with us now. But I also give much attention to that aspect of oral Black theology which might be viewed as a theology of hope.

Redemption is the core motif in this study. As we move forward, emphasis will be placed on the salvation-from-oppression dimension of redemption which has been neglected by Euro-American theologians. Attention will also be given to the confederation aspect of redemption in Black folk religious expressions which has been overlooked by Black theologians.

In chapter 2 we will review the metaphorical meaning of the term "redemption" as used by the Hebrews in their cultic practices, having borrowed the term from their contemporary commercial culture. We will also review the usage of the term in Old Testament writings. Then we will explore the understanding and usage of the term "redemption" in Black religious thought.

2

Been Redeemed

My Lord delivered
poo' Daniel,
My Lord delivered
poo' Daniel
My Lord delivered
poo' Daniel
And I know
He'll deliver poo' me.

These lines from one of the old spirituals represent a sound theological assertion about the redemptive activity of God. That the Lord had delivered Daniel was, for the creators of the spirituals, an historical certainty. That the Lord was still active in history was a certainty. And that they themselves would be redeemed was also a certainty. For more than a century Black people in this country, a country which Tom Wicker rightly referred to as "one nation, divided,"[1] have expressed in songs, prayers, sermons, and testimonies their belief in the redemptive activity of their Lord.

Redemption in the Black tradition is seen as a voluntary act on the part of the Redeemer on behalf of humankind in need of redemption. From what state, circumstances, or conditions were they

35

assured of being "redeemed"? The object of this chapter is to probe for answers to that question.

Before attempting to examine and to analyze redemption from the Black perspective, it is important that one should survey the historical-theological understanding of redemption. Since Christianity derives its biblical foundation from the Hebrew tradition, there is but one place to start with the examination—in the Hebrew tradition. I am keenly aware of the fact that in Christianity Christ is the Alpha and Omega, the Beginning and Ending, the First and Last. So, theologically and philosophically Christ is traditionally, and rightfully so, the point of departure in the Christian discussions of redemption. However, historically the Hebrews' experience and understanding of redemption were shaped prior to the historic incarnation of the Jesus (Redeemer) of history.

The Christians have borrowed the term "redemption" from the Hebrews. It is important, then, to go back to the writings of the Hebrews and examine the meaning and usage of the term by the Hebrew witnesses themselves. The next step is to survey the interpretations of the term by scholars of various Jewish groups. The use of the term in Christian theology has generally been limited to salvation from sin and guilt. It is important, therefore, to give considerable attention to the Jewish interpretation of the term, since redemption in Black thought is more analogous to the Hebrew theological position than has been heretofore granted by Euro-American Christian theologians.

The three major concerns which will be discussed in this chapter are first, redemption in Hebrew thought; second, the prevailing view of redemption in Euro-American Christian thought; and third, an introduction to the understanding of redemption in Black thought which will be the focus of the investigation throughout this book. The Black folk witnesses and interpreters of the Black religious experience and expressions assert an understanding of redemption which transcends the limited view of redemption which is promoted by most Western Christian theologians. The full meaning of redemption in Black thought which is consistent with the original meaning of redemption in Hebrew thought has the potential for correcting the distortion which has developed in the meaning of redemption in Euro-American Christian theology.

Redemption in Hebrew Thought

1. O give thanks to the Lord,
    for he is good;
    for his steadfast love endures
    forever!
2. Let the redeemed of the Lord say so,
    whom he has redeemed from trouble

. . . .

4. Some wandered in desert wastes,
    finding no way to a city to dwell in;
5. hungry and thirsty,
    their soul fainted within them.
6. Then they cried to the Lord in their trouble,
    and he delivered them from their distresses;
7. he led them by a straight way,
    till they reached a city to dwell in.

. . . .

23. Some went down to the sea in ships,
    doing business on the great waters;
24. they saw the deeds of the LORD,
    his wondrous works in the deep.
25. For he commanded, and raised the
    stormy wind,
    which lifted up the waves of the sea.
26. They mounted up to heaven, they
    went down to the depths;
    their courage melted away in their evil plight;
27. they reeled and staggered like
    drunken men,
    and were at their wits' end.
28. Then they cried to the LORD in
    their trouble,
    and he delivered them from their distress;
29. he made the storm be still,
    and the waves of the sea were hushed.
30. Then they were glad because they
    had quiet,
    and he brought them to their desired heaven.
    —Psalm 107

Biblical interpreters have not agreed upon whether this psalm is a unit or whether it is a collection from different periods and events. There is general consensus, however, that it is a hymn of salvation and lordship, and verses 1-32 advance a liturgical introduction to the presentation of thank offering. The priests take the lead in calling upon those members of the congregation who had "experienced God's salvation to bring their offering and testify to God's saving love." The summons addresses the wayfarers who had been blessed with divine guidance (vv. 4-9), "liberated *prisoners* (vss. 10-16), the *sick* who have been *healed* (vss. 17-22), and seafarers rescued from the *storm* (vss. 23-32)."[2] And God's sovereignty is emphasized throughout.

Redemption in this psalm has to do with liberation from social and physical situations, and not from sin. The priests who composed this hymn saw sin as the reason for the social and physical consequences which they were experiencing. At this point, however, the object of this presentation is to focus upon the divine acts of redemption and not upon the causes for the state in which Israel found herself and from which she needed and experienced redemption.

Donald D. Leslie, in *Encyclopaedia Judaica,* defines redemption as "salvation from the states or circumstances that destroy the value of human existence or human existence itself."[3] While sin, evil, and guilt are implied in this definition, that is, if one understands them to be destructive to the value of human existence, they are not specifically mentioned in the definition. This is a comprehensive and expanding definition that burst out of the narrow frames of a master-slave mentality which has influenced Western, Christian theology and, more specifically, American master-slave teachings. In the preface to his book *Sermons Preached on Plantations to Congregations of Negroes,* the Reverend Alexander Glennie, Rector of All-Saints Parish in Waccamaw, South Carolina, says:

> The following Sermons were written for the benefit of the Coloured portion of my flock. As the want of simple sermons, suited to the capacities of the Negroes is frequently spoken of, I have made this selection from among those which I have been writing for several years past, and publish them in the hope that Catechists and religious Masters may find them of some use.[4]

The first sermon in the book was preached on a Christmas Day. His text was from 1 Timothy 1:15 (KJV): "This is a faithful saying, and worthy of all acceptation, that Christ Jesus came into the world to save sinners. . . . " In rhetorical fashion he expands the discussion: In what condition did Jesus come? "Did he appear in the world in a state of great power and glory?" No. . . . "He who was God made himself of no reputation, and took upon him the form of a servant. . . . " He points out that Jesus Christ did not appear as a "great and rich man," but he took on the form of a servant and he came to save sinners. A theological reflection upon this Christmas Day sermon reveals that redemption for the Reverend Glennie as taught to Black folk would mean salvation from engagement in the acts of sin and from eternal punishment. All men, he declares, are descendants of Adam and Eve and are thus born in sin and are subject to the pains of hell forever. "But Jesus Christ came into the world to save sinners: to save them from living in sin in this world and from suffering the pains of hell which their sins deserve."[5]

While this position is theologically sound, it is equally conspiratorial in that it is limited to salvation from the eternal consequences of sin, meaning those consequences beyond death. The theology in this sermon intentionally neglects to admit that redemption has its genesis in salvation from the state or circumstances which destroy human values and existence in this world.

This approach was not only a distortion of the original meaning of redemption, but also it was specifically designed to keep the oppressed from rising up and claiming their God-given rights to freedom from oppression. It seems ironic that while the masters were preaching these "Servants, Obey Your Masters" sermons, the servants were holding secret camp meetings at night and giving birth to spirituals, such as: "My Lord delivered poo' Daniel, and I know he'll deliver poo' me," and "Go down, Moses, tell Ol' Pharaoh to let my people go."

The masters were successful in quashing the activities of the slaves, but they could not quash their spirit. David Shannon, who is Black and Dean of Pittsburgh Theological Seminary, gives this summary regarding the secret camp meetings of the slaves: The masters controlled their activities from sunup to sundown, but the real development and perpetuation of the world view and religious outlook of the Black fathers took place in those secret meetings between sundown and sunup.[6]

"The Cult of the Publican" is the title of chapter 2 in the book *All the Damned Angels* by William Muehl. He calls attention to the fact that the penitent publican does not stand alone in the New Testament (Luke 18:9-14). He stands among a large company of those who are glimpsed only briefly and in a moment of self-discovery. The prodigal son, the woman taken in adultery, the woman at the well in Samaria, Zacchaeus, the repenting thief on the cross, and a host of others might fall into the category of the publican in this parable. After appearing before Christ, confessing their sins and receiving salvation, they disappear into the wings. They remain there until the table of readings or the whim of a preacher brings them out to go through the same ritual another Sunday, argues Muehl. But he is not opposed to the retelling of the parable of the publican; he is against the promotion of the cult of publicanism. Here he speaks for himself:

> It is the message of Christian faith that Jesus Christ came into the world to save sinners. We believe that God was in him reconciling the world unto himself. But precisely because of this conviction we often seem to limit the Almighty to this single manifestation of love. We sometimes speak as though God is *only* in Christ and doing nothing but *reconciling*. In a significant sense we have made the Mighty One of Israel the prisoner of the incarnation.[7]

The parable is distorted in our age, declares Muehl, because it was intended to chasten the proud rather than exalt the penitent. Our age "now challenges Christian theology to speak of what lies beyond repentance. It is asking . . . questions about the content of salvation, the style of the Christian life."[8] Christian theologians, preachers, and custodians of the faith have participated in the development of the cult of a single interpretation of the many dimensions of redemption. One sometimes gets the impression that redemption has only to do with salvation from the eternal consequences of sin. It is important to point out that major Christian theologians have acknowledged the many dimensions of redemption. But until the ushering in of Black theology and liberation theology, very few treatises have been forthcoming on the this-worldly liberation aspect of redemption. It ought to be remembered, however, that Western theology unfolds in the midst of colonizing nations where, in fact, the states are superior to the church. Thus the church has been passive in the area of developing a theology that would be antagonistic to the social, economic, and political practices of the state. The theology of Dietrich Bonhoeffer is an example of the few exceptions.

We have adopted the Hebrew definition of redemption which does not negate its otherworldly outlook but neither is limited to its otherworldly benefits. Redemption means "salvation from the states or circumstances that destroy the value of human existence or human existence itself."[9]

The basic source for the following discussion is from the commentary by Donald D. Leslie, in *Encyclopaedia Judaica* referred to earlier. The words "redeemer," "redemption," and "redeem"—all related terms—appear in the Old Testament some 130 times and are all derived from two Hebrew roots, pdh [*padah*] and g'l [*go'el*]. Although these terms were used to describe divine activity as well, they arose in the setting of ordinary human affairs. It is in this context, says Leslie, that they must first be understood.[10]

H. Wheeler Robinson, a Christian theologian, finds the terms "redemption," "redeem," "redeemer," occurring 132 times in the English Old Testament (AV) and almost always derived from the Hebrew roots, *padah* and *go'el*.[11] *Padah* is the more general of the two terms, according to Leslie. It has cognates of related meaning in Akkadian, Arabic, and Ethiopic. The significant point is that it belongs to the dominion of commercial law and refers to the payment of an equivalent for what is to be released or secured. *Padah,* in its verbal form, unlike *go'el* indicates nothing about the relation of agent to the object of redemption. In the Old Testament, this object is always either a person or another living being. The usage in cultic activity does not differ from that of a normal commercial transaction. A person or an animal is released, in both cases, in return for money or a suitable replacement. Some references are Exodus 13:13; 34:20; Leviticus 27:27; 1 Samuel 14:45. In Exodus 21:7-8; Leviticus 19-20; Job 6:23, *go'el* is more restricted and does not seem to have cognates in other Semitic languages. Its connection with the family law reflects the Israelites' conception of the importance of preserving clan solidarity.[12]

The *go'el* or redeemer is the next of kin who must act to maintain the vitality of his extended family group and to prevent any breaches from occurring. He is expected to acquire the alienated properties of his kinsman "if your brother becomes poor, and sells part of his property, then his next of kin shall come and redeem what his brother has sold" (Leviticus 25:25). The *go'el* is expected to purchase the property when it is in danger of being lost to strangers (Jeremiah 32:6ff.). He is also required to support the widow of his next of kin if she is dependent (Ruth 4:4ff.). Early rabbinic authorities contested whether or not one was duty bound to perform these acts, "but it seems likely that he was expected to do so, unless there was a good reason to the contrary (cf. Ruth 4:6)."[13] "Then the next of kin said, 'I cannot redeem it for myself, lest I impair my own inheritance. Take my right of redemption yourself for I cannot redeem it.'"

Both terms make a slight shift when they are applied to divine activity; *padah* takes on the general meaning of deliverer. The notion of payment or an equivalent is not involved, since God is the Lord of the universe and everything belongs to him. Leslie reports that the only place in Scripture when such exchange is possibly suggested is obviously a rhetorical statement and *padah* is not used:

> For I am the LORD your God,
>   the Holy One of Israel, your Savior.
> I give Egypt as your ransom,
>   Ethiopia and Seba in exchange for you.
> Because you are precious in my eyes,
>   and honored, and I love you,
> I give men in return for you,
>   peoples in exchange for your life.
> —Isaiah 43:3-4

Leslie held that "God's purpose is not to retain the right of possession, but to *liberate* [emphasis mine] people, both individuals and groups, *from* their woes,"[14] as in 2 Samuel 4:9: "But David answered Rechab and Baanah his brother . . . , 'As the Lord lives, who has redeemed my life out of every adversity,'" (cf. 1 Kings 1:29). Redemption *from bondage* is found in Deuteronomy 7:8 which reads: "But it is because the LORD loves you, and is keeping the oath which he swore to your fathers, that the LORD has brought you out with a mighty hand, and redeemed you from the house of bondage, from the hand of Pharaoh king of Egypt." (See also Deuteronomy 13:5.) It must be pointed out that the oppression of the Hebrews by the Egyptians was not a consequence of any sin on the part of the Hebrews. Redemption *from oppression* is cited in Isaiah 1:27.

> Zion shall be redeemed by justice,
>   and those in her who repent, by righteousness.

And we read in Psalm 119:134,

> Redeem me from man's oppression,
>   that I may keep thy precepts.

Redemption *from death* is suggested in Hosea 13:14,

> Shall I ransom them from the power of Sheol?
>> Shall I redeem them from Death?
> O Death, where are your plagues?
>> O Sheol, where is your destruction?
>> Compassion is hid from my eyes.

(See also Psalm 49:14-15.) Both the Hebrew scholar Leslie and the Christian scholar Robinson have interpreted the meaning of redemption in Hebrew or Old Testament thought with great emphasis upon salvation from oppression.

The Deuteronomist uses *padah* in the Torah to characterize God's acts in the time of the Exodus as redemptive (cf. Deuteronomy 9:26), "You shall remember that you were a slave in the land of Egypt, and the LORD your God redeemed you . . . " (Deuteronomy 15:15; cf. 21:8; 24:18). Later writers extended this usage to describe Israel's eschatological redemption: Isaiah 1:27 (cited above) and 35:10,

> And the ransomed of the Lord shall return,
>> and come to Zion with singing;
> everlasting joy shall be upon their heads;
>> they shall obtain joy and gladness,
>> and sorrow and sighing shall flee away.

Only on one occasion is it used as deliverance from sins, "And he will redeem Israel from all his iniquities" (Psalm 130:8).

When *go'el* loses its strict judicial connotation in describing divine activities, it takes on the meaning of deliverer (Genesis 48:16). However, it still retains some of the original overtones even when referring to God; so Proverbs 23:10-11 reads: "Do not remove an ancient landmark or enter the fields of the fatherless; for their Redeemer is strong; he will plead their cause against you." The writer sees God—Redeemer—as a kind of next of kin who is duty bound to protect orphans (cf. Job 19:25). Similarly the psalmist describes God: "Father of the fatherless and protector of widows is God in his holy habitation" (Psalm 68:5). Little wonder that Isaiah was certain that God had a special reason to redeem the people of Israel; he was their *go'el*. It is pointed out that it must not be an accident that Isaiah only uses *padah* twice: 50:2 and 51:11. *Padah,* as used in both of these instances, appeared in earlier expressions concerning the Exodus.

What is important to understand about the whole discussion above is, first, that the idea of *padah* or *go'el,* "redeemer," "redemption," "redeem," belongs to the domain of commercial law—the idea grew out of the sociocultural situation of the Hebrew tradition. Secondly, the redemption idea was borrowed by the cultic movement and used metaphorically to describe the saving relationship between God and the Israelites. Thirdly, even when slight shifts occur in both the *padah* and *go'el* terms when applied to divine activity by the ancient Hebrews, the original understanding of the terms prevailed in Hebrew thought and expressions. Fourthly, and most importantly, redemption in ancient Hebrew thought applied to salvation from woes, salvation from bondage, salvation from oppression, salvation from death, and salvation from other states and circumstances in the here and now.

These points are substantiated in the many quotes and references throughout the foregoing discussion. But a further examination of the idea of redemption from the Hebraic tradition is helpful.

David Flusser, Professor of Comparative Religion, the Hebrew University of Jerusalem, points out that "while the Bible uses *padah* and *ga'al* for redemption, the *Talmud* applies *padah* to ransom . . . and *ga'al* to redemption." He asserts: "The sages know nothing of a miraculous redemption of the soul by external means." [15] Whether collectively or individually there was no failure in humanity which required special divine intervention which could not be remedied by persons themselves with the guidance of the Torah.

"The term *ge'ullah* is applied almost exclusively to national redemption and became a synonym for national freedom." So, "the main element in the yearnings of the people for the redemption of Israel" was the idea of national freedom from subjection to other states. This idea, says Flusser, became more prevalent during the period of domination by the Romans. As understood from the *Talmud*, "redemption is dependent upon repentance and good deeds." [16] While there is the "prominence of the image of a Messiah as redeemer, his role in the [whole] process of redemption [would be] no different from those of Moses" and others of the past. The Redeemer would be an instrument in the hands of God leading the Israelites to national freedom. The contrast of past redemptive events with the messianic redemption was that the former were effected by human agency and were therefore temporary whereas the latter would be accomplished by God himself and would be eternal. [17]

Flusser believes that "a quasi-transcendental and mystical element" entered "into the concept of redemption." It was the notion that redemption served the "needs of the Most High," because "wherever [Israel] was exiled the Divine Presence was exiled with them." So, in a word, "God . . . redeems Himself with the redemption" of Israel.[18]

Again it is made clear that, from the perspective of the *Talmud,* redemption for the Hebrews, from whom the Christians have borrowed the term, almost exclusively applied to national liberation and freedom. This does not negate the salvation-from-sin and guilt side of redemption, but it does point to that other side of redemption which holds great meaning for Black folk in American bondage.

The Jewish medieval philosophers building upon the foundation of the biblical and Talmudic system generally saw the finite condition of humankind as the primary state from which they needed redemption. And this "state of finiteness was not the result of human action or sin, but a cosmic circumstance ultimately due to the nature of creation." Out of his goodness and grace God created the universe, yet man was formed in a finite condition. In this state he is "subject to despair and death" and thus subject to "spiritual and physical annihilation."[19] It is from this possibility of annihilation that man needs to be redeemed. Because of the divine goodness of God, redemption is available to man, but man must participate in the process of his redemption. True beliefs and right actions make him worthy of redemption; "otherwise he is sinner and condemned either to eternal torment or physical annihilation." It is important to note that in Jewish medieval philosophy "sin does not produce the unsaved state as does original sin, for example, in the Christian view; sin rather serves to prevent the redemption of man from the spiritual or physical consequences of his finite conditions."[20]

Redemption is seen as coming in two major miraculous states: The Messianic Age and the world to come. (1) The Messianic Age will usher in the restoration of the Jewish people to the land of Israel. (2) At the end of the Messianic Age the world to come will emerge, and at that time all of the dead will be resurrected and final judgment will be rendered. The living will now become infinite in time, the righteous enjoying eternal reward and the wicked eternal punishment. The Jews are God's chosen people, but redemption is attained by all righteous people. The above is called the traditional supernatural view of redemption which incorporates the basic features of the Talmudic approach to soteriology.[21]

A second view is termed philosophic naturalism. This approach is strongly influenced by the concept of Aristotelian and Neoplatonic thinkers.[22] The medieval Jewish philosopher who is credited with being the greatest exponent of this view is Maimonides. While "the creation of the world is also the result of God's goodness . . . the universe was not created for [mankind, neither is mankind] the direct creation of the Godhead. The universe comes from God through a successive series of emanations . . . " and the world and mankind are created out of matter. Matter, then, is the principle of human finitude and redemption is achieved by mankind "overcoming his material nature." Mankind achieves this "by the actualization of the hylic intellect to an acquired intellect through metaphysical and scientific studies." Through the intellect mankind gains ascendancy over material desires, in life, and at death they achieve immortality because the "acquired intellect exists separate from the body" and is not restricted by the finitude of the body.[23]

What is discovered here is that neither of the two major Jewish philosophic approaches of the medieval period took salvation from original sin as a point of departure for the understanding of redemption.

Rabbi Reines concludes that the Christian position which says "that mankind requires redemption owing to the guilt of original sin," resulting from the consequence of the disobedience of Adam "in Eden, is completely foreign to the medieval Jewish thinkers."[24] I am not participating in the argument for or against the merits of any of the positions which have been discussed. My task is that of examining the records and reporting my findings.

The Kabbalists' original contribution to the concept of redemption would be the idea that there is an inner aspect or "mystery" in the course of redemption. Their basic teaching evolves out of the verse: "On that day the LORD will be one and his name one" (Zechariah 14:9). This is frequently interpreted in the Zohar (a theosophical work, consisting chiefly of mystical interpretations and commentaries on the Pentateuch), indicating a lack of perfection in the unity of God during the period of the exile. When iniquity has caused a fissure in the unity of the Godhead, that is, between his *Sefirot* which makes up the totality of his created beings, his name is not "One." In the opinion of the Kabbalists, the Name is the symbol of the divine *Sefirot* when the created beings are joined in complete unity. They saw the Exile as a state of creation in which this unity has become impaired. In symbolic language, exile means, for the Kabbalists, a temporary separation between the King and the queen, between God and his *shekhinah*. The union is broken.

Gershom Scholem sums up redemption as the restoration of an uninterrupted union. Israel's return to her "land at the time of redemption symbolizes the inner process of the return of the 'Congregation of Israel' or the *Shekhinah* ('the Matron') to a continuous attachment to her husband."[25] Martin Buber and A. J. Heschel are Jewish thinkers who tend to speak of redemption as the triumph of good over evil. But again this redemption is thought of in terms of a world in need of redemption. Following this same line of thinking is Mordecai Kaplan who uses the term "salvation" in speaking of redemption. From a personal point of view salvation means faith in the possibility of achieving an integrated personality.[26] Concomitant with personal salvation is social salvation since "we cannot think of ourselves except in relation to something not ourselves. . . . Social salvation is 'the pursuit of common ends in a manner which shall afford to each the maximum opportunity for creative self-expression.'"[27]

The modern Orthodox thinker Joseph B. Soloveitchik understands "redemption in terms of faith and performance of the *mitzvot*." The mitzvot is any of the group of 613 commandments or precepts which might be present in or derived from the Bible and which relate chiefly to the religious and moral conduct of the Jews. Soloveitchik believes that "human capability of renewal and self-transformation manifests itself especially in times of human distress. Being redeemed is a mode of existence, not an attribute.[28] Therefore a hermit can live a redeemed life, since redemption is an individual thing and not dependent upon society. In the words of Soloveitchik, "A redeemed life is ipso facto a disciplined life." And in contrast to the dignity which a human being feels when one triumphs over nature, redemption is a state of existence in which the human is "overpowered by the creator of nature," which is discovered in the "depth of crisis and failure."[29] The emphasis seems to be directed toward the individual in Soloveitchik's discussion, but this does not replace the communal concern in Hebrew thought.

Another aspect of modern Jewish thought on redemption is represented by the Zionists. Zionism is considered a kind of messianic movement which deals with the redemption of the Jewish people. Classical Judaism, according to A. Hertzberg, saw redemption as a confrontation between God and the Jewish people. But in the most revolutionary expression Zionism is concerned with confrontations between the Jews and other nations of the earth. "Religious Zionist thinkers saw redemption as at least beginning in temporal terms with the return of the Jews to Erez Israel and the building of the land."[30] "Redemption," writes Rabbi Y. Alkalai, "must come slowly. The land must, by degrees, be built up and prepared."[31] That hope of redemption—the returning of the Jews to the Holy Land—also served as a sustaining force for Judaism in the diaspora. Redemption thus became not only a physical reality by the return to Israel but also a metaphysical undergirding for Jews everywhere.

Even nonreligious Zionists, while not using the term "redemption," expressed themselves in concepts which were traditionally connected with redemption. From the pen of J. Klatzkin comes this statement: "Zionism pins its hopes, in one sense, on the general advance of civilization and its national faith is also a faith in man in general—faith in the power of the good and the beautiful."[32] Here, the triumph of social good implies redemption since the Jews were not full beneficiaries of the social good and the beautiful of which the writer spoke.

The origin of *padah* and *go'el,* "redeemer," "redemption," and "redeem," in biblical Hebrew grew out of the sociocultural situation of the Hebrews. They belong to the domain of commercial laws, were borrowed by the cultic movement, and were used metaphorically to describe the saving relationship between God and the Israelites. Redemption in ancient biblical Hebrew thought applied to salvation from woes, salvation from bondage, salvation from oppression, salvation from death, and salvation from other states and circumstances, primarily in the here and now.

In the *Talmud,* redemption is applied almost exclusively to the yearning for national freedom. Redemption for Israel was the idea of national freedom from subjection to other states. This is particularly true of the period of Roman domination. The finite human state which makes people subject to despair and death and to spiritual and physical annihilation is the condition from which they need to be redeemed, according to medieval Jewish philosophers. The two stages of redemption will be (1) the Messianic age ushering in the restoration of the Jewish people to the land of Israel and (2) the world to come—the final judgment.

The Kabbalists viewed the Exile as an impairment in the unity of the divine name and of the Godhead. Redemption is summed up as the symbol of Israel returning from exile to her land thus effectuating the union of God and humanity.

In modern Jewish thought, redemption means the triumph of good over evil—the eradication of human-caused evils in history. Salvation has both personal and social consequences and is very much this worldly. Redemption at least begins in temporal terms with the return of the Jews to the land of Israel according to religious Zionist thinkers.

These are the testimonies and reflections of some of those who are members of that group which brought the term "redemption" into religious usage. The next step is to give some attention to some of the traditional Christian thoughts on redemption.

Redemption in Christian Thought

Albrecht Ritschl gets into the discussion of redemption from the point of "original sin." He holds that

> the traditional doctrine of man's original state . . . implies that theology takes up its standpoint within either a natural or a universally rational knowledge of God which has nothing to do with the Christian knowledge of Him, and is consequently indifferent to the question whether the expositor who expounds the doctrine belongs to the Christian community or not.[33]

Based upon the previous discussion of the Hebrews' understanding of humankind, one must conclude that Ritschl's statement is on sound footing. And from the above statement he further concludes that the nature and extent of sin is determined by the standard of the "original" perfection: of the first human being. So, traditional Christian theology used Romans 5:12 in support of such a position. "Therefore as sin came into the world through one man and death through sin, and so death spread to all men because all men sinned." This follows Augustine's line, who, "on thoroughly rational grounds, deduced original sin from the sin of the first human pair."[34] Traditional Christian theology also takes up sin from the standpoint of universally inherited sin of the human race. This brings about the need for redemption. And this method of redemption is brought out by comparing sin with divine attributes of righteousness. This purely rational style is applied to the subject by Anselm. The third stage of theological development is that which takes into account the "knowledge of Christ's Person and work, and its application to the individual and the fellowship of believers."[35] However, Ritschl rejects the notion of traversing these three separate points of view in attempting to form a theological system since "a method which is so predominantly inspired by purely rational ideas of God and sin and redemption is not the positive theology which we need, and which can be defended against the objections of general rationalism."[36] He is not rejecting the fragmentary knowledge resulting from these separate points of view coming from the Christian community since only from the collection of these views can the worth of Christ as Revealer be employed throughout as the basis of knowledge for solving all theological problems. What Ritschl wishes to do, however, is to put Christ at the center where Luther sees that He belongs. "Luther admits no 'disinterested' knowledge of God, but recognises as a religious datum only such knowledge of Him as takes the form of unconditional trust. This knowledge, however, is so exclusively bound up with Christ, that whatever knowledge of God exists alongside of it does not . . . arrive at a neutral idea of God. . . . "[37] So any discussion of redemption for Ritschl is from the viewpoint of Christ as datum and the community of believers as the sphere of His revelation.

In the Old Testament, says Ritschl, "the concrete conception of the one, supernatural, omnipotent God is bound up with the final end of the Kingdom of God, and with the idea of a redemption. . . . that end is conceived under the limits of the national commonwealth; while the condition of the end being realised is conceived . . . as purification from sin,"[38] but it is also partly conceived as that of achieving political independence as the chosen people of God. Accompanying this independence was the achievement of outward prosperity and the perfect rule of Jehovah. But in Christianity, Ritschl sees a shift: ". . . the Kingdom of God is represented as the common end of God and the elect community, in such a way that it rises above the natural limits of nationality and becomes the moral society of nations. In this respect Christianity shows itself to be the perfect moral religion."[39] Redemption through Christ means justification and renewal. What the redeemed achieves is emancipation from evils through a spiritual process. This is specifically distinct from Old Testament anticipations. Again Ritschl asserts that

> . . . in Christianity everything is "related" to the moral organisation of humanity through love-prompted action; but at the same time everything is also "related" to redemption through Jesus, to spiritual redemption, *i.e.,* to that freedom from guilt and over the world which is to be won through the realised Fatherhood of God. Freedom in God, the freedom of the children of God, is the private end of each individual Christian, as the Kingdom of God is the final end of all.[40]

This is good Western, Christian redemption theology. It represents the prevailing view of redemption in white theology. But this purely spiritual redemption approach negates and/or neglects the full meaning of redemption by the originators of the idea—the Hebrews. It negates and/or neglects the full meaning of redemption in Black theology. A theology of redemption which speaks only to the idea of freedom from sin and guilt and omits the original idea of freedom from oppression has little relevance for Black theology.

Three points emerge in the works of Ritschl which were examined. (1) The need for redemption arises as a consequence of original sin. This contrasts with the medieval Jewish philosophical thought which understood sin as that which prevented the redemption of mankind from the spiritual and physical consequences of their finite condition. (2) Christ is the starting point for Ritschl in his discourse on redemption. Would it not have been well to have begun with the historical events of the God of the oppressed in his redemptive, historical activities from creation? (3) The theological approach to redemption based upon the Person and work of Christ does not require that the theologian deal with the Old Testament understanding of redemption as freedom and liberation from oppression.

Revelation and Redemption is the third book in his trilogy representing his life's work as a teacher and preacher, says H. Wheeler Robinson. This book "concentrates on the media of revelation and especially the redemptive act of the Cross, as based in the actuality of history."[41] Here the author announces that he is going to begin his interpretation of redemption from the event of the cross. This is the place to start for Christology, but this is not the place of the historical genesis of redemption. Implied in the title, he says, is the keynote of the book. That is to say

> the revelation made by the Gospel is that of a redemption; the redemption does not consist simply in a revelation which influences men to lead a new life; the revelation produces this (subjective) change of attitude and conduct because it reveals an (objective) redemption which God has independently wrought in Christ, which is completed in the actual transformation taking place in Christian lives.[42]

Robinson seems to be correct on this point. However, it is still true that God was in the process of "objective" redemption from creation—from the time that persons first abused their freedom. "Objective redemption" is what God has done, is doing, and will do independently as a result of his divine will in creation. Yet people are free to reject this divine offer of salvation. Again Robinson is correct when he declares that it is beyond the power of human beings to atone for the abuse of freedom which human history displays. The human being requires divine redemption, and the actuality of that redemption in Christ is the supreme revelation of God. This does not alter the fact that God's redemptive activities had begun prior to the historical Jesus. In spite of Robinson's stated position that the actuality of history supplies a line of approach to which sufficient attention has not been given, he does not deal with the Old Testament meaning of redemption until chapter 12 in his book. But here he offers some helpful information on redemption from its historical perspective.

Redemption, like most great terms in our religious vocabulary, conceals a metaphor; it means buying back by payment of a price; it comes from the same root as "ransom," according to Robinson. The word "redemption," becoming somewhat old-fashioned, is now giving way to such terms as "atonement," "salvation," and "reconciliation," which are preferred as expressions of what Christ has done for humanity. All of these terms tend to imply the more subjective side of man's deliverance from sin than the word "redemption" does. It is for that reason, says Robinson, that he here prefers the more objective term—"redemption." He warns that we are dealing with metaphors in the discussion of "sacrifice" and "penalty" and neither "should be interpreted as the payment of a price, and thus confused with the idea which underlies 'redemption.'"[43]

He asserts: "The ransom paid for a slave or prisoner by which he obtains his freedom, is not a sacrifice or a penalty, except in a very loose and metaphorical use of these terms." Ransoming (in theology) implies a definite activity which is independent of any action or response on the part of the person affected.[44] Salvation, throughout the history of our faith, in Christian conception, refers to what God has done in an objective sense through Christ. The idea of "objective" redemptive acts of God was the position of Leslie in our earlier discussion. He said the notion of payment or an equivalent is not involved when the term *padah* is applied to divine activity since God is Lord of the universe and everything belongs to him. Thus, it seems that here Robinson is in agreement with Leslie's understanding of redemption as an "objective" act of God. This does not mean that people do not participate in the redemptive process. The Jewish medieval philosopher, David Flusser, contends that although the goodness and grace of God are available to people who need redemption from their finiteness, they must participate in the process of redemption by true belief and right action.

It is clear in Robinson's further discussions that redemption in Hebrew thought was this worldly. He points out that *padah* originally denoted an equivalent in real or assumed value given for the release from some bond or taboo. In its figurative sense, which is the concern of theology, it "naturally denotes the activity of God in delivering man from *any disability* or *constraint*" (emphasis mine). Actual payment is usually dropped out of sight and attention is fixed on the *result,* that is, the deliverance or escape from the constraint. Some supports are offered by Robinson: "He has redeemed my soul from going down into the Pit, and my life shall see the light" (Job 33:28). ". . . the Lord has brought you out with a mighty hand, and redeemed you from the house of bondage, from the hand of Pharaoh king of Egypt" (Deuteronomy 7:8*b*). And "'He who scattered Israel will gather him, and will keep him as a shepherd keeps his flock.' For the LORD has ransomed [*padah*] Jacob, and has redeemed [*go'el*] him from hands too strong for him" (Jeremiah 31:10-11).

Robinson concludes that "we can no more insist on actual payment as essential to ransom or redemption in such metaphorical use than we could insist on the literalness of the accompanying metaphor of God as a shepherd, and ask what the shepherd's staff did in this rescue."[45] This is a kind of key statement in coming to grips with the metaphorical understanding of the redemptive activity of God in history and through Jesus Christ. Literary Black theology, which is being developed from the oral folk expressions in the Black tradition, is not primarily concerned with this matter of "to whom the ransom was paid." That has been dropped out of sight and the emphasis is fixed upon the hope, activity, and result of redemption—deliverance and rescue from disabilities and constraints.

Redemption from what? Nowhere is the word *padah* used for redemption from sin alone, according to Robinson; "it always means deliverance from some tangible and visible menace, which may or may not be regarded as a consequence of the suppliant's sin."[46] "Even the death of Christ," he suggests, "is conceived in the New Testament as redemptive and as saving man from a number of evils to which he is exposed."[47] In conclusion, he advances this statement:

Our answer, therefore, to the question "Redemption from what?" is, broadly speaking, to assert a twofold need. On the one hand, each of us needs new power to live, that is, deliverance from all the evils that threaten us in actual living, whether from within or from without. On the other hand, though in closest relation with the inspiration and maintenance of this new power, we need, as a race and as the individual members of it, redemption from the burden of our guilt, which means our responsibility for the temporal defeat of the divine purpose.[48]

It seems that this is a sound approach in answer to the question. Redemption, in its original meaning, and when used metaphorically in theology, meant deliverance from all the evils which threaten humankind in actual living and secondly from their guilt for participating in the forces which tend to defeat the divine purpose. The oppressors in this country need redemption from the guilt of dehumanizing Blacks. The oppression of Black people is a temporal defeat of the divine purpose. Black folks need redemption from oppression. They need an Exodus out of the state and circumstances of dehumanization.

J. Deotis Roberts, Sr., sees the beginning of redemption in the Exodus of the Old Testament. From that point forward an awareness of redemption is upon the hearts and minds of the Israelites. This awareness is centered in faith in the divine Covenant which Yahweh made with Israel. The Covenant became a binding relationship between God and the Israelites rather than a simple contract. Israel was wayward, but God became the "Redeemer who acts through the history of people and in individual lives."[49] Roberts points out that the idea of redemption in the Old Testament stresses God's initiative in restoring mankind to a saving relationship to God. Deliverance from material and spiritual perils and constraints is the meaning. The basic concern is the redemption of Israel as a people, although the individual receives some attention.[50]

H. F. Davis's statement in *The Theology of the Atonement* also admits that the Old Testament usually speaks of redemption in conjunction with the Exodus. The religious experience which Israel enjoyed at the time of the Exodus enabled her to appreciate the idea of redemption. And, thus in Jewish consciousness the Exodus cannot be separated from the Covenant. God delivers his people from slavery in order to bind them to himself. God instructs Moses to say to Israel: " . . . I am the LORD, and I will bring you out from under the burdens of the Egyptians, and I will deliver you from their bondage, and I will redeem you . . . and I will take you for my people, and I will be your God; . . . And I will bring you into the land . . . " (Exodus 6:6-8). Here the idea of redemption goes beyond the limits of liberation from bondage; it also means confederation, coming into community, as discussed in the introduction of this study. Davis gives us a quick glimpse of the development of the redemption/atonement theories of the church fathers: Ignatius, Iranaeus, Justin, Origen, Athanasius, Augustine, Anselm, and Thomas. Generally, all of them dealt with redemption/atonement from the christological point of view. And although Davis asserts that redemption in the Old Testament translates God's act of saving or liberating his people from earthly or spiritual bondage, when he turns to the witnesses in the Scripture, he is heavily spiritual and christologically centered.[51] That is, that Christ came to save sinners is uppermost in the argument. That He also came to liberate the oppressed from human-caused suffering fades into the wings of the discussion.

Ritschl, Robinson, and Davis are all aware of that dimension of redemption which has to do with salvation from the states and circumstances of this-worldly oppressions. But they have elected to accentuate the otherworldly dimension, which is legitimate but not complete. This reveals the imperialistic, cultural influence upon these scholars.

In one of his sermons, the late Dr. Martin Luther King, Jr., detected the tendency by various groups down through the ages to overstress certain aspects of the Christian doctrines. There developed a concept prior to the Reformation, he declares, which stipulated that if people waited submissively upon the Lord, in his own good time He alone would redeem the world. This concept was prominent in the Reformation; it overstressed the corruption of mankind. "The Renaissance was too optimistic and the Reformation too pessimistic. The former so concentrated on the goodness of man that it overlooked his capacity for evil; the latter so concentrated on the wickedness of man that it overlooked his capacity for goodness."[52]

The Reformation theology tended to emphasize otherworldly religion. It stressed the utter hopelessness of this world and called upon individuals to concentrate on preparing their souls for the world to come. King concluded that religion ignored the need for social reform and divorced itself from the mainstream of human life. He said the idea so filtered its way down into our time that a pulpit committee listed the following as the first essential qualification of a new minister: "He must preach the true gospel and not talk about social issues." The one-sided emphasis, he said, of disregarding the fact that the gospel deals with man's body as well as with his soul creates a "tragic dichotomy between the sacred and the secular."[53] As I see the situation, this is the tragedy of Christian theology as it relates to the idea of redemption. Gayraud S. Wilmore quotes John Wesley from *Explanation Notes Upon the New Testament*. The focus was upon 2 Corinthians 3:17, ". . . where the Spirit of the Lord is, there is freedom." The explanation: "There is liberty from servile fear, liberty from the guilt and from the power of sin, liberty to behold with open face the glory of the Lord."[54] It is not surprising, explains Wilmore, to find this kind of spiritualization of Christianity in the eighteenth century. What is important, however, is the fact that white biblical commentators interpreted the Scriptures dealing with freedom as freedom from sin and guilt, for Blacks, but freedom also applied to political independence for themselves. It should be remembered that the otherworldly teachings of the Reformation were followed by the this-worldly practices which characterized the era of expansionism, industrialization, and American slavery.

Any Christian theology must have among its components an otherworldly element since it must be anchored in the resurrection of Jesus and adhere to the idea of immortality of the soul and eternity with Christ. In spite of the fact that the otherworldly aspect of theology has been used for devious purposes on the part of the slave masters and thus, in a way, has become polluted, this does not mean that it must or can be abandoned by Black theologians. (See chapter 9.)

The task of Black literary theology is to bring that balance which is inherent in the genesis of the term "redemption" to the fore. Generally all those who have "talked" about redemption in the past have been white theologians. And James Cone is correct when he said in an address at Goucher College in Baltimore (November 6, 1974): "Any 'God talk' or 'talk about God' generally reveals more about the talker than it does about the One talked about." Those who have been talking about redemption (in literary theology) belong to that group of people who have a background in colonialism. Black theologians must deal with the idea of redemption as it is understood by those who talked about it in their folk expressions. Black religious expressions seem to have greater affinities with the Exodus than with the Bethlehem story. They seem to have more affinity with Moses in the Exodus, the delivery of Daniel from the den of lions, and the saving of the "Hebrew boys" from the fiery furnace than they have with Peter, James, and John. There is a need, then, for a new examination of redemption by Blacks in America.

Redemption in Black Thought

Throughout this book the object will be to continue to examine the understanding of redemption in Black thought. James D. Tyms offers a kind of summary of the understanding of redemption from the Black tradition. In his book *The Rise of Religious Education Among Negro Baptists,* Tyms addresses himself to these three questions about redemption which were put by Dr. Henry Nelson Wieman:

> What is the evil from which man needs to be saved?
> What is the good to which he can be saved?
> What are the conditions which must be met before this saving power can operate effectively?

His answers, he says, are from the perspective of religious education among "Negro" Baptists. His response to the first question is that the "Negroes" have in the past and still need to be saved from those pathological influences of the social process which tend to reduce them to subhuman status in society. They need to be saved from the "psychology of unconscious self-hatred" which tends to rob them of the creativity needed for the emergence of an approved self-image. "Negroes" also need to be saved from the "demoralizing effects of second-class citizenship" which limits cultural enhancement and spiritual fulfillment.[55] Tyms does not see the evil from which Black people ought to be saved only from the lopsided view of sin and guilt. Blacks need to be saved from *all* of the evils which rob them of their creativity.

"The good to which the Negro needs to be saved," says Tyms, ". . . is a deep sense of self-acceptance, a transforming and transcending self-image, . . . a sense of self-esteem—worthship—a basic requirement for high moral conduct, ethical character, and high ideals in the upswing of personality development."[56] The conditions which must be met before the saving power can operate effectively have two foci, according to Tyms. The first has to do with the general secular acculturizing processes and agents, that is, the home, school, church, etc., plus the conditions of economics in the process of human development. These institutions must reflect an *"unqualified commitment to the centrally great ideals which undergird the democratic philosophy of life.*" [57] And the second focus has to do with a dynamic religious experience. [58]

The major contribution of Tyms in his elaborate discussion is his clear focus upon the neglected aspect of redemption. Salvation transcends to narrow limits of being saved from sin and guilt. It includes the deliverance of Black people from the socioeconomic ills which tend to reduce them to subhuman status in society. And the conditions conducive to the full salvation of the Black people include a humane and equitable social order as well as a dynamic and creative religious experience.

Tyms quotes from a 1959 address by O. Clay Maxwell, late president of the National Baptist Sunday School and Training Union Congress: "The greatest weakness of the religion of our time, and time past, is that it draws circles around the areas of life where the religion of Jesus belongs and shuts him out of vital areas of human interest and activity." [59] Maxwell called to the attention of the delegates the fact that somebody had engineered the fallacy that Jesus belongs to the area of religion (the redemption of people from sin) and is not concerned with human interests.

Personal and communal development and deliverance from the ills in this life are and always have been an undergirding reality in the understanding of redemption in the Black church. Sometimes it was evident in overt expressions and actions; at other points the force of human-caused oppressions hushed those open expressions and quashed those actions by which Blacks attempted to participate in their physical and social redemption in this world. But whenever Blacks sang,

> My Lord delivered
>   poo' Daniel,
> My Lord delivered
>   poo' Daniel,
> My Lord delivered
>   poo' Daniel,
> And I know
>   He'll deliver poo' me,

the theological implication had/has far deeper meaning than is generally understood in traditional and current Western theology.

One point which was made clear from the research and report in this chapter is that the Hebrew witnesses and theologians have understood redemption to be both this-worldly as well as otherworldly. Redemption means salvation from oppression as well as salvation from sin and guilt. It has also been discovered that Western, Christian theologians were also aware of the this-worldly emphasis of redemption in the Old Testament. But Western, Christian theologians in general have elected to participate in a cult which emphasizes only the otherworldly dimension of redemption.

In the last section of this chapter James Tyms shows that the Black understanding of redemption transcends the narrow limits placed around the term as used in white theology. Tyms is a Black scholar, but his conclusions are based upon the ideas of the masses of Black folks. It is important to note that the witness he brings in to support his claim is O. Clay Maxwell, a Baptist pastor, who was making a presidential address to the largest organized body of Black, lay religious workers in this country. This is the approach which will be used in order to analyze the understanding of redemption in Black theology.

The object of the next chapter is to outline the historical development of Black religion in America and to identify the manifestation of the redemption theme in Black theology. Redemption for Blacks means, as it does for the Hebrews, prosperity, posterity, and victory over oppressions, as well as salvation from sin and guilt.

3

Soul Looks Back and Wonders

How I got over
Oh, how I got over
My soul looks back and wonders
How I got over.

These lines from a song still heard in the Black church today give a clear indication that history plays a major role in the theology of Black people in America. From the day that the colonizers unloaded their first Black human cargo on the shores of Jamestown, Virginia, in 1619, Afro-American history was in the making. This involuntary importation of Black human beings into the mainland was to continue as a legal enterprise for the next two hundred years. Illegal smuggling of Blacks into this country continued for a number of years after the law went into effect outlawing the importation of slaves on January 1, 1808.

Historical Periods

In her book, *The Development of Negro Religion,* Ruby F. Johnston divided the development of Negro religion into three stages based upon what she referred to as shifts of interest in Negro

61

religion.[1] The first period she labeled "The Inceptional Stage." This period extends from the beginning of Negro religion in America to the Civil War. The first phase of this period was marked by supernaturalism, simple rudiments of Christianity, and emotionalism. The second phase of the first stage was marked by the rise of the Negro consciousness of race and efforts of Negro leaders to secure freedom of worship and freedom to *be* persons. Emphasis and objectives were directed and centered toward heaven. The second period of Johnston's scheme is called "The Developmental Stage." This stage begins with the Emancipation Proclamation and extends to World War I (from 1863 to about 1914). Steady growth and development with emphasis shifting from freedom toward civil and social rights and active participation in government and social life characterized this period. The heavenly elements were still central in Black religion, but somewhat diminished. The third period for Johnston was "The Transitional Stage." This stage begins in 1914 and continues to the writing of her book in 1945. Characteristic of this period, according to Johnston, is the tension arising as a result of both the decline and the struggle to return to emotionalism in Black religious practices. She also sees a wane in traditional religious attitudes and a transference of religion to this world. This was seen in the political activities of the Negro churches, the social activities, with emphasis upon recreation, and the Negro philosophies of American society as expressed in the church.

The third period outlined by Johnston comprised the main portion of her study, and throughout she was preoccupied with the degree and shifts of emotionalism in Black religion. This approach is helpful in tracing the shift in emotional expressions in Black religion, but it is totally inadequate for an understanding of the theology which undergirded any and all Black religious expressions. This is the problem of most studies of Black religion until recently. The researchers were so blinded by white stereotypes of Black religion that most studies dealt with whatever generally are considered to be the negative aspects of Black religion, for example, the emotional expressions. There is a need for an updated outline of the development of Black religion and a study which describes the positive aspects of Black religious thought and not just the emotional expressions.

The development of Black religion and Black theology which we discuss spans a period of one hundred years—from the end of the

Civil War to the present. But it is my position that the mold of Black theology had been cast during the half century from the end of the Civil War to the beginning of the Great Migration, about 1914. The dynamic theologizing which has taken place since the beginning of the Great Migration is only a matter of refining and restating the views of the founding fathers of Black religion.

Very little academic reflection from a Black theological perspective was permitted to make its way through the oppressors' resistance and through the printing presses in this land. The reason is simple: The oppressors owned and controlled all of the facilities and means of printing, production, and distribution. Even though today ownership, control, and access to the means of production and distribution of literature are in the hands of the oppressors or those who are the beneficiaries of oppression, Black publications saw an unprecedented upsurge in the sixties and early seventies. (Black publications are now in a waning period.) The first widespread Black literary reflections upon the Black experience took place during the 1920s and early 1930s, a period referred to as the Harlem Renaissance. It ended during the Great Depression. The second Black literary period had its beginning concurrent with the civil rights movement of the 1950s and is now in decline.

The literature of both periods, the Harlem Renaissance and the civil rights era, are reflections of the prevailing thoughts in the Black community. The redemption theme saturates all of the literature.

The century of Afro-American history covered in this investigation divides easily into five periods, namely: (1) the Formative Period—from the end of the Civil War through the era of Reconstruction, 1877; (2) the Maturation Period—after the era of Reconstruction to the beginning of the Great Migration, *ca.* 1914; (3) the Expansion-Renaissance Period—from the beginning of the Great Migration to the beginning of World War II; (4) the Passive Protest Period—World War II to 1955; (5) the Radical Reassertion Period—from 1955 to 1973.

Prior to the Formative Period lie two hundred years of Black presence in this land. Religiously this might properly be referred to as the Transitive Period for Blacks. Definitely it was not a period when the African slaves gave up their gods and religious beliefs and adopted those of the oppressors as has been erroneously taught and believed. The Transitive Period is a fascinating period which needs to be revisited and reinvestigated, and the religious adjustments in the lives of the slaves must be reinterpreted. Obviously this work cannot cover everything that was involved in the period. But a few things must be said in passing.

Transitive Period

An African scholar, Osadolor Imasogie, has concluded that the terms "animism," "fetishism," "polytheism," and "primitive monotheism" are inadequate as blanket terms in reference to African traditional religions. He concludes that despite the Western view that Africans believe in the embodiment of spirits in material objects, such as charms, amulets, and talisma, these objects only serve as a subordinate part of the African religious complex. He argues that "all religions which uphold the doctrine of sacramentalism" could logically be reduced to fetishism. The images on the African altars, he asserts, function as aids in worship in the same way that the icon and the crucifix function in the Christian churches.[2]

Polytheism would have to be ruled out as an adequate term to refer to African religions since polytheism, in reference to Greek, Babylonian, and Egyptian gods meant gods of equal status, with no Supreme God. This is not the case, he says, in traditional African religion.[3] Imasogie holds that whatever degree of differences there might be among African religious expressions, "a belief in the Supreme being remains the one golden thread running through the heart of their religious experience."[4] He quotes John S. Mbiti in defining the African notion of God as the Supreme Being: "He is self-sufficient, self-supporting, self-containing just as He is self-originating."[5] "Bureaucratic Monotheism" is the term which best describes the African traditional religion for Imasogie. It reflects the sociopolitical pattern of African societies and the cultural patterns of the people which are also expressed in their religious practices. In their sociopolitical experiences, their day-to-day dealings were generally with the local chiefs and ministers although the king had absolute power.

This new perspective challenges the old heathenistic, paganistic idea of the religious views of the imported slaves. The slaves did not have to give up their bureaucratic monotheism views in order to accept the Christian religion. On the one hand, they did not have to give up their Supreme Deity, who, like their cultural, tribal king, was generally inaccessible to the ordinary villagers and to the bushpeople. On the other hand, they could readily accept Jesus Christ as an intermediary in the bureaucratic hierarchy, since they already possessed a bureaucratic, hierarchical religious perspective into which he could be fitted.

The induction of the African slaves into Christianity was more a matter of religious transition and modification than it was a matter of a complete break with something old and useless and the acceptance of a religious way of life that was completely new and useful. In this process of religious transition and modification, the slaves retained much of their African modes and expressions. These modes and expressions were never appreciated or adopted by white Christians in America; thus, the Black religious style and expressions among the masses are different from those of whites.

One must remember that during this transitional period, Blacks had no opportunity to continue to practice their religion in the African tradition. In South America the slaves were grouped in large masses and were permitted to retain their drums and much of their material culture. This was not the case in North America. Slaves who spoke the same dialects were usually separated. The drums and percussion instruments were also denied to those slaves. Ortiz Walton tells us that because slaves in Trinidad, Haiti, and Jamaica were permitted to retain their percussion instruments, they also retained the African music and orientation. But "the enforcement of anti-drum laws in the United States made it necessary to transfer the function of the drum to the feet, hands and body by way of the Spirituals during the slave era and by way of instrumental music after the Civil War in the new form of black music called jazz."[6]

Another problem which hampered slave cohesion in North America was the fact that slaves were held on relatively small plantations when compared to those in South America. In the states of Alabama, Mississippi, Louisiana, and Arkansas the median slave holding did not reach twenty, and in the agricultural regions of Kentucky, Maryland, Missouri, North Carolina, South Carolina, and Tennessee, the median slave holding was even smaller.[7]

So the slaves had a difficult task, that of using their ingenuity to adapt themselves to the religion of their masters. They did, bringing to the situation their own religious perspectives and fashioning a new thing. The slaves were ingenious in that they could go through the motions which were necessary to please the masters while thinking and planning something different all the time. This is evident in the following lines:

> Got one mind for white folks to see
> 'Nother for what I know is me;
> He don't know, he don't know my mind,
> When he see me laughing
> Just laughing to keep from crying.[8]

I recall that once in 1966 a white person reminded me that his gardener, who was an elderly Black man, told him that he did not support or endorse the Black civil rights activities of the 1960s. Meeting with various groups in my political campaign for election to the Maryland House of Delegates that year, at one meeting I reported what this white man had told me. Another elderly Black gentleman interrupted my speech and said: "Reverend! I am a senior citizen, too, and I work for white people, too. I know what they ask us, and we tell them what they want to hear. But we want you young people to continue your protests; we stand with you."

Efforts to Christianize the slave took many forms. E. Franklin Frazier reports that "from the beginning of the importation of slaves into the colonies, [Blacks] received Christian baptism." There was initial opposition to Christianizing the slaves until "laws made it clear that slaves did not become free through the acceptance of the Christian faith and baptism."[9] Although the Anglicans were the first to attempt to Christianize the slaves, in the early 1970s there were still only approximately 80,000 Blacks in that denomination. The St. Thomas Episcopal Church, which was founded by Absalom Jones in 1794, was not accepted into the white Episcopal parent body until 1865. St. Thomas was still the largest of the twenty-eight predominantly Black Episcopal churches when it celebrated its 175th anniversary in April, 1969. Its original charter contained a "Black only" clause which was not changed until 1965.[10]

The Quakers were in the forefront in the battle against slavery. They worked largely among the free Blacks in the North. The Black population in the North constituted only about 10 percent of the nation's Black population prior to the Civil War. The Quakers made comparatively few lasting converts. One reason for the lack of attraction to the Quaker religion by Blacks might rest in the style of worship. The Congregationalists, concentrated largely in New England, were out of touch with the masses of Blacks and made few converts. The Presbyterians' work was in areas where Blacks were scattered and this had little effect.

Some of the impediments affecting the Christianization of the slaves were: First, they had to break with their traditional African style of religious expressions. Second, the spiritual state of whites was low. One should remember that it is not true that all of those who came to this country came in search of religious freedom as white history might have us believe. Many of them were the "scum" of the land of Europe. John Hope Franklin reminds us that when the supply of those who had indentured themselves for a period of years became insufficient, the Englishmen resorted to more desperate tactics. "They raided the prisons of England in search of workers." Then he quotes Benjamin Franklin as saying "dumped 'upon the New World . . . the outcasts of the Old.'" Out of their desperation came the "widespread practice of kidnapping children, women, and drunken men." Again John Hope Franklin draws from Eric Williams who indicated that the horrors experienced by these people "in the trip to the New World equaled those experienced by any group before or after." [11] (Note the reference is to the experience of capture and the "trip to the New World." It has already been pointed out that the Black experience in this land is equaled by no other race or ethnic group.) The fact of the matter is that there were whites among the enslavers who were of very low spiritual state.

A third impediment was a belief that to Christianize the slaves would unfit them for slavery. A fourth impediment was the inability of the slaves to read the English language. Fifth, there were not enough missionaries to minister to all of the slaves, and travel was difficult.

During the great revivals led primarily by the Presbyterians and the Congregationalists during the mid-eighteenth century, Christianity among the slaves did increase. However, the overwhelming number of Black converts went into the camps of the Baptists and Methodists. There is general agreement among scholars that the absence of strict liturgy among these two groups and the freedom of emotional expressions are the major factors which drew Blacks into those denominations. Later the Episcopal, Presbyterian, and Congregational churches were considered "high churches" while the Baptist and Methodist churches were considered "low churches," and Blacks who were members of either group disassociated themselves from the other. Louis Lomax quoted his grandfather, who was a Baptist firebrand of the late nineteenth and early twentieth centuries, as saying: "If you see a Negro who is not a Baptist or a Methodist, some white man has been tampering with his religion." [12] The

Transitive Period culminated with the slaves, who had been denied the opportunity to practice their native religion, moving largely into the camps of the Baptists and Methodists where they could retain some of their traditional style of expressions.

That the God whom they continued to serve now through the Christian faith would redeem them was an eternal hope. In the work of the Abolitionists they saw the hand of God at work. But in the edict of the United States Supreme Court in 1857 they felt the blows of oppressors who were determined to deter the process of redemption. Dred Scott, a slave who had lived with his master in free territory for a period, later sued for his freedom on the grounds that once living in free territory he ought to be henceforth free. The Supreme Court issued its decision in 1857. Chief Justice Roger B. Taney declared that the Constitution was made by whites for whites, and Blacks, whether free or slave, "had no rights which a white man was bound to respect." Redemption from these human-made edicts was and is the hope of Black Americans. The investigation of this redemption motif in the development of Black religion will be the object of the discussion in five periods outlined below:

The Formative Period: From the End of the Civil War Through the Reconstruction

Except in the few free Black churches in the North where only 10 percent of the Black population resided, Blacks had virtually no opportunity to organize any public religious institutions of their own. Of course they had their secret meetings in their camps at night where they worshiped God in their own style. But remembering that the plantations in the colonies had an average of twenty or less slaves, there was little opportunity for any widespread religious development in these camp meetings. The secret meetings did provide the opportunity for the slaves to formulate their secret codes so that they could communicate with each other during their work in the fields with other slaves from sunup to sundown. For example, the old spiritual

> Meeting tonight,
> Meeting tonight,
> Meeting on the old camp ground.

is now known to have been the secret code call to the community of field slaves to meet for secret worship and for the discussion of their plight of enslavement. They also planned many of their escapes in these secret meetings. Out of these camp meetings came the "invisible" Black churches of the South.[13]

There were three distinct modes of Black church membership during slavery, according to William L. Banks.[14] First was that of white churches with Black membership. This group consisted of the Blacks who attended the churches of their masters. These Blacks were not really welcomed as brothers and sisters in the Christian faith even though some masters permitted them to worship in the religious services. They were tolerated; their presence served as an opportunity for the masters to keep their eyes on the slaves to prevent them from using the time when the masters were in church as an opportunity for planning insurrections and revolts. In most instances the slaves were relegated to segregated sections of the churches.

The second type of Black church membership was that of Black congregations led by whites. The rise of cotton production and the rise in the importation of Blacks soon made it impractical to accommodate all of the Blacks in white churches. But there were strict Black codes. These Black codes were expressly designed to place restrictions on Blacks and to insure the maximum protection of the white population. They were designed to maintain discipline among the slaves. Some of the prohibitions were as follows. The slaves could not leave the plantations without permission. They could not possess firearms, and, in Mississippi, they could not beat drums or blow horns; they could not hire themselves out; they could not visit homes of whites or of free Blacks; they could not entertain such persons in their quarters, and they could not receive or transmit any incendiary literature.

They could not assemble themselves together for religious worship or for any other purpose without permission and without the prescribed number of white persons present.[15] Banks reports that in Mississippi in 1823 a law was passed making it "unlawful for six or more Negroes to meet for educational purposes. Meetings for religious purposes required the permission of the master. Even then a recognized white minister or two reputable whites had to be present." Then, in 1831, Delaware passed a law making it unlawful for more than twelve Blacks to assemble after 12 o'clock midnight unless three respectable white persons were present. The same law prohibited Negroes from calling any meeting for religious worship which had not been previously "authorized by a judge or justice of the peace upon the recommendation of five respectable white citizens." [16]

It was these kinds of laws which made the second type of Black church relationship—Black congregations with white leadership—more widespread than the other two types of Black church membership. The kind of teaching and preaching which took place in these settings was "servants, obey your masters" in intent and in content.

The third type of Black church membership was that of Black churches led by Blacks. These congregations were in the North. The first was the Bethel African Methodist Episcopal (AME) which was founded in 1794, by Bishop Richard Allen, who along with Absalom Jones was ushered out of the St. George Methodist Episcopal Church in Philadelphia in 1787 when they insisted on praying at the altar with all other members rather than going to the balcony which was reserved for Blacks. Allen's movement spread to Baltimore, Pittsburgh, and as far south as Charleston, South Carolina. In 1796, two years after Allen's organization of the AME Church in Philadelphia, Peter Williams, Sr., in New York, having had a similar experience to that of Allen, left the John Street Methodist Church and organized the African Methodist Episcopal Zion (AMEZ) Church in New York. The AMEZ also grew into a denomination and spread south. [17] It was the few free Black churches in the North which constituted the third group—Black churches led by Blacks without white overseers and/or observers. These churches were the vanguard of the Black churches which would be organized in subsequent years, particularly after the Civil War.

There were a few Black churches in the South led by Blacks prior to the Civil War, but they were under strict scrutiny and surveillance by whites. Thus in many of the Black churches led by Blacks the sermons had to be carefully worded so that the masters would not get the impression that the preachers were inciting the slaves to a belief in redemption in the here and now. But the record is clear; the Black slave preachers were ingenious in that they seized every opportunity to incorporate the redemption message into their sermons. And those sermons with reference to Moses and the Exodus were strictly designed to let the slaves know what God had done in history and will do again in the present and in the future. God will redeem them out of the hands of the Pharaohs of their day and bring them into a community of brotherhood. Excerpts from "An Ante-Bellum Sermon," in poetic form, by Paul Laurence Dunbar, follow:

We is gathahed hyeah, my brothahs,
  In dis howlin' wildaness,
Fu' to speak some words of comfo't
  To each othah in distress.
An' we chooses fu' ouah subjic'
  Dis—we'll 'splain it by an' by;
"An' de Lawd said, 'Moses, Moses,'
  An' de man said, 'Hyeah am I.'"

Now ole Pher'oh, down in Egypt,
  Was de wuss man evah bo'n
An' he had de Hebrew chillun
  Down dah wukin' in his co'n;
'Twell de Lawd got tiahed o' his foolin',
  An' sez he: "I'll let him know—
Look hyeah, Moses, go tell Pher'oh
  Fu' to let dem chillun go."

"An' ef he refuse to do it,
  I will make him rue de houah,
Fu' I'll empty down on Egypt
  All de vials of my powah."
Yes, he did—an' Pher'oh's ahmy
  Wasn't wuth a ha'f a dime;
Fu' de Lawd will he'p his chillun,
  You kin trust him evah time.

An' yo' enemies may 'sail you
  In de back an' in de front;
But de Lawd is all aroun' you,
  Fu' to ba' de battle's brunt.
Dey kin fo'ge yo' chains an' shackles
  F'om de mountains to de sea;
But de Lawd will sen' some Moses
  Fu' to set his chillun free.

An' de lan' shall hyeah his thundah,
  Lak a blas' f'om Gab'el's ho'n
Fu' de Lawd of hosts is mighty
  When he girds his ahmor on.
But fu' feah some one mistakes me,
  I will pause right hyeah to say,
Dat I'm still a-preachin' ancient,
  I ain't talkin' 'bout to-day.

But I tell you, fellah christuns,
  Things'll happen mighty strange;
Now, de Lawd done dis fu' Isrul,
  An' his ways don't nevah change,
An de love he showed to Isrul

Wasn't all on Isrul spent;
Now don't run an' tell yo' mastahs
Dat I's preachin' discontent.

'Cause I isn't; I'se a-judgin'
  Bible people by deir ac's;
I'se a-givin' you de Scriptuah,
I'se a-handin' you de fac's.
Cose old Pher'oh b'lieved in slav'ry,
  But de Lawd he let him see,
Dat de people he put bref in,—
  Evah mothah's son was free.

An' dah's others thinks lak Pher'oh,
But dey calls de Scriptuah liar,
Fu' de Bible says "a servant
  Is a-worthy of his hire."
An' you cain't git roun' nor thoo dat,
  An' you cain't git ovah it,
Fu' whatevah place you git in,
Dis hyeah Bible too'll fit.

So you see de Lawd's intention,
  Evah sence de worl' began
Was dat His almighty freedom
  Should belong to evah man,
But I think it would be bettah,
  Ef I'd pause agin to say,
Dat I'm talkin' 'bout ouah freedom
  In a Bibleistic way.

But de Moses is a-comin',
  An' he's comin', suah' and fas'
We kin hyeah his feet a-trompin,
  We kin hyeah his trumpit blas'.
But I want to wa'n you people,
  Don't you git too brigity;
An' don't you git to braggin'
  'Bout dese things, you wait an' see.

But when Moses wif his powah
  Comes an' sets us chillun free,
We will praise de gracious Mastah
  Dat has gin us liberty;
An' we'll shout ouah hallehuyahs,
  On dat mighty reck'nin' day
When we'se reco'nised ez citiz'—
  Huh uh! Chillun, let us pray! [18]

Even though Blacks were involved in churches in many ways prior to the Civil War, it was not until the end of the war that Black religion in America really became organized as an independent institution on a massive scale. The era of Reconstruction was also an era of a third Great Awakening—religious evangelism and revival. Blacks formulated a religious tradition which was transmitted orally from generation to generation.

The Black population in the United States in 1860 was 4,441,830, and by 1880, two decades later, it had reached 6,580,793.[19] This is an increase of approximately 48 percent. At the same time, the Black Christian population increased from about 300,000 to more than 900,000. This is at least a 200 percent increase.[20] There was a concerted evangelistic thrust among Blacks. It is true that with four million freed, Blacks were caught with no organized ministry to baptize their children, to perform their marriages, and to bury their dead, and thus they had to create a ministry out of the material which they had at hand. But the fact of the matter is they already had a cadre of underground preachers and ministers. The white folks were not aware of their existence, but they had been preaching and ministering to their people in secret camp meetings from sundown to sunup for years. It was now merely a matter of their coming from underground and assuming legitimate leadership. The new, openly affiliated Black members brought with them their African religious traditions which, although they had not remained intact, had not been so contaminated that they could not be revived in bits and incorporated into their oral Christian, religious thoughts and expressions.

What of the doctrines? The Black denominations adopted the doctrines of their white counterparts; i.e., the Black Baptists adopted the doctrines of the white Baptists and the Black Methodists adopted the doctrines of the white Methodists. But Blacks took these doctrines and made them their own in usage just as they were doing with the Old and the New Testaments. There was a tremendous and ingenious process of reinterpretation. The redemption theme replaced the "servants, obey your masters" as a point of departure throughout the Black churches. Black religionists have not written sets of new creeds and doctrines to this day. But the songs, prayers, sermons, and testimonies coming out of the oral Formative Period reflect a new interpretation of both Scriptures and denominational doctrines.

The Formative Period, then, was that era of Reconstruction

when the Black churches and denominations saw unparalleled formation and growth. It was that era when Black churches and denominations organized and supported all types and sorts of benevolent societies and enterprises. The Black church led the Black community in the area of political involvement. It sent a preacher, the Reverend Hiram Revels, as its first Black United States senator from Mississippi.

A real resemblance of Black Power existed during the Reconstruction era. From 1870 to 1901, twenty Blacks served in the Congress of the United States and two Blacks served in the Senate. In fact, Blacks served in the state legislatures of every southern state. In some states Blacks served as school superintendents, postmasters, state treasurers, state secretaries, and lieutenant governors. In Louisiana, P. B. S. Pinchback, a Black man, served as acting governor for a period. South Carolina was perhaps the only state with a majority of Black delegates to the constitutional convention. In 1872 all of the constitutional delegation to the United States Congress from South Carolina were Black men.[21] A reporter was describing the first South Carolina legislature of the Reconstruction era when he wrote:

> The Speaker is black, the Clerk is black, the doorkeepers are black, the little pages are black, the chairman of the Ways and Means is black and the Chaplain is coal black. At some of the desks sit colored men whose types it would be hard to find outside of the Congo.... It must be remembered also that these men, with not more than half a dozen exceptions, have been themselves slaves, and that their ancestors were slaves for generations.[22]

It is important to note that it was in this Formative Period that the Black church began to assert its own understanding of the Christian faith—its own theology. This Black theology has not been put down in writing, but one can hear it in the oral tradition of any mass Black church on a Sunday morning. It might be in the form of a song: "It's no secret what God will do, for what He has done for others He will do for you," meaning what God did in delivering the biblical characters from their earthly woes, he would also do for those who are inflicted with earthly woes today. It may come in a prayer: "Lord, I know that you are still pulling down mountains and elevating valleys." This redemptive understanding of the Christian faith was well formulated by the end of the Reconstruction era. The historical incidents of widespread oppression and segregation following the era of Reconstruction provided the necessity for the maturation of Black religion and Black theology in the succeeding period.

The Maturation Period: From the End of Reconstruction to the Beginning of the Great Migration, About 1914

The social, economic, and political events in the life of Blacks, from the end of Reconstruction to the beginning of the Great Migration, about 1914, forced the Black church into a period of maturation.

The aspiration of Rutherford B. Hayes to become president of the United States in 1876 compromised the Republican party's support for Black causes, and thus the Blacks received their most drastic setback in American history. Blacks were used as a political football. After the election of Hayes the state legislatures in every state of the Union passed laws stripping Blacks of rights they had gained during the era of Reconstruction. Civil Rights Acts were struck down by the Supreme Court. Jim Crow laws went into effect in many states. Federal troops were withdrawn from the South. The abolitionists lost interest in and/or effectiveness with the Blacks of the South. The Freedmen's Bureau became less and less effective. There was a loss of white missionary zeal and effectiveness. By the end of the century, Black politicians were virtually weeded out through various and devious means. And measures were taken to make sure that none got elected again. It was more than a half century later, in 1963, before another Black was elected in Georgia. Disfranchisement was effectuated through such measures as poll taxes, literary tests, previous voting records, grandfather clauses, and knowledge of the Constitution. What happened in Louisiana sums up what happened elsewhere: There were 130,334 Black registered voters in Louisiana in 1896; by 1904, that state had only 1,342 registered Black voters.[23] It might be interesting to note that it was in 1896 that the Supreme Court came out with its separate but equal decree which set a pattern of legal separation of the races for the next half century.

During this period the Black church stood fast; its growth and expansion did not keep pace with that of the Reconstruction era, but maturation took place. The Black church was about the task of refining its own interpretation and understanding of Scriptures and doctrines. It went about the task of refining its understanding of the revelation of God in the movement of Black history. The redemption theme which had been central in the prior era was still at the core of Black beliefs. Expressing the thought of the Black masses, in 1895, Paul Laurence Dunbar wrote:

We Wear the Mask

We wear the mask that grins the lies,
It hides our cheeks and shades our eyes—
This debt we pay to human guile;
With torn and bleeding hearts we smile,
And mouth with myriad subtleties.

Why should the world be overwise
In counting all our tears and sighs?
Nay, let them only see us while
        We wear the mask.

We smile, but, O great Christ, our cries
To Thee from tortured souls arise.
We sing, but oh the clay is vile
Beneath our feet, and long the mile;
But let the world dream otherwise,
        We wear the mask.[24]

To the oppressor, Blacks wear the mask, but they can tell Christ the truth because it was he who said that he came to set the prisoners—oppressed—free. Total segregation of the Black and white churches had been completed, and Blacks had become fully mature theologically. "By 1900," states Benjamin Quarles, "Christianity had divided along the color line even more markedly than ever before." He quotes W. E. B. Du Bois: "There may be in the South a black man belonging to a white church today. But if so, he must be very old and very feeble."[25]

Du Bois, writing in 1903, asserts that, at least in the South, "practically every American Negro is a church member. Some, to be sure, are not regularly enrolled, and a few do not habitually attend services; but, practically, a proscribed people must have a social centre, and that centre for this people is the Negro church."[26] Using the United States Census of 1890, he reports that there were nearly twenty-four thousand Negro churches in the country with an enrolled membership of more than two and a half million. There were ten enrolled church members for every twenty-eight Black persons. In some southern states, he reports, one in every two persons was an enrolled member. Again, he reports that a large number of the nonenrolled persons attended the churches and took part in the activities. "There is," declares Du Bois, "an organized Negro church for every sixty black families in the nation, and in some States [there is a Black church] for every forty families, owning, on an average, a thousand dollars' worth property each," for a total of nearly twenty-six million dollars. At that time there were a million and a half Black Baptists and nearly one million Black Methodists.[27]

It is clear that the Black church had reached full autonomy. It was virtually totally separated from the white churches. It surrounded and shaped every area of the Black life. During this period the Black church reached its theological maturation. And anything which happened in the Black church's theological understanding of redemption since its era of maturation is only a matter of shifts in emphasis. For example, during the period of Radical Reassertion there was greater emphasis upon this-worldly redemption than that which characterized the immediately preceding period, but redemption was always the core motif. During the following three periods the Black church built upon that unshakable religious foundation which was anchored in redemption.

The following statements are offered in support of this thesis. (1) By the end of the Maturation Period segregated Sabbaths were the prevailing practices for Blacks and whites. The Black denominations were autonomous. (2) Blacks had fully developed their modes and styles of worship which were not monolithic but in all variations highly tempered with African survivals. (3) Adaptations and reinterpretations of doctrines and Scriptures by Blacks were fully developed. (4) The songs, prayers, testimonies, and the orientation behind the sermons during the first two periods, though varying in some degree, served as a basis for Black religious expressions and application down through the years. They still serve as the basis of Black religion among the folk today. The variations are limited almost exclusively to the realm of grammatical structures and presentations. The redemption motif had now become the central factor in Black religion. And it is the theology—the Black religious thought—developed largely in the South during the Formative and the Maturative periods that the Black masses took to the North during the Great Migration.

The Expansion–Renaissance Period: From the Beginning of the Great Migration to the Beginning of World War II

The Black invisible church expanded from plantation to ghetto.

There are several reasons why this expansion took place. Blacks were pushed out of the South by the force of white hostility and inhumanity. By 1914 a combination of boll weevils and floods played havoc with the crops. So survival for Blacks in the South became more and more difficult. Blacks were pulled into the North by the rise of northern industries. World War I was in progress in Europe, and the United States was soon to become actively involved in the war. This gave rise to industrialization. Blacks were pulled into the North in search of better economic prospects, housing, and social living conditions.

During and shortly after World War I, report Meier and Rudwick, nearly a half million Blacks left the old South. The Black population in Chicago jumped from 44,000 to 110,000 between 1910 and 1920 while the Black population in Cleveland quadrupled, rising from 8,000 to 34,000 in numbers.[28] Gilbert Osofsky shows in his book, *Harlem: The Making of a Ghetto,* that the Black population of New York City grew 66 percent from 91,709 to 152,467 between 1910 and 1920; and it rose 115 percent from 152,467 to 327,706 from 1920 to 1930.[29] "There were more Negroes in the city in 1930 than the combined Negro population of Birmingham, Memphis and St. Louis." Osofsky quotes Rev. Dr. Adam Clayton Powell, Sr., as saying: "There was hardly a member of Abyssinian Church who could not count on one or more relatives among the new arrivals."[30] This era is properly called the era of the Great Migration. The exodus was of such magnitude that a Black minister declared in his sermon that the exodus and migration had been "inspired by Almighty God."[31]

It is evident that Blacks saw the whole movement as redemption in process. They could easily compare what was happening to them with the Exodus of the Hebrews. So, it was the hand of the Almighty God guiding them through the Exodus experience. However, unlike the Hebrews in the Moses story, upon arriving in the Promised Land—the North—it was not so promising after all. God did redeem them out of one land of bondage, but God did not bring them into a land flowing with milk and honey, not for Black people anyway. In the North, Blacks found themselves under the domination of New Pharaohs. They found themselves crammed into ghettos with very limited opportunities to earn a survival-living wage.

The established Black churches of the North could not absorb the flood of newcomers. Although many Black Baptist and Methodist churches expanded by leaps and bounds, there was still a lack of space to accommodate all of the newcomers. Then, too, the established Black churches of the North tended to be more ritualistic and formal in worship style than the mass Black churches of the South. Thus the newcomers were not at home in many of the Black churches of the North. This lack of space and tendency toward a more formal worship style on the part of the Black churches in the North gave rise to new Black sects, cults, and the storefront churches.

Appearing on the scene was Father Divine whose movement quickly amassed thousands of followers. The Daddy Grace Movement—the United House of Prayer for All People—came into focus. Then came also the Nation of Islam—the Black Muslims, the Black Jews, and a host of other groups. The religious views and practices of these groups, particularly the storefront variety of the Baptist and Holiness or Pentecostal denominations were, with little modification, a continuation of what they brought up from the South. A brief word might be said here about the Black Holiness or Pentecostal groups.

Joseph Washington holds that a "number of whites motivated by the hundreds of unconverted in the churches, and by the drastic decline in vital piety," which permeated the total society, created an alternative in the Holiness movement in 1867.[32] Some Blacks left independent Black denominations to join the Holiness movement, and others who were never converted by other evangelistic ventures were captured by the Holiness revivals. But overall, the number of Blacks going into the Holiness churches was small. The Holiness movement was not directed at Blacks and generally supported the Ku Klux Klan and other anti-Black organizations. "In some cases," says Washington, "the Holiness movement brought poor whites and blacks together in interracial fellowships." And having a membership drawn from the bottom rung of society, the Holiness sect would remain longer with Blacks because they would stay longer at the bottom of poverty.[33]

The marks of this group include an emotional experience at conversion, sanctification, the need to strive for perfection, fundamentalism in beliefs, strict puritan morality, and speaking in tongues as evidence of having the blessings of the Holy Ghost. Historically, Black Holiness or Pentecostalism had its beginning shortly after the dawn of the twentieth century. One Reverend Sister Lucy Farrow shared in a Pentecostal experience with the Reverend Charles Parham (white) in Topeka, Kansas, in 1901. She carried the

Pentecostal message to Houston, Texas, "paving the way for Parham to establish a short-lived, racially integrated Bible school there in 1905. . . . From Houston, it was a black preacher, W. J. Seymour, who took the message to Los Angeles." It was that movement in a storefront church on Azusa Street to which nearly every charismatic denomination must point when tracing its beginning. A Wesleyan body in Memphis heard of the Pentecostal movement in Los Angeles. It sent its overseer, C. H. Mason, to investigate. It is reported that Mason returned to Memphis speaking in tongues.[34] The body was reorganized as a Pentecostal denomination which was the birth of the Church of God in Christ.

As Blacks migrated North, Black religion expanded and was expressed in a variety of ways in a variety of church structures from storefronts to cathedrals. The bond which united them all was the redemption motif. All doctrines and expressions revolved around that single hub of redemption.

This era also saw the birth and development of several organizations including the Negro Business League, the NAACP, and the National Urban League. Hopefully, these would be organizations committed to the physical and social redemption of Blacks. Then came Marcus Garvey, born in Jamaica, West Indies, in 1887. He left the Wesleyan Methodist denominational school at the age of sixteen and worked as an apprentice in a printing plant. After discovering his ability to influence people, he used that skill as a political agitator to work for the rights of Blacks on the island. He attended London University from 1911 to 1914 and traveled over North Africa observing the social conditions. Returning to Jamaica, he organized the Jamaica Improvement Association. In 1916 he came to Harlem, traveled south, and later organized the Universal Negro Improvement Association, better known as the "Back to Africa Movement." In 1920 he claimed four million dues-paying members, and by 1923 he claimed six million members. Obviously he was doomed to fall into disfavor with the "system." Then, in 1923, he was convicted of using the mail to defraud, was sent to the federal penitentiary in Atlanta in 1925. In 1927 he was pardoned and left America.[35]

But during his sojourn on these shores Garvey lifted the redemptive vision of Blacks. The idea which stood behind the "Back to Africa Movement" was indeed a parallel to the "Back to Canaan Movement" in the Moses story. When Garvey founded the African

Orthodox Church, he again sounded the redemption note. In that church all of the angels were Black while Satan and all of his imps were white. The worshipers could glorify the "Black Man of Sorrows" and the "Black Virgin Mother," says Benjamin Quarles.[36] This arrangement of Black angels, white Satan, and white imps was designed to liberate the mind of the Black worshipers from the bondage of white purity and superiority and to bring Blacks into a state of self-respect and self-pride—the arrangement was redemptive in design.

While Black religion was expanding in the North during the Great Migration, something else was also happening. Although religion was not regarded as the point of departure, redemption was still the undergirding factor of this movement. It has been referred to as the era of "The New Negro," "The Black Renaissance," or "The Harlem Renaissance."

The Renaissance was generally a post–World War I movement which saw the expression of the Black folk's soul in the outpouring of creative literature, art, and music. The Renaissance was the articulation of the discontent of Black people in their situation of oppression and the condition of the ghetto. It was also a new approach on the part of Blacks who were seeking to liberate themselves from the shackles of oppression. Alain Leroy Locke, who is credited with being the midwife of the Renaissance movement, wrote in 1935:

> The intelligent Negro of today is resolved not to make discrimination an extenuation for his shortcomings in performance, individual or collective; he is trying to hold himself at par, neither inflated by sentimental allowances nor depreciated by current social discounts. For this he must know himself and be known for precisely what he is, and for that reason he welcomes the new scientific rather than the old sentimental interest. . . . Now we rejoice and pray to be delivered both from self pity and condescension.[37]

It is clear that Blacks were seeking to come into their own through the power of the pen. Quarles sees a kind of agreement on one canon among the Black writers of the Renaissance: "the use of dialect was taboo."[38] They were not objecting as much to the dialect tradition as to the literary and topical limitations it imposed. The writings about Blacks, generally done by whites heretofore, were saturated with stereotypes. Somehow Black writers felt that writing poetry, fiction, and prose in the best English tradition would hasten the day of redemption of Blacks and bring about some kind of equality among the races. The error in this dream was grounded in the fact that the white people's race pride and race prejudice had so distorted their minds that they would never come to accept the Black people on grounds of equality no matter how well Black people wrote literature or participated in any of the other cultural activities.

Paul Laurence Dunbar, the Black, pre-Renaissance poet, partly out of economic necessity and consideration, wrote in the Black dialect. And the outpouring of his works in Black dialect accounts for his rise to fame. It was true that the Black writers of the Renaissance came to face the stern realities that only through the use of the dialect could they reach the book-buying public which was primarily white. But generally they tried to stick to "standard" English as their point of departure. Jean Toomer's *Cane*, which is considered by many literary critics as the single best Black work of the Renaissance, sold only five hundred copies during its first year, according to the report of its publisher, Horace Liveright, in March, 1924.[39]

Claude McKay, Langston Hughes, and Countee Cullen were leading writers of Black poetry. Hughes' poem "Feet o' Jesus," written in Black dialect, sums up the redemptive mood of the poetic writers.

> At the feet o' Jesus,
> Sorrow like a sea.
> Lordy, let yo' mercy
> Come driftin' down on me.
>
> At the feet o' Jesus
> At yo' feet I stand.
> O, my little Jesus,
> Please reach out yo' hand. (1927)[40]

Jessie Faucet, Jean Toomer, and Rudolph Fisher led in the writing of Black novels in the twenties. Just the titles of two of Fisher's writings reveal the redemption theme which characterized the Black novels of the Renaissance. One is *The City of Refuge* and another is *The Walls of Jericho*.

The names of Willis Richardson, Charles Gilpin, Paul Robeson, and Roland Hayes are among the playwrights and entertainers. The list of those who contributed to the Renaissance in all aspects of Black culture goes on and on. Bessie Smith became a superstar singing the blues; W. E. B. Du Bois, the first Black Ph.D. of Harvard University, wrote extensively and served as editor of *Crisis* magazine;

Carter G. Woodson, another of the few Harvard Ph.D.'s of his time, was producing volume after volume on the subject "Negro" history.

The Renaissance was a definite step in the Black redemptive process; the wealth of Black literature gave rise to Black culture and Black pride. What the Renaissance failed to achieve was its objective of assuaging the furor of white racism. So the force which directed Blacks to participate with God in the process of their redemption from human-caused afflictions was still at work in the Black community.

While the activities of the Blacks during the Renaissance were done largely outside of the church, the views of the writers and participants were molded in or by the Black church, and the course they traveled was mapped in the Black church.

The Renaissance began to decline in the depression years of the 1930s, and there was not to be another rise in the production of Black literature until the period of Radical Reassertion, beginning in 1955. This also led to the period when the active involvement in the push for redemption became somewhat passive on the part of Blacks. Some of the reasons the era of Passive Protest emerged will be examined in the following section.

The Period of Passive Protest: World War II to 1955

In spite of the many points in which this investigator finds himself in disagreement with Joseph R. Washington, Jr., in his book *Black Religion,* Washington was correct when he said:

> Born in slavery, weaned in segregation and reared in discrimination, the religion of the Negro folk was chosen to bear roles of both protest and relief. Thus, the uniqueness of black religion is the racial bond which seeks to risk its life for the elusive but ultimate goal of freedom and equality by means of protest and action.[41]

Washington argued that Black religion is just a protest religion rooted in secularism. It is not authentic Christianity. This is a distorted view focused through the white frame of reference in this country. Black religion is authentically Christian religion. The situation of racism and all of its fallout brought redemption into the center of Black religion. Protest and action against oppression is of divine appointment. Beginning with Moses and following through the prophets and on through Jesus and his disciples, redemption, in its many facets, including protest and action, has been at the center of the Judeo-Christian religion. That aspect of the redemption theme which had to do with protest and action had been intentionally shunned by the oppressors and those who benefited from oppression for so long that Joseph Washington mistook protest and action as unauthentically Christian in his first major writing.

One should understand, however, that Washington was born, reared, and educated during the era of passive protest on the part of the Black church. This accounts for his misguided views of Black religion in his early writings. There is a radical shift in his views of the Black church and Black religion in his later writings. This is the result of the enlightenment which lighted the paths of all open minds during the period of Radical Reassertion, which is to be discussed later.

The degree of Black church leadership in the process of redemption varied from one period to another depending upon the social and economic conditions of the time and the degree of overt and covert hostilities against Blacks on the part of the oppressors. The two major factors which forced the decline of the Black Renaissance were (1) the national depression of the late 1920s and the 1930s and (2) the intense hostility on the part of white oppressors who themselves were suffering from the afflictions of the depression. Black suffering multiplied during the depression, and the Black church, the only institution controlled by Blacks, was forced to give more attention to the survival of the people than to their liberation. The churches were used as distribution centers for government food. The late Reverend L. A. Williams, who was pastor of a Black Baptist church in Baltimore during the depression, told me that in the 1930s his church was one of those distribution centers. Cornmeal, flour, grits, and peanut butter were among the products distributed. He related, with a bit of humor, that those who, for one reason or another, did not get their allotment during the week would "beat me to church on Sunday mornings to collect their allowance of food." One can understand, then, that the Black church, so preoccupied with human survival, could not at the same time carry out its aggressive opposition to oppression. It would have meant suicide for masses of Black folks. Blacks were not fools. They always knew that it is one thing to be a martyr for a cause, but it is another matter to commit suicide. The genius of Black survival in this country is inherent in the Black people's ability to shift to Passive Protest when active protest borders on suicide.

During the period of the Great Migration and the Renaissance, the Black church flourished and reached its peak of rapid growth in the North as it had done in the South during the Formative and Maturative Periods. In this period of Passive Protest the Black church levels off. It is preoccupied with human physical survival. Roosevelt came on the scene with his New Deal and massive public works programs. Blacks thanked God for sending President Roosevelt. World War II came, and with the rise of industrial productions Blacks were able to find more jobs and improve, to some degree, their economic conditions. While Roosevelt's Executive Order 8802 marked a turning point in job opportunities for Black folks, the primary reason for the Executive Order was to avoid the national shame of massive active protest against oppression on the part of Black folks in this country while she was at war with other nations. The Executive Order was issued to avoid what Robert H. Brisbane referred to as "The Original March on Washington."[42]

In the early stages of World War II the defense industries refused to hire any appreciable number of Blacks or to upgrade the few they did hire. A. Philip Randolph, then president of the Brotherhood of Sleeping Car Porters, led in the mobilizing of a protest movement called the "March on Washington." Brisbane puts it this way:

> In short order, buses were hired and special trains were chartered for a demonstration of fifty thousand people to take place in Washington on July 1, 1941. The Negro press and pulpit played its part in whipping up sentiment. Pullman porters carried the word to the Negro communities throughout the country. Mayor Fiorello LaGuardia and the President's wife pleaded, without success, with the Negro leaders to call off the movement. Just a few days before the critical date, Randolph and other leaders were called to Washington.[43]

They were demanding an executive order prohibiting discrimination. The first draft of the order by the president and some of his ranking cabinet members was rejected by the Black leaders because it did not include governmental agencies. Finally Executive Order 8802, which was acceptable to the Black leaders, was issued. This became the first such presidential action affecting Black people in this country since Lincoln's Emancipation Proclamation.[44] The "March" was called off, and the President's Committee on Fair Employment Practice was formed.

Two important points surfaced in the brief discussion of the Randolph/Roosevelt encounter. First, in this effort to redeem Black folks from economic oppression, the Black pulpit was actively involved. Secondly, the oppressors in this country have always had a way of controlling the degree of overt protest on the part of Black people. In this case, massive, overt Black protest was aborted by Executive Order 8802, which was a war edict and nothing more. In the Expansion-Renaissance Period, one will recall, the oppressors controlled the Black literary protest through their control of the printing presses and their selective buying of Black literature. Jean Toomer's *Cane,* referred to earlier in this chapter, sold only five hundred copies in the first year of its publication.

By the coming of the Korean War, Blacks had been in a state of virtual Passive Protest for a decade and a half. And just as they had erroneously thought that their achievements in the literary and artistic circles would have won for them respect in the total American community during the Black Renaissance, they had now come to believe that economic security would bring about a change in white attitude toward Blacks.

So some Blacks were so busy trying to achieve Black bourgeois status that there was not much active protest against the evils of oppression. Two lessons were learned from this bourgeois striving on the part of Blacks: (1) Proportionately, very few Blacks were able to make it through the pressures of white power to achieve real bourgeois status, even though many others lived in a make-believe world, as if they had achieved bourgeois status. (2) Those who had achieved bourgeois status and those who made believe that they had achieved some found out that, in racist America, they were still just "a Negro" or "a colored person" or "a nigger," depending upon who was making the reference, which really means a Black person is not equal in personhood to a white person. So the need for redemption was still the ultimate concern. And the expression of that concern took a new turn in 1955.

The Period of Radical Reassertion: 1955 to 1973

The Black church has withstood many damaging indictments. Such indictments have accused the Black church of being too opiate or too militant, too spiritual or too secularist, too emotional or too ritualistic.

But whatever the accusations, the Black church has been the center of redemption for the dispossessed. During the civil rights and Black Power movements the Black church has been accused at once of being both too opiate and too militant. But a sober look at the facts is revealing.

It was largely the members of the militant student camp who charged the Black church with being an opiate institution. They argued that the Black church was an instrument in the hands of the white oppressors designed to keep Black people under the control of whites, hiding behind religion as a shield. The fact of the matter was that those students were more concerned with recognition than with reason. And one can agree that there is not much room for reason when one is at the bottom in every walk of life. In such a state it is time for revolution. But again there must be some distinctions between conducting a revolution and committing suicide.

Those young people, in the main, had just arrived on the campuses. They had their certifications in the experience of segregation and discrimination. But having been born in the era of Passive Protest, they had little knowledge of the active protest which was intertwined in the history of the Black church. They did not know that the note sounded by the Reverend Highland Garnet at the National Convention of Colored Citizens held in Buffalo, New York, in 1843 had been a constant factor in the Black church. Quotations from this address which he wanted sent to all slaves in the United States follows:

"Let us view this demon, which the people here worshipped as a God. Come forth, thou grim monster, that thou mayest be critically examined! There he stands. Behold him, one and all. His work is to chattelize man; to hold property in human beings. Great God! I would as soon attempt to enslave Gabriel or Michael as to enslave a man made in the image of God, and for whom Christ died. Slavery is snatching man from the high place to which he was lifted by the hand of God, and dragging him down to the level of the brute creation, where he is made to be the companion of the horse and the fellow of the ox. . . . Our poor and forlorn brother whom thou hast labelled 'slave,' is also a man. He may be unfortunate, weak, helpless, and despised, and hated nevertheless he is a man. His God and thine has stamped on his forehead his title to his inalienable rights in characters that can be read by intelligent beings. Pitiless storms of outrage may have beaten upon his defenseless head and he may have descended through ages of oppression, yet he is a man. God made him such, and his brother cannot unmake him."[45]

This idea advanced by the Reverend Garnet has been evident in rhythmic fashion throughout Black church history. And Black people were now ready to follow Martin Luther King, Jr., in radically reasserting the redemption of themselves in a nonviolent manner.

While young Blacks were accusing the Black church of being too passive during the early part of the civil rights movement, white segregationists were charging the Black church with giving leadership to the new uprising and resistance on the part of Blacks. Whites expressed their belief that the Black church was at the center of this new revolution by bombing and burning Black churches across the southland.

The students were wrong about the Black church being a kind of opiate of the people. The white segregationists were correct in one point, that is, in their belief that the Black church would be the enduring and leading institution in the new revolution. History has now proved them correct. The role of the Black church in the civil rights movement is so well known that it need not be repeated. But a few events might be mentioned in passing.

When Rosa Parks was arrested on Thursday, December 1, 1955, for sitting on a bus in a seat reserved for "whites only" in Montgomery, Alabama, it was the Black church which took the lead in the following successful bus boycott. At a meeting on Friday evening, December 2, the clergymen were the ones who promised to take to their pulpits on the following Sunday morning the request to call upon seventeen thousand Blacks to stay off the buses on Monday morning. Martin Luther King, Jr., assumed leadership in the task of mimeographing and distributing printed materials to the fifty thousand Black citizens of Montgomery. When the buses moved through the Black section of Montgomery on Monday morning, they were empty.[46] The Southern Christian Leadership Conference (SCLC) was born out of this event. This was largely a Black church movement. Many other civil rights groups sprang up during this period; they served nobly and valiantly. They played great roles in bringing down many of the "walls of Jericho"—segregation. But many of them have faded away. Today SCLC stands as one of the viable organizations which was born in the period of Radical Reassertion. Two other viable organizations emerging out of this period are (1) "People United to Save Humanity" (PUSH), led by the Reverend Jessie L. Jackson, and (2) Opportunities Industrialization Center (OIC), led by the Reverend Leon Sullivan. Both of these organizations of redemption are led by Black clergymen, who, incidently, happen to be Baptist preachers. This indicates the degree of commitment of the Black church to all areas of human redemption. (The NAACP, which is still the strongest civil rights organization today, had its beginning long before the coming of the organizations developed during the Radical Reassertion era).

The Black church provided financial undergirding for many of the civil rights organizations. The Black church provided meeting, eating, and sleeping accommodations for civil rights workers. The civil rights workers from every walk of life borrowed the songs of the Black church to drive away the evils of humiliation and the burdens of exhaustion. The theme song "We Shall Overcome" had been lifting the broken spirits of Blacks long before the coming of the civil rights movement. It is a theme song about Black redemption. The "pray-ins" originated not with the civil rights movement, but with Richard Allen back in 1787. That pray-in was the genesis out of which the African Methodist Episcopal (AME) Church evolved.

There is no doubt about it, the folk, the masses in the Black churches, saw the events of the civil rights era—the Radical Reassertion Period—as the redeeming acts of God in history. The statement of one Black woman in Montgomery is typical of Black understanding of God as Redeemer from human-caused oppression. Robert Carter, legal counsel for the NAACP, argued the case against segregated seating in the Federal District Court in Montgomery; and on June 6, 1956, the court ruled in favor of the plaintiff and against segregated seating on municipal buses. Four months later, the Supreme Court of the United States upheld the district court's decision. Thus, segregated seating on buses in Montgomery came to an end. Louis Lomax reports that one woman was heard to say: "Praise the Lord, God has spoke from Washington, D.C."[47] This is the redemption hope from the lips of one from among the masses.

The fourth line of a familiar hymn sums up the black theme of redemption:

E'er since by faith I saw the stream,
   Thy flowing wounds supply,
Redeeming love has been my theme,
   And shall be till I die;
And shall be till I die,
   And shall be till I die;
Redeeming love has been my theme
   And shall be till I die.[48]

Even though this hymn had its genesis in the white religious tradition, Blacks have adopted it and reinterpreted it because of its redemptive message to those in bondage.

Black Theology in Historical Perspective

Africans have always been a religious people. They did have an idea of a supreme deity—the "Pure King"—which was expressed in varying degrees depending upon the variations in tribes and clans. Upon being brought to this country the Africans went through a period of religious transition. Jesus Christ, the Holy Spirit, the angels, and the devil in Christianity replaced some of the lesser deities and intermediaries in their traditional African religions.

Blacks made virtually no progress in the establishment of independent Black churches in the South prior to the Civil War. But there were a few Black churches in the North, where less than 10 percent of the Black population lived, prior to the Civil War. After the Civil War, independent Black churches and denominations sprang up and grew by leaps and bounds all over the southland. The history of the formation and the maturation of these Black churches and denominations over the half century following the Civil War is the source for the research into the development of Black theology. What happened in the transmission and further refinement of Black theology in the succeeding periods of Black history is in direct proportion to the norm of Black theology—the situation and degree of racism and oppression. In all cases redemption has been at the heart of Black theology.

The object of the following chapter is to examine the relationship between the concepts of humankind and redemption in Black thought.

4

Poor Pilgrims of Sorrow

"O! that there might be breathed anew in the nostrils of the Negro that primeval breath of Godhood. The Negro must believe that he is the Son of God and heir and joint heir to the divine patrimony. The rights of humanity are inalienable, of which no human creature can be divested by reason of race, color, condition, creed, or clime. Although recognition may be withheld and privileges denied for the while, they can never be effaced or taken away."[1]

Black people are indeed a pilgrim people who are inflicted with human-caused sorrows. But Kelly Miller, author of the above statement, is clear in his ideas about the Negroes. They are the "Sons of God." They are heirs to divine patrimony and their rights of humanity are inalienable. Recognition of these rights are indeed withheld and privileges are denied, but they can never be ultimately taken away because the Redeemer is against oppression. In this chapter we shall explore the understanding of the human-Redeemer relationship in Black theology. It seems that Black theology moves from man/woman to God rather than moving from God to humankind.

Humankind to God Theology

Beginning with humankind and moving to God is the proper procedure for Black theology since the norm for Black theology is shaped by Black people's situation of oppression. The temporal process of history is the place in which Black people find themselves. It is also the place where Black people meet God working out the revelation of himself as the Alpha and Omega. In doing theology, spiritually and/or philosophically, one might start with God. But Black theology is akin to practical theology. It is not a matter of philosophical propositions. J. Deotis Roberts, Sr., is correct when he declares that "It is possible for theology to begin with man and move to God."[2] James Cone is also right when he raises the rhetorical question in his latest book, *God of the Oppressed:* "What difference does it make if one should 'prove' a philosophical point, if that point has nothing to do with the spreading of freedom throughout the land?"[3]   •

The theology arising out of Black religion has an abiding propensity toward existentialism. Training for reconnaissance in the United States Army, members of the company were told that, if any of them became lost while on a mission, the first thing to do was to try to determine where he was—his existing location—before attempting to figure out where he ought to go. This holds true for Blacks in their expression of the Christian faith. Before one can look up to God, back to creation, or forward to last things, one must have some idea of who one is. When I mentioned this approach to a fellow student during my seminary days, he replied: "Before I become concerned with who I am, I must first be concerned about the source of my being." One can sympathize with this spiritual and philosophical approach. But who is this "I" in his statement? He admits the "I" before God—the source of his being.

Nels Ferré in deciding where to start in the development of a Christology concludes that one should not start with human experience because human limitations and self-centeredness may distort the truth which one perceives. Thus, what one discerns as truth may not be truth at all. He further concludes that "Only Christ himself as the truth, illuminating, judging and fulfilling all other truths, can be the adequate starting point methodologically for Christology."[4] Again philosophically this methodology is adequate, but practically it is a person who is doing the christological development and one cannot escape bringing self, culture, and human limitations to the situation even when one takes the leap and starts with Christ. The Christian existentialist approach evolving out of the works of Pascal and Kierkegaard is the methodological way to the development of a Black theology. Bernard Ramm summarizes the existential approach this way:

> The fundamental thesis of existentialism is that existence is prior to essence. This thesis means that my personal existence, my problem of being, my concern with my selfhood, my situation in the world is prior to and more fundamental than any theory about the world or reality. Man cannot begin with a theory of reality, a metaphysics or ontology; he can begin only where he is, as a human being in the midst of all the contingencies of human existence. To attempt to begin anywhere else is to attempt the fantastic.[5]

It is out of this concept and background that I proceed with the examination and description of Black theology beginning with humankind.

Humankind As Fallen Creature

Ontologically, humankind in Black theology are beings who have an heir-like relationship with the Being who lets them be. People are pilgrims experiencing states and circumstances which are designed to press them into nonbeings. But the Being who permitted people to be in the first place is also active in history, redeeming humanity from those states and circumstances which are designed to destroy the value of human existence and from those things which are designed to destroy human existence itself.

Black people came out of an African background which is ontologically anthropocentric. African scholar John S. Mbiti makes the following declaration:

> . . . African ontology is basically anthropocentric: man is at the very center of existence, and African peoples see everything else in its relation to this central position of man. God is the explanation of man's origin and sustenance: it is as if God exists for the sake of man. The spirits are ontologically in the mode between God and man: they describe or explain the destiny of man after physical life.[6]

A close examination of Black religious expressions will reveal that there is an element of this mode of African belief surviving in Black religion in America. It does seem as if God exists for the sake of persons. Philosophically and theologically, for Christians, God is the Alpha and Omega; he exists over and above humankind; he is self-existing and does not need human beings in order to be. But the revelation of himself at the highest point in his Son strongly suggests that, not his existence, but the revelation of himself is for humanity. John makes this declaration when he says: "For God so loved the world that he gave his only Son, that whoever believes in him should not perish but have eternal life" (John 3:16).

In the "We Shall Overcome" theme song of the civil rights movement, which was borrowed from the Black church, there is a line which says:

God is on our side,
God is on our side,
Down in my heart
I do believe
We shall overcome some day.

The very title of Cone's last book, *God of the Oppressed,* is suggestive of his position concerning the importance of people, particularly the oppressed, in the eyes of God. J. Deotis Roberts, Sr., attempts to combine the ontological and the existential into a dual construct in his interpretation of the Black experience. "Existentialism," he declares, "is an introspective humanism or a theory of man which expresses the individual's intense awareness of his contingency and freedom."[7] Roberts further asserts:

> Whereas existentialism is preoccupied with meaning, ontology is concerned about reality. Through their ability to survive under conditions which would have driven most whites to insanity or suicide, Blacks have indicated the ontological basis of their experience. In spite of everything, we have touched base with the realities of our existence.[8]

He concludes that "our reflection is based upon the realities of our existence. It is ontological-existential reflection. Black thinking is always practical."[9] Roberts is correct on this point, but the point ought to be carried a step further. While Blacks were existentially trying to make sense out of their experience and were ontologically touching base with the realities of their existence, there was another dimension to this drama. Black religionists were certain that the Being who lets them be was concerned about their redemption and indeed was in the process of redeeming them. The meaning of their existential situation and their very being were bound up with the Being of creation and redemption.

Blacks knew that they were made in the image of God, and God was in the process of redeeming them. Lines from a gospel song disclose this awareness:

> I've heard the story of David
>   I've heard of Daniel in the lion's den,
> I've heard of Job with his affliction,
>   how they all kept the faith to the end;
> And when all hope had seemed to fail,
>   God's power did prevail
> I know, I know prayer changes things.[10]

Humankind is made in the image of God which means that they are related to God in a way in which no other being is related to God. Blacks assert this in another familiar song, "He Knows How Much We Can Bear."

> We are our Heavenly Father's children
> And we all know that He loves us one and all.
> Yet there are times when we find we answer, Another's voice and
> call; If we are willing, He will teach us,
> His voice only to obey no matter where, and He knows.
> Yes, He knows just how much we can bear.

> ### CHORUS
> Tho' the load get heavy
> You're never left alone to bear it all.
> Ask for the strength and keep on toiling
> Tho' the tear drops fall.
> You have the joy of this assurance,
> The heavenly Father will always answer prayer, and
> He knows, yes, He knows just how much you can bear.

The fundamental relationship to God is one of father-children relationship, as revealed in the song above. D. M. Baillie came to a very similar conclusion in a refined theological statement:

> The "sacred story" begins with God's eternal purpose for man, as faith perceives it. His eternal purpose was that mankind should be "one body," with the unity of a perfect organism: a higher kind of organism, indeed, than any that we know. . . , a free and harmonious fellowship of persons united in the love of God. . . . the true life of mankind is found in the corporate enjoyment of God, a life of complete community with God and man. That is true human nature, created in the image of God. That is God's plan for mankind: that it should be "one body."
>
> But something has gone wrong. The organism has somehow failed to function as one body.[11]

Exercising their freedom, people elected not to maintain a right relationship with the Creator. They appropriated to themselves authorities which ought to have been the dominion of God, the

Creator. This caused a broken relationship which only could be understood mythically. It is something which is suprahistorical, inflicting all our history. The understanding of the "Fall" can be examined only from what Black religion has to say about humanity in need of redemption. There is no logical explanation of the "Fall" in Black religious expressions. Black theologizing begins from a point of humanity in need of redemption.

Personally, I have concluded that I cannot accept the story of the "Fall" in a literal sense. Neither do I believe that sin is passed on in the genes from one generation to another. This would make all responsible for the sin of one, which seems difficult to justify theologically. This would negate individual human dignity. The "Fall" story, then, must be mythically descriptive of fallen human nature evolving out of the risk of freedom which the Creator voluntarily bestowed upon human beings in creation. This would make every person the Adam of his or her own soul—every person is thus created with freedom and responsibility.

Humankind is neither inherently good nor inherently evil. Every person has potentials for good and potentials for evil. There are many arguments on the subject. I hold that the "Fall" story is a mythical genesis of fallen human nature. The story derives from the misuse of human freedom. Therefore, the image of God in humanity was distorted and sets all of humanity in the midst of a struggle between good and evil. However, despite the fallen human nature, people are left with sufficient grace which, if responsibly appropriated, will evoke efficacious grace through which they can be saved. Dr. Martin Luther King, Jr., puts it this way:

> Man is no helpless invalid left in a valley of total depravity until God pulls him out. Man is rather an upstanding human being whose vision has been impaired by the cataracts of sin and whose soul has been weakened by the virus of pride, but there is sufficient vision left for him to lift his eyes unto the hills, and there remains enough of God's image for him to turn his weak and sin-battered life toward the Great Physician, the curer of the ravages of sin.[12]

God and people belong together since people are the crown of God's creation. This is evident in the fact that even though there were fallen angels, God made no provision for their redemption. But God did provide for human redemption. People were intended to be in a unique relationship with the Creator. This was spoiled by the misuse of freedom on the part of the created. God willed to be the *go'el* and to make provisions whereby this creature could be restored to the previous relationship. Here, God is the *go'el*. He is the Father; he is the next of kin, who redeems his children from their fallen or spoiled state. Since he is Lord of the universe, the notion of payment or its equivalent is not involved, because everything belongs to the Father. There is no doubt about it; in Black religious thought, "we are our heavenly Father's children," as declared in the folk song quoted earlier, even though we are fallen creatures and sinners before our Maker. But God is redeeming the fallen.

Sinners Before God

Wine, women, and whiskey were sinful involvements, according to the teachings of the white masters. Movies, card-playing, and dancing were also religious taboos for Blacks, according to the white masters. These prohibitions did serve to minimize all possibilities of Blacks coming together for social events which might provide the opportunity for them to plan rebellions against the oppressors.

Prohibitions against wine, women, and whiskey coming out of the European puritanical mold, intentionally or unintentionally, became effective weapons in the hands of white racists in the battle of oppression against Blacks. This was social morality based upon white mores. Lying, lynching, lust, and exploitation of the dispossessed on the part of white power were overlooked as sins by the oppressors and those who benefited from Black oppressions, including some white preachers and theologians.

In Black theology sin is understood to be the fallout of the initial distortion of human nature—the sordid relationship between Being (the Creator) and being (the creature)—when beings attempted to appropriate for themselves elements of the domain which Being reserved for Himself. ". . . 'You will not die. For God knows that when you eat it your eyes will be opened, and you will be like God, knowing good and evil'" (Genesis 3:4-5). So the original distortion of human nature and the relationship with God evolved from human gullibility and lust to put oneself in the place of or to be equal to God. This is the sin of humankind down through the ages. The lust for omnipotence which the Creator has reserved for himself is the sin of humanity.

In his wise providence God did not make people to be puppets. He blessed them with dignity and allowed them the freedom to venture out on such a suicide mission but not before warning them of the consequence: "but of the tree of the knowledge of good and evil you shall not eat, for the day that you eat of it you shall die" (Genesis 2:17). Both Roberts and Cone view sin as estrangement of people from the source of being. Roberts sees sin as both vertical and horizontal estrangement. The former is a broken relationship with God; the latter is estrangment from one's brother. [13] Cone says, "Sin is living a lie, that is, trying to be what we are not." [14] But Cone goes further; sin for him is to deny the values that make a community what it is. It means living in accordance to one's own private interest and not in accordance with the goals of the community. [15] He is reflecting upon sin from both the white and the Black perspective. He is correct when he writes that sin is a theoretical idea and not a concrete reality in white theology. But he might have overlooked some white theologians when he said that no white theologian has been able to relate sin to the Black/white encounter in America. [16] There are a few white theologians who have addressed themselves to the matter of sin in the Black/white encounter. [17] Again Cone writes, "In a word, sin is whiteness—white people's desire to be God in human relations." [18] This seems to be a just indictment against many whites. Experiences have taught Black folks that many whites do desire to play God in human relations with people of other races in America. Observations have also taught Blacks that some white people desire to be God in their relations with other people of the world.

Cone's reference to sin from the Black perspective presents some problems. He makes this declaration:

> Because sin is a concept that is meaningful only for an oppressed community as it reflects upon its liberation, it is not possible to make a universal analysis that is meaningful for both black and white people. Black Theology believes that the true nature of sin is perceived only in the moment of oppression and liberation. [19]

If he means that it is impossible to make a universal analysis of sin that is meaningful for both Blacks and whites on the basis of what most white theologians have done in their theoretical approach to sin which negated Black reality, he is correct. On the other hand, his own statement that "Sin is living a lie, that is, trying to be what we are not" is quite universal. This definition of sin encompasses both Blacks and whites. There are Black sinners and white sinners—those who play God in their relationship to other human beings. And I make no apologies for the sins of Blacks. But Blacks are not guilty of the sin of oppression as a people. In Black religious expressions there is acknowledgment of sin. It is evident in this spiritual:

Somebody's knocking at your door,
Somebody's knocking at your door;
O sinner, why don't you answer?
Somebody's knocking at your door.

Here, Blacks do have a sense of sin in the Black community. Cone's view, in the quote above, that the true nature of sin in Black theology is perceived only in the moment of oppression and liberation and his further claim that sin is inseparable from revelation which takes place in the moment of liberation from oppression forces him to the conclusion that knowledge of the sinful condition cannot be achieved except in the movement of an oppressed people claiming their freedom. One will concede that the true nature of the sin of the oppressor was perceived by Blacks in the moment of oppression and liberation. But Cone goes too far in his claim that sin is inseparable from revelation and that there can be no knowledge of sinful condition except in the movement of an oppressed people claiming their freedom. Sin—trying to be what one is not—is sin whether it is understood as sin by the sinner or not. It may or may not be bound up with revelation. Cone's conclusion, then, that there can be no knowledge of the sinful condition except in the movement of an oppressed people claiming their freedom must be restated. All that one can say is that the public awareness of the sin of oppression has come about primarily in the moment of liberation from oppression. That this is the only way to knowledge about sin is still an open question.

Black religion confirms a universal understanding of sin—it is the estrangement from the Source of one's being and the appropriation of privileges to one's self which belong only to the Source of one's being. The symptoms of the sins of the oppressors in this country are evident in racism and bigotry—white power or overlords in their human relationship with nonwhites, denying them their humanity. They also commit the sin of exploitation and misuse of God-given natural resources. The sins of Blacks are expressed symptomatically first in the Black people's capitulation to white power and their attempt to become what they are not—like white folk—assuming their socioreligious standards and customs of morality which, in most respects, do not affirm the being of Black folks. The second symptom of Black people's sins is their attempt to become lord in their relationship with other Black brothers and sisters. The third symptom arises out of their failure to participate in God's redemptive movement. In order to come into the Promised Land, the Israelites of Egyptian bondage had to participate in a struggle against the forces they encountered in their wilderness journey. In many instances they were chided by Moses for their complacency. God expects Black people to be active participants in the struggle for their own redemption from human-caused states and circumstances. Black theology assumes that all persons are sinners before God and stand in need of redemption. The redeemed people are God's chosen people. In the situation of racism and oppression in America, the chosen people also happen to be suffering servants.

Chosen People and Suffering Servants

To be sure, neither from Old Testament nor from Black religious expressions is there anything close to conclusive evidence that "suffering servants" are tantamount to "chosen people." Suffering people might happen to be the chosen people of God, or the chosen people of God historically have experienced suffering. This does not mean, however, that chosenness and suffering or the converse must of necessity follow each other in an eternal nonvariable sequence. Historically, peoples of every nation have experienced suffering, but the peoples of every nation can make no claim to be chosen people of God.

This is not to say that Blacks are not chosen people of God; they might well be. The assertion is that the reason given for the conclusion that Blacks are chosen people is not valid. The title of one of Albert Cleage's sermons in *The Black Messiah* is "We Are God's Chosen People." Throughout the sermon he makes his case for chosenness on the part of Black people on the basis of suffering. He points out that the Babylonians required of the Israelites a song "just as today in the Gentile nightclubs they say, 'You black people have such a talent for singing. Sing us your spirituals.'" Then he remembers seeing the Clara Ward Gospel Singers on television entertaining in a Las Vegas nightclub. He declares: "They were singing the very songs which our people sang in their suffering and misery, while the white folks laughed." [20]

Joseph Washington, Jr., also makes a correlation between chosenness and suffering among Blacks in America. Declaring that the "Negroes do not perceive themselves as the people chosen by God to be His suffering servants for the 'transgression' of all God's people in America, if not elsewhere. . . ," he proceeds to say:

Precisely because the Negro has not called his people "chosen," it is in keeping with the faith and Negro Spirituals to perceive them as chosen. The idea of "chosen" is a religious interpretation of a people's experience. Indeed, Negroes would not wish to be called—and would actively resist being—the "chosen people" were they consciously to understand and accept the biblical meaning of being chosen by God: inflicted, stricken, grieved, chastised, an offering poured out as "intercession for the transgressors." But just as they have neither known nor accepted it, this is their history. For it is through their experience that the presence of God in all our midst can be affirmed. Through their suffering "we are healed"—black and white together.[21]

This is a long quote, but it was necessary to quote the whole statement in order to get the full impact of Washington's thought. There is no question about it; Washington is linking the chosenness to the suffering as if they of eternal necessity belong together. An examination of the election of Abram and his descendants shows that there is no indication of suffering as a necessary complement to his chosenness:

Now the Lord said to Abram, "Go from your country and your kindred and your father's house to the land that I will show you. And I will make of you a great nation, and I will bless you, and make your name great, so that you will be a blessing. I will bless those who bless you, and him who curses you I will curse; and by you all the families of the earth shall bless themselves" (Genesis 12:1-3).

Neither was there any indication of necessary suffering in the statement of the election of Isaac. The Lord said to Isaac:

"Sojourn in this land, and I will be with you, and will bless you; for to you and to your descendants I will give all these lands, and I will fulfil the oath which I swore to Abraham your father. I will multiply your descendants as the stars of heaven, and will give to your descendants all these lands; and by your descendants all the nations of the earth shall bless themselves" (Genesis 26:3-4).

Major Jones points out that basic to the struggle of Black people to liberate themselves from their oppressors is the "age-old idea of God's chosen people. This idea," he states, "has occurred among many peoples, both privileged and oppressed, in quite different ways and for many different reasons," from the Old Testament times to now. So, since Black awareness has picked up this hope, he sees the task of current Black theologians as that of interpreting "such a hope from a black theological frame of reference."[22] Jones makes the right appeal, but his brief attention to the matter of chosen people and suffering servants seems to suggest an inevitable linkage.

"One needs to be aware of the perils as well as the promises of the idea of a chosen people," declares Roberts.[23] He believes that the "promises outweigh the difficulties." Real questions are raised in his mind, he says, whenever the suggestion is made that perhaps the clue to the Black person's chosenness is suffering. This led him to the crucial question which is also the crucial question for me: "Is it necessary that such oppression and undeserved suffering continue in order that grace may abound?"[24] James Cone seems to be saying "yes" to that crucial question. He says that Israel's election is a real call to share in Yahweh's liberation, which is not a position of privilege but a terrible responsibility. To participate in Yahweh's liberation means suffering, because liberation means a confrontation between evil and the will of the One who directs history.

Cone proceeds to suggest that "the existence of Jesus Christ also discloses that freedom is bound up with suffering. It is not possible to be for him and not realize that one has chosen an existence in suffering."[25] He defends this statement with a statement of Jesus: "Blessed are you when men revile you and persecute you . . . falsely on my account" (Matthew 5:11). But there is a question as to whether the persecution which Blacks have undergone in this country was on account of their allegiance to Jesus Christ. If the answer is "no," then Cone might have misused this passage in support of his views of necessary perpetual suffering on the part of Blacks in order for them to be numbered among the free—the chosen people of God. If freedom is bound up with suffering, the question which arises is: "Why are white people free?"

Roberts is correct; our suspicion is aroused by the fact that the affirmative attitude toward human suffering comes from the side of the oppressor and not from the oppressed themselves. So whatever understanding of our chosenness emerges in a Black theology must take into serious account the fact that the experience of Black people has been purged in the fires of suffering. But at the same time chosenness must hold up the promise of a better day. "The uses of our past must be for the redemption of our future."[26] Redemption from human-caused oppression, particularly non-Christ-related suffering, is the work of the *go'el* in Black thought.

This leads me to some positive assertions about the chosenness of Blacks in the history of their sojourn in America. First, Blacks, in their religious expressions, do see themselves as chosen people of

God. And Blacks are chosen people of God. This chosenness arises out of the fact that God has elected to choose them and not out of necessity resulting from their circumstances of suffering. Many other people in this world also suffer, but this does not make them a chosen people. Conversely, God elected to choose the Israelites before they fell subject to Egyptian bondage and experienced undeserved, human-caused suffering. God elected Blacks as his chosen people amid their experiences of human-caused and human-inflicted suffering.

Rabbi Richard L. Rubenstein offers a challenging argument in his book *After Auschwitz.*[27] He cannot reconcile the idea of a God who is Lord of history, directing the course of history toward the fulfillment of his own purpose, and yet allowing six million of his chosen people to be executed in Germany. One must remember that when God granted to human creatures freedom, they were free to do good or to do evil. The Germans, under Hitler, misused their freedom, and they directed this evil against a people who happened to have been the chosen people of God. God did not deprive Hitler of that freedom to do evil. But God did intervene, and as a consequence Hitler and his host went the way of Pharaoh and his army. The debate on the subject goes on, but the Hitler episode does not negate the fact that God does intervene in history.

Secondly, God made Blacks his chosen people because, as a mass of people, they said "yes" when he asked whom shall I send and who will go for us as agents of redemption in America. This took place during the Transitive Period when, after Blacks were introduced to Christianity, they modified their African traditional religions and accepted and reinterpreted the Christian faith. Thus, Black people in general and Black Christian religionists in particular assumed a posture in humanity which affirmed the right to be for all people and for all of God's creation. One is aware of the fact that since people were created in freedom, even the oppressed could say "no" to right and righteousness. It might also be remembered that suffering does not evoke election by God since many peoples who have experienced suffering throughout the world made no such claim.

Thirdly, in Judeo-Christian theologies God has always had a remnant through whom he challenged the nation to return to a life of right and righteousness. What Christian group in America today has a history of exemplifying an abiding humanity and a love of God and neighbor, even those who oppressed them? Black people. This humanity anchored in a belief in God is characteristic of Black religion which touched all of Black life. Black humanity and love of God and neighbor were exhibited as the "Magna Charta" in Martin Luther King, Jr.'s, nonviolent protest movement. This idea of humanity and love, even in protest, was not a new idea around which Black folk rallied at the call of King. It was a latent truth embedded in the religious fibers of the Black Americans. The call of King to an involvement in nonviolent protest with love as a core motif brought to the fore that which had been the bedrock of Black Christianity.

The practice of humanity and love which is the inevitable and abiding center of Black Christianity puts Blacks in close proximity with the expression of the righteousness of life on the part of the chosen people of the Old Testament and of the early Christian church. There is no other group of Christians in America which operates with as much humanity and love as a praxis. Black Christians in general have been and are a people who affirm the dignity of human beings and practice the love they preach. If the majority element of white America is to be redeemed from her sins of oppression and exploitation of other human beings and natural resources, it must look to the Black religious community—the chosen people of God in this age—for guidance. It is through them that God's plan of redemption is being carried out in America today. Blacks have also rightfully identified themselves with the chosen people to whom Jesus addressed himself when he said:

> "The spirit of the Lord is upon me,
> because he has anointed me to preach
>   good news to the poor.
> He has sent me to proclaim release to
>   the captives
> and recovering of sight to the blind,
> to set at liberty those who are oppressed,
> to proclaim the acceptable year of the Lord" (Luke 4:18-19).

This is a kind of New Covenant in the New Testament between Jesus Christ and a new people—the Blacks in this land.

Why do the righteous suffer? This is the question of theodicy raised by William Jones and to which he says he does not find adequate answers in existing treatises on Black theology. He suggests that oppression and suffering (among humankind, not just the righteous) exist because God is not active in human history; thus, the desires of some people to lord over others results in human suffering.[28] We have disagreed with his premise that God does not intervene in human affairs, which is a deistic approach to the problem. One might admit with him that in large measures much of the suffering which exists in the world is human caused. But the question still persists: why does God not do something about it if he is all-powerful and all-merciful?

Constructing a balanced theodicy is not the object of this book. Black thought has not been very *analytic* and *explicative* on this count, but it has been very clear in its reflections that God is both omnipotent and merciful. In passing, a word, which seems to get to the heart of the matter, might be said about this problem. The full revelation of God and of his plan of redemption, from creation to the last things, has not been totally disclosed to humankind. The data are still coming in. The problem of Black suffering is still veiled in eternal mystery and the theological answers which have been advanced are inadequate. Much more research needs to be conducted in the problem of Black suffering.

The following three points constitute an approach in response to the problem of undeserved human suffering. First, God does not will that people must, as an eternal nonvariable, experience undeserved suffering. In creation he willed that people would be free. This freedom created a risk that they might misuse this freedom. And it is this misuse of human freedom on the part of groups of people down through time which has resulted in untold human-caused suffering upon other groups of people.

Secondly, there is a mystical and transcendental—a beyond human comprehension and God's will to reveal—entity in unde-served, human-caused suffering which is without adequate theologi-cal explication. This has baffled religious thinkers from creation to the present. The cause for the oppression of the Israelites under Egyptian bondage presents major theological problems. Certainly the suffering was not to prepare them for election, for they were elected the chosen people long before the Egyptian encounter. Was it to prepare them for a future life of righteousness? If so, that four hundred years of preparation did not have much of a lasting effect once the Israelites were again settled in the land of Canaan. Why the Egyptian oppression then? The Egyptians were created in freedom; they misused that freedom in the oppression of the Israelites. But the Exodus is evidence of God's plan of redemption.

Theologians like to think that they can reason through all of the theological problems. But if humans could reason the way to all eternal truths, then they would be equal to their Creator, and there would be no need for the continuing existence of the Creator. There comes a time in theological reasoning when human beings must take the Tillichian leap. They must say, "Whatever the reason is for this problem, God has not yet chosen to reveal it to us; but we know he has a reason for permitting things to be the way they are at a given time." The question arising out of this position is inevitable: "Then, why must a people work in rebellion against oppression if this is the way God is permitting things to be at a given time and place?" God is against the deprivation of the full existence of his created beings. He is Redeemer, and he calls his people as agents of redemption. Blacks must fight oppressions and all attempts to reduce human beings into nonbeings, for one knows not the day nor the hour when God will intervene in history and change the course of events as he did in the Exodus after four hundred years of Hebrew suffering. Blacks must be found engaged in their portion of the work of redemption when He comes. The Black masses were on sound theological footing when they sang:

> He may not come
> when you want Him
> But He's right on time.

This does not mean the abandonment of the theological inquiries into the meaning of Black suffering. The search for meaning goes on. God does intervene in the affairs of human history, and there is an overabundance of references in Old Testament history to support Cone's position that God intervenes in history in situations of oppression. It means that Blacks, being oppressed, do identify themselves with the oppressed in the Old Testament on whose side God seems to be always at work. The Exodus, the story of Daniel and his deliverance from the den of lions, and the deliverance of the Hebrews from the fiery furnace are all stories about God's interventions into human affairs as Redeemer on the side of the oppressed. And these stories occupy a central focus of oral theology in the mass Black community. Only the story of Jesus as Redeemer and Lord of lords takes a place more central than the Old Testament redemption stories in Black theology.

The discourse above was not intended to solve the theodicy problem, but it gives direction to my position on the matter. And these thoughts were shaped by the thoughts as orally expressed in the Black religious community.

Black Cry for Redemption

The masses of Black folks in this country have walked always in the shadow of death. They have never been free from the pressures which were aimed at reducing them into a state of nonbeing. And, like the oppressed of Old Testament times, their pilgrimage has been replete with cries directed to the Great Redeemer. Any Black theology which will reflect the thought of the Black masses will have to take into serious consideration the cries and shouts of the dispossessed to the Almighty—the Redeemer.

White Christian theologians had no real need to deal with this matter of crying out to God as a religious concept, because usually their theological reflections emerged out of the background of the religious views of the oppressors. Black theologians have also generally overlooked crying or weeping as a meaningful religious concept in Black theology. Roberts did bring crying into focus as a Black religious concept when he asserted: "The other side of the Barthian 'God speaks, man listens' is 'man cries, God hears.'"[29] However, Roberts did not develop the concept.

Every religious expression has theological implications. The concept of "cry" in this book means those verbal and nonverbal expressions which include weeping, groaning, moaning, humming, chanting, singing, and praying individually or in communal settings, both ceremonial and nonceremonial. It is the sincere outpouring of the desires of the heart before the Redeemer. In William H. Pipes' book, *Say Amen, Brother!*, a Black preacher in a sermon entitled "Pray!" sums up in his definition of prayer what the overall understanding of the concept of cry in Black theology really means:

> . . . a prayer is a sincere desire. A prayer come up outta the heart, wid a meaning into it. Yeh, meaning.
> Prayer is a light on the bench. When yore way gits dark in this world, travelin' thru in a Christian manner, prayer will shine and den prayer will show you ter git out uv it. Just use prayer and God—exercising prayer—will lead you out.[30]

The concept of crying unto the Lord in Black theology is Black people's sincere desire coming out of their hearts with meaning. That meaning is understood by the Redeemer. So when the way gets dark as Blacks travel through this world, they are directed to pray—cry—

unto the Lord, the Redeemer. And they are assured that he will lead them out of their distress.

The concept of crying out for redemption plays a major role in Old Testament religious expressions. The psalmist, depicting the state of the Hebrews and their religious expressions while in that dreadful state, says:

> Some wandered in desert wastes,
>   finding no way to a city to dwell in;
> hungry and thirsty,
>   their soul fainted within them.
> Then they cried to the LORD in their
>   trouble,
>   and he delivered them from their distress.
> —Psalm 107:4-6

These Hebrews, according to the psalmist, were at their wits end; they were in a state of not fully being in the eyes of their oppressors. Oppressions had apparently spoiled their opportunities for full participation in life. It was at that point that they cried, they wept, which could have extended to the point of adorning themselves with sackcloth and ashes to express their mourning because of their oppressed condition. It was at this point that Yahweh heard their cries and the redeeming event took place in their historical situation.

The Black experience of oppression and redemption has been much more akin to those experiences reported in the Hebrew tradition than to those of their masters whose theology has left much to be desired when it comes to relevancy for Black Christians. The pouring out of cries—the sincere heart's desire—to the Redeemer and the experience of his response on behalf of the oppressed find little place in white theology.

The cry also had to do with duration. When Black folks came into confederation in order to place their sincere hearts' desires on the invisible altar before the great Redeemer, time was of little significance. The time needed to make their cases before the Eternal presented no problems. They were not afflicted with the time consciousness which afflicted their oppressors as a European survival. It took time to tell God about their experiences of humiliation and dehumanization and to implore him to redeem them from the hands of the oppressors. The cry was an important element in their total religious expressions. One learns from Black oral history that it was not uncommon for Black folk to stay in an ordinary prayer meeting half of the night during the Formative and Maturative periods of Black religion in America. By ordinary prayer meeting is meant those meetings which were set aside for singing, testifying, and praying only. No other element of worship was conducted during these meetings. There were times, too, when these prayer meetings went on until the early hours of the morning. Tradition informs us that it was not uncommon for one person to pray for a half hour. There is no question about it; they were crying for salvation from the states and circumstances which were destroying the values of their human existence and were indeed destroying their human existence itself.

The very fact that Blacks did physically and mentally survive the crucial blows of slavery and an Emancipation experience which had little real survival potential is reason for them to conclude that God was hearing their cries and that his eternal, redeeming love was active in their midst. So they felt both the necessity for and the results of their cries. In white American experience, there is no parallel for this concept of crying.

The concept of crying has influenced the total sphere of Black religious worship and expressions. It is still present in most Black religious services in the mass Black churches today. It is evident in the length of time and the frequency of meetings for worship. The frequency of meetings specifically for worship is greater among Black churches of the denominations mentioned than that of white churches of the same denominations. What does this mean? It means that Blacks still feel the need to spend adequate time presenting their cases before the Redeemer in a communal setting.

It might be revealing to some readers to know that in Baltimore there are still some Black churches whose pastors preach nearly one hour every Sunday. There are some Black churches which have not less than five choirs singing every Sunday during the regular Sunday worship. There are some churches whose Sunday worship services run for three hours or close to it every Sunday—from 11:00 A.M. to 2:00 P.M. Churches with these arrangements, any combination, or any single aspect of these activities generally have large crowds in attendance. Why? Because there is still that need among the oppressed to take adequate time to express their frustrations in religious worship. According to their own testimonies, in the past their forefathers or they themselves cried unto the Lord out of their oppression, and he heard their cry. The cry is evident not only in the duration and frequency of Black worship, but it is also evident in the words of the songs, prayers, sermons, and testimonies.

In an interracial national gathering in 1974 a young Black preacher was selected to offer an extemporaneous prayer during one of the sessions. The following lines were part of his prayer:

> I love the Lord
> who heard my cry
> and pitied every groan.

This kind of redemptive assurance comes fresh out of the Black church experience and belief. There is no question about the affirmation here. It is the human creature who cries. It is the Redeemer who hears. He not only hears, but also he responds to the cries. He pitied (past tense) every groan. It is suggested here, too, that the cry might have flowed upward not in articulate words but in simple groans out of the sincere heart of the oppressed. In the mass Black church the terms "groan," "moan," and "hum" are loosely used, overlapping each other. But they all mean the expression of the heart's sincere desire to God. When a congregation has sung all of the verses to a familiar hymn, and when the church atmosphere is charged with the presence of the Holy Spirit, just before the last few words of the hymn are sung, the preacher might say, "Let's groan it; let's groan it!" or "Moan it!" The congregation understands what he means and immediately unites in humming the last stanza of the hymn. It is a kind of crying out to God. It has both a transcendent and a healing—redeeming—effect upon the participants. Often, after such experiences one might hear another say, "The Lord surely met us in this place today!"

The cry in Black theology is a valuable leftover from the Formative and Maturative days of Black religion. Black people are pilgrims who cry out for redemption. Their *Go'el* —Redeemer— intervenes in history on their behalf and rescues them from their afflictions. While living and experiencing redemption, they have an eternal right to live in dignity.

Pilgrims with Dignity

James Cone quotes ex-slave Anthony Burns: "God made me a *man*—not a *slave,* and gave me the same right to myself that he gave to the man [who] stole me to himself."[31] Burns was articulating what has always been the understanding and the teaching of the Black church. Blacks knew that they were children of God and had the same rights to be as those whose object it was to crush them into nonbeings and to deprive them of their dignity as human beings and as children of God.

The oppressors in this country did create an abundance of stereotypes about Black people which have had the effect of psychological brainwashing. These stereotypes are too well known to need listing at this point. In summary they convey the idea that "if you are white, you are right and if you are Black, get back" because you are not as fully human as whites. This also means that any custom or behavior which does not derive from white folks is not fully human custom and behavior. Thus it must be rejected. Living under such conditions they did develop, psychologically, a degree of self-hatred.

In his book *Pedagogy of the Oppressed,* the Brazilian scholar, Paulo Freire, has this to say: Only as the oppressed discover themselves to be "hosts" of the oppressors can they make a meaningful contribution to the midwifery of their liberating pedagogy. "As long as they live in the duality in which *to be* is *to be like,* and *to be like* is *to be like the oppressor,* this contribution is impossible."[32] But this is the kind of mentality which was pressed upon Black folks in North and South America: "To be is to be like white folks." This led James Tyms, Professor of Religious Education at Howard University School of Religion, to write:

> ... the Negro has needed to be saved, and still needs to be saved, from the pathological influences of the social process which have tended to reduce him to a subhuman status in society, and from the psychology of unconscious self-hatred which has tended to rob him of the creativity needed for the emergence of an approved self-image as a condition of self-esteem and high personal idealism.[33]

The Black church is the only institution which has kept Black people on their feet amid the crushing blows of the oppressors. The Black church never ceased to promote the idea of the worth and the dignity of the Black people. But the powers and the pressures of the masters had their psychologically damaging effects. So Blacks are called upon to save themselves—join the Redeemer in the activity of redemption—from those social processes which tended to reduce them to subhuman status and unconscious self-hatred.

In their book, *The Jesus Bag,* William H. Grier and Price M. Cobbs, both Black psychologists, have a chapter entitled "Black Psychology." Here, they point out that Blacks have long been told that they were blocking their own progress, that they were their own worst enemies, lazy and preoccupied with superficialities, and that this was the cause of their wretched state. Blacks always knew better, they argued; but threatened by the power of hatred in the nation, blinded by fear, and weakened by the feeling of inferiority, they could not lay hands on the villain. They saw the spirit of Black identity as helping to allay this psychological impotence. Grier and Cobbs saw Blacks who were embracing blackness for the first time experiencing a feeling of a lifting of the spirit "as if they have been freed of a burden. . . . The white man who once was feared can now be called a son-of-a-bitch, and all because of changes *inside* the black man." [34]

It was during the Black awareness movement that Blacks, for the first time, on a massive scale, publicly criticized every form of racism and white oppression in spite of the inhumane reprisals. Despite the charges that they were their own worse enemies, Blacks always knew better. They knew better, we believe, because they knew that they were heirs of the Creator. They knew that they were made to live in dignity. So the outbursts of Black Power, Black pride, Black identity, and Black dignity openly expressed during the Black awareness movement were only the bursting out of the frame of repression of that which was always understood to be of divine appointment—human dignity. That is, Black people are endowed with eternal rights to *be,* and to *be* meant to *be* as fully human and as autonomous as any other human being on the face of the earth. So, down through their pilgrimage of oppression Blacks fought against every odd because they knew that the Redeemer was on their side. Black people had reached the oral, theological position that all human beings have a right to live in freedom.

The historical situation in which the Black people found themselves could not contain them because they were created for a higher purpose. So they continued to rise above the historical circumstances, to transcend the given situations, and to reach for the new possibilities which are the inheritance of every child of God. Since humanity is created in the image of God, and since God as Redeemer is active in the process of redeeming people from human-caused states and circumstances which distort that image as well as from sin and guilt, Black people have come to know God through his acts of redemption.

Christopher Hill, author of *The World Turned Upside Down,* borrows a quote from Edward Burrough, of the seventeenth century, which seems to be an appropriate summary of the stance of the Black oppressed in America, who knew that they were the object of God's redeeming love, over against the oppressors. Edward Burrough told the all-powerful restoration government of England in the 1660s: "If you should destroy the vessels, yet our principles you can never extinguish, but they will live for ever, and enter into other bodies to live and speak and act."[35]

Langston Hughes affirms the dignity of the Black man in his poem "I, Too, Sing Amerca":

> I, too, sing America
>
> I am the darker brother.
> They send me to eat in the kitchen
> When company comes,
> But I laugh,
> And eat well,
> And grow strong.
>
> Tomorrow,
> I'll be at the table
> When company comes,
> Nobody'll dare
> Say to me,
> "Eat in the kitchen,"
> Then.
>
> Besides,
> They'll see how beautiful I am
> And be ashamed—
>
> I, too, am America.[36]

This hope emerges out of the experiences of a pilgrim people—poor pilgrims of sorrow—who realize their state of sinfulness arising out of their distorted relationship with the Creator. They understand themselves to be the chosen people of God; so they cry out for redemption while at the same time they walk before him in dignity. Their hope was and is anchored in the God who continues the process of revelation and redemption.

5

Revelation and Redemption

Far above the strife and striving
And the hate of man for man,
I can see the great contriving
Of a more than human plan

And day by day more clearly
Do we see the great design
And day by day more nearly
Do our footsteps fall in line.[1]

In spite of the strife and struggling and the experience of "hate of man for man" through which the Black people were passing, Benjamin Brawley could perceive a more than human plan which was being unfolded more and more day by day. Two points are made clear in this excerpt from his poem: (1) the revelation of the plan of God is gradually unfolding, and (2) the Redeemer is disclosing himself to those who are experiencing strife and striving and the "hate of man for man."

In this chapter we shall examine and discuss the meaning of God's revelation as it relates to redemption in Black theology. Our investigation will be centered upon the understanding of God's self-disclosure in the Black community, his promise and the goal toward which he is directing history.

Grace Unfolding

The concept of revelation in Black theology encompasses the general theological understanding of the meaning of the self-disclosure of God, which we shall discuss in these pages. But Black theology goes further in its assertion about revelation. Revelation in Black theology—Black folk expression—is the divine self-manifestation or self-disclosure of God as Redeemer. Revelation in Black theology is grace—the unmerited favor of God—unfolding amid Black suffering.

This idea of revelation as the self-manifestation of God as Redeemer—grace unfolding amid Black suffering—is unique to Black theology. God's self-manifestation as Redeemer, specifically as Redeemer from human-caused suffering, is given little attention by white Christian theologians. God reveals himself, according to Euro-American theologians, as the One who is omnipotent, omniscient, and omnipresent, and this is correct. These terms speak to the theoretical problem of his essence, but they do not answer the practical question of what in the world he is doing or what he is doing in the world which is the practical question raised by those trapped in the wilderness of oppression.

The revelation of God which has been received on the Black frequency in the situation of racism in America has revealed him as the One who is first and foremost the Redeemer. James Cone is correct in his assertion that, "According to Black Theology, revelation must mean more than just divine self-disclosure. Revelation is God's self-disclosure to man *in a situation of liberation.*" More clarification is needed with respect to Cone's further statement which says: "There is no revelation of God without a condition of oppression which develops into a situation of liberation. His revelation is only for the oppressed of the land."[2] To say that God *only* reveals himself in situations of oppression is putting limitations on God. This is not necessary in order to support his argument in the previous statement which asserts that according to Black theology "revelation is God's self-disclosure to man *in a situation of liberation.*" This is a fact which can stand upon its own merits.

It is true that the history of God's self-disclosure in the Old

Testament, in Jesus Christ, and in the Black experience has been in situations of oppression and liberation. But it is not our aim here to show that God has never revealed himself in another situation.

To say, however, that there is no revelation without a condition of oppression and liberation is to establish a dogmatic concept of revelation. This makes the Black theologians bedfellows with the white theologians who assume that they have the whole truth on the matter of revelation, even though both groups have a different truth. To limit the revelation of God only to situations of oppression and liberation also limits the ways in which God can reveal himself.

We cannot be certain about how or to whom God will reveal himself except as we look back from beyond the *eschatos,* that is, beyond the end of time. And obviously that is not where we are. Again these words from the writer of Hebrews are helpful: "In many and various ways God spoke of old to our fathers by the prophets; but in these last days he has spoken to us by a Son . . ." (Hebrews 1:1-2*a*). Today, we might say that "in many and various ways God revealed himself through the prophets, and later through his Son, and in these days through his redemptive presence among us."

We do want to make it clear that we do agree with Cone who holds that in *Black Theology* revelation must mean God's self-disclosure in a situation of liberation. He has revealed himself as God on the side of the oppressed. This position is affirmed from Old Testament writings, from the person and works of Christ, and from the testimonies of oppressed Blacks during their centuries of human-caused suffering in America. Our basic disagreement with Cone is that we cannot limit the possibility of revelation to oppression and liberation. We are only free to say what is revelation for us. Another missing link in Cone's assertion is his lack of attention to the other dimension of redemption in Black theology, namely that of being drawn into community by the same One who is also Liberator.

Revelation, as grace—unmerited favor—unfolding again makes it clear that salvation to Blacks which comes through the redemptive intervention of God is not earned by the condition of suffering. Without any merit on the part of Black people, Black theology says God reveals himself to Black people who happened to be in a situation of suffering in America. In the midst of their suffering God elected to choose the Black people of this country to be redeemed to himself and as agents of redemption. The Black people said "yes" to God in words and in deeds.

J. Deotis Roberts, Sr., offers a succinct definition of revelation when he writes:

> Revelation is the process of unveiling. Revelation is the divine self-manifestation or self-disclosure. God's word is for man. . . . Revelation, in order to complete its process, must have a revealer and a revealee. Revelation is transcendent and immanent; it is ontological and existential; it is objective and subjective. Revelation comes to the human order from the divine order which is the Beyond within.[3]

This statement is all encompassing and at the same time limited as it relates to Black theology. It does not specify the practical means by which it is transcendent and immanent; the ontological and the existential are conceived in the Revealer-revealee relationship in Black theology. The praxis—practice as distinguished from theory— of Black theology demands that the definition of any theological concept must not only be implied, but it must also be stated. Any definition of revelation in Black theology, then, must say that God discloses himself as Redeemer of suffering Black people in this country. This is not intended to limit his self-disclosure to Redeemer only. It is to say that is the primary way in which he has disclosed himself to Black people in America. We cried to the Lord out of the midst of our troubles and he heard our cries. The unfolding grace of God has been revealed in his acts of redemption; so Black people created a song entitled "Grace Is Sufficient" which tells that story:

Grace—Grace—God's Grace—His
Grace—is—sufficient—for me—
Grace—Grace—God's Grace—His
Grace, will give you victory.

I

Grace woke me up this morning—
Grace started me on my way.—
Grace—Will make you love your enemies—
Above all it'll brighten up your day.

V

Grace will help you bear your burdens
When your strength is almost gone—
Grace will keep you from falling—
Grace will take you safely home.[4]

This expression in Black religious songs encompasses the general feeling of the Black community about the revelation of God. Here God's unmerited favor, his grace, is sufficient. It will give victory to those in battle against those things and persons who would treat them like nonbeings or at least not fully human. Grace will also assist them in burden bearing and will keep them from falling when their personal strength is almost gone. God reveals himself to every people in their own language. And Blacks have testified of God's revelation from what they have seen and heard. Their position is akin to that of Peter who declared: ". . . for we cannot but speak of what we have seen and heard" (Acts 4:20).

Such testimony grows out the fact that God is Revealer to every people in their own life situation and in their own language. Luke reminds us of this when he states that on the day of Pentecost the revelation of God was of such nature that peoples from various nations raised the question: "'And how is it that we hear, each of us in his own native language?'" (Acts 2:8).

We hold first that God does reveal himself to humankind in historical events. God has a plan for humanity which has its genesis in creation and transcends all of the ages. While it is not fully revealed, it is, through grace, constantly unfolding. Secondly, the dynamic self-manifestations of God are universal but appear differently in various life situations among diversified peoples. Thirdly, God's self-manifestations are comprehended differently among those of the mass Black impoverished community than they are comprehended by the masses of white Americans. Revelation must have both transmitter and receiver. Reception depends upon the tuning of the receiver. When revelation is being sent out on one frequency and groups of people in their life situations are tuned in on other frequencies, this means that this revelation is not received by all groups of people at the same time. Through human-caused segregated sabbaths and other segregated arrangements in this country, Blacks and whites have never been on the same religious frequency. And it is this fact of Blacks coming to know God as Redeemer in their own life situation which gave rise to the development of Black oral theology.

Paul Tillich's "Marks of Revelation" are helpful for the articulation of revelation in Black theology. One mark is the phenomenological method. "The significance of this methodological approach," he says, "lies in its demand that the meaning of a notion must be clarified and circumscribed before its validity can be determined, before it can be approved or rejected."[5] This is precisely what we are saying about revelation perceived as redemption in Black religion. Before white theologians begin to reject any theological concept which is reinterpreted in Black theology, the very existential meaning of the notion itself to Black religionists must be examined. Otherwise, as Tillich puts it: "In too many cases, especially in the realm of religion, an idea has been taken in its undistilled, vague, or popular sense and made the victim of an easy and unfair rejection."[6] In the current Black-white theological discussions, this would mean that Black reinterpretation of theological concepts has been made easy victim of rejection because the concepts have been taken by most white theologians only in the popular theological sense which has been fashioned out of white culture. Tillich offers another statement on the matter of the phenomenological approach which is apropos for Black-white theological understanding. "The test of phenomenological description is that the picture given by it is convincing, that it can be seen by anyone who is willing to look in the same direction. . . ."[7]

The object of Black theology is to give a picture of the Black understanding of the revelation of God in his redemptive acts in the situation of oppression. It is our further objective to make the picture convincing enough so that it can be seen by those who are *willing to look* in that direction.

The aim of Black theology is not to discard the existing definitions of revelation. Black theology will trace back through the traditional understanding of revelation testing the multiplicity of interpretations which have appeared, relating them where possible to the reality of revelation in the Black religious experience. Black theology is forming new constructs from existing materials combined with the Black realities of revelation which have not been made before about the unfolding grace of God in the Black community.

Revelation in Community

From their African survivals there is a deep propensity among Blacks to understand and to relate theological concepts in relationship to the total community. This is not to say that each and every individual in the community has lived out his or her life in compliance with the hopes and aspirations of the majority of the members of the Black community. However, since no racial or ethnic group makes the claim that every individual member lives in harmony with the wishes of a total group, we need not account for the fact that some Blacks have said "no" to God and to the ideals and

aspirations of the Black community. Not all conform to the norm.
The concept of "we"—communal concerns and expressions—is a central concept in Black folk religious thoughts and expressions. While salvation from sin and guilt is an individual concern, salvation from woes and earthly tribulations is also an ongoing, communal activity in the plan of God. Salvation from earthly woes and tribulations is for the entire community of the suffering; it is not individual salvation. God, as Redeemer of the "we" in Black thought, is reflected in the following poem by Fenton Johnson. It comes out of the period of Passive Protest and also reflects the feeling of the absence of active redemptive activities on the part of God, but it also correctly reflects the hope that the redeeming activities of God would some day become accelerated. It did happen when Rosa Parks, in what some Black religionists believe to have been a God-directed act, sat in a seat reserved for whites only on a city bus in Montgomery, Alabama, on Thursday, December 1, 1955. This is what Johnson wrote in 1949:

The Old Repair Man

God is the Old Repair Man.
When we are junk in Nature's storehouse he takes us apart.
What is good he lays aside; he might use it some day.
What has decayed he buries in six feet of sod to nurture the weeds.
Those we leave behind moisten the sod with their tears;
But their eyes are blind as to where he has placed the good.
Some day the Old Repair Man
Will take the good from its secret place
And with his gentle, strong hands will mold
A more enduring work—a work that will defy Nature—
And we will laugh at the old days, the troubled days,
When we were but a crude piece of craftsmanship,
When we were but an experiment in Nature's laboratory . . .
It is good we have the Old Repair Man.[8]

This is a beautiful understanding of redemption. It is "we" whom God will mold with his gentle strong hands. And it is "we" who will laugh at the old troubled days when we were just experiments in nature's (or the oppressor's) laboratory.

The revelation of God in the history of Black folks is similar to his revelation of himself to the Israelites as reflected in the statement of Johnson above and in the following statement of Bruce Vawter: "Somehow, when time and time again it appeared that Israel was done for spiritually and morally, it rose from its own ruins to live again. Somehow, despite internal corruption and external oppression, it preserved its integrity and it survived."[9]

Vawter reminds us that other nations came and went and only Israel remained. Largely responsible for the survival of Israel under these circumstances, he says, was the institution we call prophetism.[10] Obviously it is that institution we call the Black church which helped Black people to rise again and again with integrity from the ruins of their own corruption and from depression and oppression. The Black church, like the prophets, kept pointing Black people to the One who was constantly disclosing himself as Redeemer.

Revelation in Black theology has to do with experiencing, witnessing, and responding. It was the experiencing of the presence of God giving life and meaning to life in rhythmic fashion, individually and collectively, which gave rise to the witnessing. The experience of indices of the revelation of God often broke into the Black community in the Tillichian sense of ecstasy. Tillich says the so-called "ecstatic" movements have saddled the term "ecstasy" with unfortunate connotations. This happened in spite of the fact that prophets and apostles spoke of their own ecstatic experiences time and time again in a variety of terms. Then he advances a definition:

> "Ecstasy" ("standing outside one's self") points to a state of mind which is extraordinary in the sense that the mind transcends its ordinary situation. Ecstasy is not a negation of reason; it is the state of mind in which reason is beyond itself, that is, beyond its subject-object structure. . . . This is the state mystics try to reach by ascetic and meditative activities. But mystics know that these activities are only preparations and that the experience of ecstasy is due exclusively to the manifestation of the mystery in a revelatory situation. Ecstasy occurs only if the mind is grasped by the mystery, namely, by the ground of being and meaning. And, conversely, there is no revelation without ecstasy.[11]

In the Black situation of oppression they sang:

> Nobody knows the trouble I see
> Nobody knows but Jesus
> Nobody knows the trouble I see
> Glory, hallelujah!

The "glory, hallelujah" here depicts a state of ecstasy in which the mind is extraordinary in the sense that it has transcended the ordinary situation of troubles. The revelation of God as Redeemer is so prevalent that the mind is beyond itself. The mind takes a mysterious leap and sees a way out of a desperate situation.

Because of the many ecstatic experiences in the Black community, witnesses to the revelation of God spring up everywhere. This witnessing is followed by the community responding to the revelation of God. By responding, we mean the development of a style of life in harmony with what is understood to be the will of God communicated through his self-disclosure in revelation. Revelation in the existential situation, then, points to ontological reality. Cone was correct when he concluded that "Revelation . . . is the epistemological justification of a community's claim about ontological reality." [12] The revelation of God as Redeemer of the oppressed is a Black community concept. It is also a Hebrew concept. This community's understanding of revelation was not expressed in literary creeds, confessions, or doctrines, but it was disclosed to individuals and to groups; it was refined in the religious community, and it was transmitted orally through the prayers, preaching, songs, and testimonies of the communicants in the Black church. The Black folk's understanding of revelation was also transmitted from one generation to another through nonchurch oral and literary expressions. God had revealed himself and is still revealing himself as the One who is redeeming the world and humankind.

Black religion influenced all of Black life; so when we speak of nonchurch expressions, there is not that clear distinction which we are accustomed to think exists between the sacred and the secular. African survival plays an important role in the Black folk idea about religion. African religion influenced and touched every area of African life. This idea about religion and life was not totally erased with Black acculturation into Euro-American Christianity. This is why the blues and the spirituals have so much in common. They both speak of the real life struggles, and they both speak of some hope of mysterious redemption from such struggles. The following comparison shows the similarity of the expression of struggle in blues and in the spirituals as they tell of the hard realities of life:

> Sometimes I feel like nothin', somethin' th'owed away,
> Sometimes I feel like nothin', somethin' th'owed away,
> Then I get my guitar and play the blues all day.
>
> Money's all gone, I'm so far from home,
> Money's all gone, I'm so far from home,
> I just sit here and cry and moan.[13]

Then we turn to the church and we hear them singing:

> Sometimes, I feel, just like a motherless child
> Sometimes, I feel, just like a motherless child
> Sometimes, I feel, just like a motherless child
> Then I started to fold my arms and cry.

These are cries of despair, but not utter despair because the Redeemer continues to reveal to them the needed ray of hope time and time again. So the bluesmen sang:

> My burden's so heavy, I can't hardly see,
> Seems like everybody is down on me,
> An' that's all right, I don't worry, oh, there
> will be a better day.[14]

From the church we draw these lines:

> Though the path you tread may be so dark and dreary,
> Laden with care, no light anywhere,
> Beneath your heavy load you may become so weary
> He will come and answer prayer.[15]

The "better day" which closed the lines from this blues, says Cone, "is not naive optimism." It is an expression of the will to be.[16] It is also the expression of a nonchurch song of the redemptive hope of the larger community influenced by the church. In fact, it is the redemption theme of the Black church sung in a nonchurch setting. It reflects the overflow of the revelation of God into the total Black community. The blues and the spirituals were derived out of the same situation of racism in America.

It would be misleading to convey the idea that Blacks did not make any spiritual or ethical distinctions between the blues and the spirituals during the Formative and Maturation periods and thereafter. The idea of the sacred and the secular was imposed upon Blacks by their captors. They were forced to adopt the notion of the sacred and the secular through the process of Christianization.

So, theoretically the blues were the music of the devil, and there developed a whole body of activities which was viewed by Black church folks as secular and was to be shunned by church folks. This created a dichotomy in the Black community which was not known by their African ancestors. But a reexamination of the spirituals and the blues reveals that in expression and aspiration the Blacks were speaking of suffering and redemption both on Saturday night in the blues and on Sunday morning in the spirituals. Redemption was the transdivisional phenomenon uniting the dreams and lives of the Black people on Saturday night and on Sunday morning. This made them a community in spite of the outside imposition of the idea of sacred and secular. We must remember, too, that in many instances the same people who sang the blues on Saturday night also sang the spirituals on Sunday morning.

Historically, in the Black community, in both the sacred and the secular segments, God was known as Redeemer. God had revealed himself through his acts of salvation in their historical situation as Savior. Independently of Tillich, Blacks have reached the position which Tillich articulates:

> The history of revelation and the history of salvation are the same history. Revelation can be received only in the presence of salvation, and salvation can occur only within a correlation of revelation. . . . any attempt to separate revelation and salvation . . . must be rejected.[17]

In his article "The Concept of Revelation in Ancient Israel," Rolf Rendtorff says "Jahweh himself becomes visible in his powerful acts of salvation. He becomes known through these acts; whoever sees or experiences them can know God in them. He becomes revealed in them."[18] The history of the revelation of God is a history of salvation in Black religion. As Rendtorff understands God's revelation, Yahweh, God, has become known in the Black community through his acts which Blacks have seen and experienced. Not only does God make himself known in his acts in history, but he also discloses the fact that history is moving from his promise toward his preordained goal.

God's Promise and Goal

God's promise includes redemption for nations and for individuals. We read in Deuteronomy:

> ". . . it is because the LORD loves you, and is keeping the oath which he swore to your fathers, that the LORD has brought you out with a mighty hand, and redeemed you from the house of bondage, from the hand of Pharaoh king of Egypt. Know therefore that the LORD your God is God, the faithful God who keeps covenant and steadfast love with those who love him and keep his commandments, to a thousand generations" (Deuteronomy 7:8-9).

While the Deuteronomist speaks of national salvation resulting from the promise of God, Job speaks of individual salvation:

> "He has redeemed my soul from going down into the Pit,
> and my life shall see the light."
> —Job 33:28

There is no doubt about God's promise of redemption in the Old Testament, the New Testament, or in Black religious thought. The full revelation of God is the goal toward which each revelatory event in history points. The goal is to bring persons back into full and unspoiled relationship with himself. Pannenberg puts it this way in his second thesis on the doctrine of revelation: "Revelation is not comprehended completely in the beginning, but at the end of the revealing history."

He continues:

> The linking of revelation with the end of history is related to its indirect character. It follows directly out of the indirectness of the divine self-vindication, and without this presupposition revelation cannot be understood.
> We have seen that the revelation of God is the defined goal of the present events of history. And only after their occurrence is God's deity perceived. Thus, placing revelation at the close of history is grounded in the indirectness of revelation.[19]

Pannenberg's argument seems to be convincing at this point and apropos for Black theology. While Blacks experience the acts of God in history and recognize them as the self-disclosure of God, they still sing "We'll understand it better by and by." "It is only in the time of the eschatological inauguration of the new aeon," declares Pannenberg, "that the meaning of the present time is revealed." He sees "the destiny of man, from creation onward . . . to be the unfolding according to a plan of God."[20]

The destiny toward which God's self-disclosure is directing mankind is the restoration of the unimpaired unity between Creator and creature. The contribution of the Kabbalists to the concept of redemption (discussed in chapter 2) is helpful at this point. The Kabbalists hold that when iniquity has caused a fissure in the unity of the Godhead, that is, between his *Sefirot* which makes up the totality of his created beings, his name is not one. The Name of which they speak is the symbol of the divine *Sefirot* when they are joined in complete unity. The exile of Israel created a state in which this unity was impaired. In symbolic language the exile meant a temporary separation between the King and the Queen, between God and his *Shekhinah*. The union was broken. The return of Israel to her "land at the time of redemption symbolizes the inner process of the return of the 'Congregation of Israel' or the *Shekhinah* ('the Matron') to a continuous attachment to her husband."[21] Thus, the goal of the revelatory events of God in Black history is redemption—the liberation of Blacks from oppression and from sin and the confederation of Blacks into community in this world and the final restoration of them into a state of unimpaired unity with himself.

Black theology must interpret these historical events. Cone believes that the goal of Black theology is to interpret the activities of God as he is related to the Black oppressed community.[22]

He contends that while special revelation, which has occupied the central role in Christian theology, means that God has made himself known in biblical history and decisively in Jesus Christ, there is also *general* revelation. He writes:

> To summarize general revelation from the perspective of Black Theology, to say all men know God means that human oppression is contradictory to the idea of the holy, and every blow for liberation is the work of God. God has not left himself without a witness.[23]

Cone's view here seems to be in harmony with the Kabbalists. His view that human oppression is contradictory to the idea of the holy is in harmony with the Kabbalists' view that iniquity caused a fissure in the Godhead. Redemption is the process of mending this broken unity. The latter part of the statement of Cone seems to suggest that the oppressed must take the initiative in striking blows for liberation since the blows for liberation are understood by many Blacks to be of divine appointment. We think this is a correct interpretation of Black religious thought. We have a case history in the writings of Black abolitionist and author David Walker who in his famous *Appeal,* said:

God is on Our Side

> "Fear not the number and education of our enemies, against whom we shall have to contend for our lawful right; guaranteed to us by our Maker; for why should we be afraid, when God is, and will continue, (if we continue humble) to be on our side?
>
> "The man who would not fight under our Lord and Master Jesus Christ, in the glorious and heavenly cause of freedom and of God—to be delivered from the most wretched, abject and servile slavery, that ever a people was afflicted with since the foundation of the world, to the present day—ought to be kept with all of his children or family, in slavery, or in chains, to be butchered by his cruel enemies."[24]

The Reverend Henry Highland Garnet saw *Walker's Appeal* as an overflow of the religious views of Black oppressed people in America, and the call to participate in striking blows for freedom was understood by Garnet to be the revealed will of God.[25]

The Civil War and the resulting Emancipation were understood by Blacks to be the revelation of a redeeming act of God in history. Henry Mitchell quotes one Sallie Paul as saying:

> *God* set de slaves free. De Lord do it. It just like dis, I believes it was intended from God for de slaves to be free en Abraham Lincoln was just de one what present de speech. It was revealed to him en God was de one dat stepped in en fight de battle.[26]

Further illustrations of Black witness to God's revealing acts in history are offered by Mitchell. He points out how slaves saw a merciful God providentially setting them free in the experience and report of one Josiah Hanson. On an alleged journey serving as an Underground Railroad conductor, Hanson reported that he had been the recipient of God's help in rapid sequences. They went as follows: "On landing (at Maysville, Kentucky), a wonderful *providence* happened to me. The second person I met in the street was Jefferson Lightfoot, brother to James Lightfoot . . . who promised to escape if I would help him."

Then, while en route from Maysville to Cincinnati the boat "sprung a leak before we had got half way, we got to the shore before the boat sunk." But when their party had arrived at the Miami River overland, they were unable to cross over into Cincinnati until they were assisted by a divine Exodus-like intervention:

> This was a great barrier to us, for the water appeared deep, and we were afraid to ask the loan of a boat, being apprehensive it might lead to our detection. We went first up and then down the river, trying to find a convenient crossing place, but failed. I then said to my company, "Boys, let us go up the river and try again." We started, and after going about a mile we saw a cow coming out of a wood, and going to the river as though she intended to drink. Then said I, "Boys, let us go and see what the cow is about, it may be that she will tell us some news." I said this in order to cheer them up. . . . The cow remained until we approached her within a rod or two; she then walked into the river, and went straight across without swimming, which caused me to remark, "The Lord sent the cow to show us where to cross the river!" This has always seemed to me to be a very wonderful event.[27]

There is no question about the understanding of the self-disclosure of God in Black history as Redeemer. In the above legend, quoted by Mitchell, the Lord uses a variety of media in his acts of redeeming the distressed in Black thought, even the cow.

What God had done and does in the Emancipation and in these

continuing events are merely what Ulrich Wilkens calls "proleptic" revelations.[28] That is to say, the fulfillment of the redemptive experience in any one of these single events is only a microcosm of the macrocosm of full redemption which can only be completed at the end of time. These individual revelatory events were ordered from the very beginning of God's plan of history, and they are proleptic in that the fulfillment which is derived from any single revelatory event points to or anticipates the complete fulfillment—the redeeming of the oppressed into a state of unimpaired relationship with the source of being. Redemption is seen here to mean both liberation from states and circumstances of distress toward the final union with the Eternal.

As God acts in history, these acts are perceived by the Black community of faith as God's revelation. Cone is correct in his argument that revelation in biblical perspective is inseparable from the community with faith to perceive it. Thus faith is the perspective through which people recognize God's act in human history. And faith is something other than an ecstatic feeling present in moments of silent prayer, or an acceptance of inherent propositions.

> Faith is the community's response to God's act of liberation. It is saying Yes to God and No to oppressors. Faith is the existential element in revelation, *i.e.*, the community's perception of their being and the willingness to fight against non-being.[29]

The expression of this communal faith is summed up in the lines which Alain Locke collected from a "young Negro" (Langston Hughes) during the era of the Black Renaissance:

> We have tommorrow
> Bright before us
> Like a flame.
>
> Yesterday, a night-gone thing
> A sun-down name.
>
> And dawn today
> Broad arch above the road we came
> We march![30]

Here Black faith points to a bright tomorrow which the Black community, traveling through the darkness of oppression, sees as a radiant flame. So "we march!" is the call of the "young Negro." The night of yesterday which is gone only came about because of the acts of God in history. Amid the sufferings of life, life has meaning because God is revealing himself day by day in one event after another. The Blacks have faith in the God who has promised redemption, both social and spiritual, and his interventions in the course of history in his self-vindication. Black faith says the course of historical events is moving from God's promise to his final goal of creation—an unimpaired union between Creator and creature. Revelation is not only God's self-disclosure of what he has done in the world and what he is doing in the existential situation, but revelation also points to what God will do and what he wills that people ought to be doing in the process of redemption.

Revelation in Black thought is seen as grace unfolding in the Black community which reveals God's promise and the goal toward which he has everything moving. God had made many aspects of his will known to man throughout human history. But God has not spoken his last word. He is the "Old Repair Man" who, through his Son Jesus Christ, is molding us into a more enduring people who will forever defy the powers of oppression.

6

Walk with Me, Jesus

I want Jesus to walk with me,
I want Jesus to walk with me;
All along my pilgrim's journey
I want Jesus to walk with me.

In my trials, walk with me,
In my trials, walk with me;
When the shades of life are falling,
Lord, I want Jesus to walk with me.

He walked with my mother, he'll walk with me.
He walked with my mother, he'll walk with me.
All along my pilgrim's journey
I know Jesus will walk with me.

In Black religious thought Jesus is Redeemer of humankind from the this-worldly states and circumstances which diminish the fullness of his people as well as Redeemer of humankind from sin and guilt. This chapter will examine some of the ways in which Black folks have expressed themselves in relationship to Jesus Christ.

The Pilgrims' Journey

In Black theology Jesus is the prolepsis of the end of God's redeeming activity in human history. This means that what God has done in the historical events in the life of Jesus is an anticipation of what he is bringing to completion in history. In the lines cited from the folk spiritual above, several points stand out. First, those who shared in the singing were a confederation of believers on a pilgrims' journey. This means that they saw themselves as wanderers and sojourners moving in the direction of a fixed destiny. Secondly, the pilgrimage was made difficult by trials. Thirdly, since they knew Jesus to be their burden bearer, they cried out, "I want Jesus to walk with me." There was no question as to whether he would walk with them. Looking back to the historical-divine experiences and the reports of their predecessors, they asserted, "He walked with my mother, he'll walk with me." This affirmation and hope are still sung in the mass Black church today, particularly during prayer and testimony services and during the devotional services held prior to the ordered worship services.

The Jesus who has walked with their mothers and who will walk with them is their Alpha and Omega. But Black theology understands that God elected to give humankind a history which is replete with his rhythmic and redeeming events, including the liberating event of the Exodus and the confederating event in the land of Canaan. These historical events preceded the coming of the historical Jesus. The unwillingness of most Euro-American theologians to deal with the reality of the biblical Old Testament meaning of redemption—liberation and confederation of the oppressed in this world—forced them to center redemption in Christology.

In doing so they made two errors. The first error rests in the fact that they have neglected the Hebrew understanding of redemption which tended to be more weighted on the side of salvation from human-caused oppression than from sin and guilt. Of course it is not difficult to understand why the oppressors and/or those who benefit from oppression would overlook the Old Testament liberation aspect of redemption. The second error of those who put Christology at the center of redemption is evident in the fact that, as they reflected upon redemption in the New Testament, they made Jesus the redeemer of humanity from sin and guilt and óverlooked the fact that one of the persistent characteristics of the historical Jesus was his identity with the oppressed and the dispossessed of the land.

For these reasons Black theologians might suggest that any theology with redemption as the core motif (and redemption is at the heart of Black theology) ought to bypass the Euro-American approach and start with the literal meaning of redemption, moving through its metaphorical usages in the Old Testament and then on to a christological meaning of redemption in Black theological perspective. This is not to suggest that it is impossible to start with Jesus in doing theology from the perspective of redemption. It is possible to start with Jesus and look back through time since he is Alpha as well as Omega. However, it is a delusion to start with Jesus and construct a Christology which changes the theology of the revelatory events of God prior to the advent of the historical Jesus. Jesus himself said, "Think not that I have come to abolish the law and the prophets; I have come not to abolish them but to fulfil them" (Matthew 5:17).

Just as Jesus declares that he did not come to abolish the law and the prophets, neither did he come to abolish the horizontal dimension of redemption and to refocus it into a single vertical dimension. The horizontal dimension of redemption here means the saving of humankind from human-caused states and circumstances of oppression while the vertical dimension means the saving of human-kind from their own sins and guilts arising out of their acts resulting from their spoiled or broken relationship with the Source of their being. Jesus said he did not come to abolish the law and the prophets. He did not come to change the Hebrews' understanding of redemption either. He came to fulfill and to expand the existing metaphorical meaning of redemption. This idea is made clear in his statement:

> "The Spirit of the Lord is upon me,
> because he has anointed me to preach good news to the poor.
> He has sent me to proclaim release to the captives
> and recovering of sight to the blind,
> to set at liberty those who are oppressed,
> to proclaim the acceptable year of the Lord."
>
> —Luke 4:18-19

Jesus came to extend and to fulfill the horizontal as well as the vertical dimensions of redemption which his father had begun after the event in the Garden of Eden and had made more explicit in the Exodus.

Black religion affirms the classical Christian view of the role of Jesus in the vertical dimension of redemption. Jesus is the One who brings fallen humanity and sinful human beings back into a right relationship with the Eternal. The atonement took place on the cross of Calvary. Black religion has grown out of a childlike faith. It has not been engaged in any extended theological debate on the matters of how one man could atone for the sins of all or to whom the ransom was paid, or why it was necessary that a human life be sacrificed in order that God might redeem humanity from sin and guilt if God is all powerful and thus could have wrought human salvation by some other means. The discussion of these and other such christological concerns from the Black religious perspective must be reserved for future work. The aim of this chapter is to lift up the horizontal—the this-wordly—understanding of the redeeming work of Jesus which is central in Black theology, and which has been neglected in most Euro-American theologies.

In our discussion of redemption we did not start with Jesus as the point of departure; our aim is to point out the correlation between the literal and mythical Old Testament meaning of redemption and that of Black religion. We must also refuse to be caught up on the theoretical and philosophical meaning of Jesus as Redeemer, because in Black religion Jesus was a practical deliverer of the oppressed, whose goal it was to bring them into a community of children of God. Racial cultural biases have been the dark glasses which have kept a majority of white theologians from seeing Jesus as the Redeemer of the oppressed as well as the Savior of humankind from sin and guilt.

It was the separating of the historical Jesus from the Christ of faith that led to docetism. This is a belief which arose early in the third century which held that Christ did not really suffer but only seemed to have suffered. This doctrine overstressed the divinity of Christ. Cone calls for a "dialectical relationship between the historical Jesus and the Christ of faith."[1] This dialectical relationship of the Jesus of history and the Christ of faith is the way Black pilgrims have expressed their Christian faith. James Cone is correct when he says:

> We do not have to choose between a Christology either "from below" or "from above." Instead we should keep both in dialectical relation, recognizing that Christ's meaning for us today is found in our encounter with the historical Jesus as the Crucified and Risen Lord who is present with us in the struggle of freedom. Indeed, it is Jesus' soteriological value as revealed in his past, experienced in our present, and promised in God's future that makes us know that it is worthwhile, indeed necessary, to inquire about his person.[2]

I would not go so far as to say Black theology "inquires" about the person of Jesus. It is more appropriate to say that in Black folk thought it is Jesus' soteriological value as revealed in the experiences of the Black pilgrims' journey that makes them aware of his person as well as his divinity. In all cases redemption through Jesus Christ in Black theology is understood both vertically and horizontally. Most of Euro-American theology which is deeply influenced by cultural imperialism has neglected the horizontal dimension of the redeeming acts of the Jesus of history.

In the foreword to Jóse Míguez Bonino's book, *Doing Theology in a Revolutionary Situation,* William H. Lazareth quotes Ruben Alves who rejects Thomas G. Sanders's view that Latin American liberation theology must be understood from the perspective of Christian realism. Alves concludes "'in irritation,' that the Christian Realism [of which Sanders speaks] is indebted to its own 'silent agreements' with positivism and pragmatism." He continues:

> And when we say this, we are saying that traditional ways of doing theology must recognize their ideological bias, their rather unambiguous relationships with colonialism, racism, and economic exploitation. We believe that your theology to a great degree—although it does not want to recognize this—is part of cultural imperialism.[3]

Alves is correct, and the recognition of this basic right which frees the oppressed of Latin America to do a theology of liberation which need not bow to the strictures of the methodology evolving out of the culture of imperialism is also the basic right which frees Blacks in America from bowing to the strictures of existing main-line Euro-America theological approaches. It might be well worth noting here, too, that there must be something transmundane behind the fact that there is this rise of the this-wordly aspect of redemption taking place concurrently, yet somewhat independently, among the oppressed in both Latin America and North America.

In continuing this discussion on the subject of Jesus as Redeemer out of the praxis—practice rather than theory—of Black religion, we shall examine the following concerns: (1) Jesus as an historical reality, (2) Jesus as Redeemer of the oppressed, (3) Jesus as the resurrected Lord and, (4) Jesus as the One who walks with the oppressed.

Jesus As Historical Reality

One thing which is unnecessary in the development of Black theology from the historical expressions in Black folk thought is the quest for the historical Jesus. Black religion in America has always presupposed the reality of the historical Jesus as well as the Christ of faith. This is what Black people had to say about Christ's birth:

> Go tell it on the mountain,
> Over the hills and everywhere;
> Go tell it on the mountain,
> That Jesus Christ is born.[4]

They had a literal understanding of Jesus' acts and deeds:

This Man Jesus
I
Jesus walked the water and so raised the dead
He made the meats for those saints—He multiplied the bread
The blinded eyes he opened and cleaned the lepers too
Then died to save sinners—Now what more could Jesus do.

Chorus
This man never will leave you—This man will not deceive you
This man waits to relieve you—When troubles are bearing you down
Oh this man when danger is near you—This man is ready to cheer you
This man will always be near you—He's a wonderful Savior I've found.[5]

The first stanza of this gospel song points to the earthly and physical presence of Jesus and to his acts and deeds and redemption in earthly historical settings. The chorus, however, speaks of the transcendent qualities of the person of Jesus. Although he is not physically present, there is a certainty that "this man never will leave you." "He's a wonderful Savior I've found." The author of the song knows this because he has personally found it to be so. Here, Black theology sees Jesus as the unique Son of God who was an historical figure. Jesus was fully man in the sense that we understand the term, but he was more so. He was also fully divine in our fullest understanding of the term.

For Black theology, Jesus was an historical figure and the divine Son of God. Neither James Cone nor J. Deotis Roberts gets into the debate about historicity of Jesus. Both moved forward from the presupposition of the once-present historical Jesus, but they know that these quests are ventures of many white Euro-American theologians. These quests have never appealed to the Black Christians in America. Black Christians have accepted the testimonies of the New Testament witnesses concerning that fact of his physical presence.

The Reverend Albert B. Cleage, Jr., has stimulated another kind of quest which has been given much attention in Black theological circles. This quest is for the Black Messiah. Cleage makes a strong point for a new understanding of the historical Jesus as a Black Messiah in the literal sense. In his "An Epistle to Stokely" he quotes lines from the hymn "Fairest Lord Jesus" and makes the following comment:

> I only mention it to point out the very simple, but very obvious fact that black Christians have a whole lot to do to rewrite much of the ritual and songs that are used by Christian churches. It's kind of ridiculous for us to be sitting here singing about "Fairest Lord Jesus." We might sing about "Darkest Lord Jesus" or something else.[6]

Cleage argues that it was through the Hebraic genealogy that we received the historical Jesus and that we might sing "Darkest Lord Jesus" because an inherited anatomical characteristic of the Hebrew people was dark skin. Cleage begins with Abraham, the father of the Israelite nation, and points out that the father of Abraham was a Chaldean. Answering the call of God, Abraham left his city and, for a time, lived in Egypt. In Egypt, he dwelt with the Egyptians, says Cleage, where the extant Sphinx, drawings, and inscriptions attest to the fact that the Egyptians were Black people. It was among the Egyptians that the people of Israel had their early beginnings, although they were not yet considered a nation. That Abraham took Hagar, his Egyptian servant, as a second wife and had children with her is a biblical fact. The son of Abraham and Hagar, Ishmael, became the father of the Ishmaelites. They became a separate people from the Israelites, but we must remember that they sprang from a single father.

Moses, says Cleage, was half Egyptian and half Jewish, which made him unquestionably nonwhite. He married a Midianite woman (not a Hebrew woman), and they had children. The Hebrews came from among the Chaldeans, mixed with the Egyptians, the Midianites, and the Canaanites. Thus, the conclusion that the nation, Israel, was nonwhite. They could not have picked up any white blood wandering around in Egypt. Even when they were taken captives into Babylon, they mixed with the Babylonians—a people who were already mixed. Cleage declares: "It was as impossible to separate the Jews from the people of the land as it was to maintain segregation [in America] in the South after nightfall. . . . The Jews were scattered all over the world. In Europe and Russia, they converted white people to

Judaism. The Jews who stayed in that part of the world where black people are predominant, remained black." There is some conflict, today, he contends, between Black Jews and white Jews in Israel. And most of the Jews in America today are descendants of white Europeans and Asiatics who were converted to Judaism about a thousand years ago.[7]

So goes Cleage's argument in his "An Epistle to Stokely." It was this argument that led me to do further research into the ethnic background of the people of Israel.[8] I began the investigation from the prehistoric movements. W. E. B. Du Bois quoted Charles Darwin as saying, ". . . it is somewhat more probable that our early progenitors lived on the African continent than elsewhere."[9] Du Bois quotes Griffith Taylor as saying that Negro culture existed in an "uninterrupted belt" and that it extended from Central Europe to South Africa as early as the close of the Paleolithic Age. Du Bois also quotes G. Massey as follows: "The one sole race that can be traced among the aborigines all over the earth or below it is the dark race of a dwarf, Negrito type." Du Bois then says, "It seems reasonable to suppose that Negroids originating in Africa or Asia appeared first as Negrillos."[10]

Carter G. Woodson, an eminent Black historian, believed that a people called the Bantu probably reached Africa about 30,000 years ago and after 20,000 years mixed their blood with the Hamites. About 6,000 years ago the Arabs filtered south. They mixed their blood with the Negroes and the Hamites about 3,000 years ago.[11]

Records of the Negroes beyond the sixteenth century B.C., according to Woodson, are extinct except for a few rare Arabic works which are largely legendary and contradictory. What is reasonably known of the Africans is that a branch of the Negroid race lived in Burma and the sea islands and traveled through Mesopotamia. Upon doing so, they left among the people of Mesopotamia "their curly hair, dark complexion, as a distinguishing mark of the Jew, Syrian, Assyrians, and Southern Europeans."[12]

My investigation went into the ethnic backgrounds of the people of the Hittites, the Habiru (Aprue), the Egyptians, the Ethiopians, and the Hysksos to Abraham. My conclusion confirms Cleage's position. A complexity of ethnic stock went into the "melting pot" out of which the Hebrews emerged. And from the time that God called Abram (Genesis 12:1), the Hebrews have been a wandering people upon the face of the earth and accommodators of other ethnic blood and cultures. Thus, since Jesus is a descendant of the Hebrews, if Albert Cleage ever elects to sing "Darkest Lord Jesus," scholars might be forced, by historical evidence, to join in the chorus.

For too long the majority of Euro-American artists have been giving us a white Jesus with which to decorate our altars, churches, and Christian facilities while most white theologians and religionists have been saying color does not matter. If it is true that color does not matter, these white theologians and historians ought to tell their artists to tell the truth about the historical Jesus in their paintings—they ought to add a little darkness to him.

It is true that physical color has little to do with redemption. But what we are calling for here is the truth about the historical Jesus; and if he happens to be one whose complexion is more akin to the oppressed group in America than it is to that of the oppressor, why should this fact be withheld? Is this a cover-up? It is not the complexion of the historical Jesus which has the redeeming qualities; it is the *truth* that sets humanity free.

It is truth which is sought by both Cone and Roberts in their discussions of the Black Messiah. Cone asserts that "the historical Jesus emphasizes the social context of Christology and thereby establishes the importance of Jesus' racial identity. *Jesus was a Jew!*"[13] Beyond this assertive stand, Cone sees the Black Christ as

> an important theological symbol for an analysis of Christ's presence today because we must make decisions about where he is at work in the world. Is his presence synonymous with the work of the oppressed or the oppressors, blacks or whites? Is he to be found among the wretched or among the rich? . . .
>
> The definition of Christ as black means that he is the complete opposite of the values of white culture. He is the center of a black Copernican revolution. . . .
>
> Blackness is a manifestation of the being of God in that it reveals that neither divinity nor humanity resides in white definitions but in the liberation of man from captivity. The Black Christ is he who threatens the structure of evil as seen in white society, rebelling against it, thereby becoming the embodiment of what the black community knows that it must become.[14]

So what Cone means by the Black Christ is symbolic of Christ taking sides with the oppressed, most of whom happen to be the Blacks in this country. He does not develop the facts of the historicity of a nonwhite Christ or the Black Messiah.

Roberts does not take the figure of the Black Messiah in a literal, historical sense. Of course, we have shown in our presentation above that there is no reason why one should not. For Roberts, the figure of the Black Messiah is a symbol or a myth. He declares, "My use of *symbol* and *myth* in the understanding of the black Messiah does not mean that I am prepared to give up a historical-literal understanding of the incarnate Lord." [15] By myth he means a "traditional story of historical events that serves to unfold part of the world view of a people or explain a practice, belief, or natural phenomenon." Its description of a person or a thing might have "only an imaginary or unverifiable existence." [16]

> A symbol participates in that which it symbolizes while it also points beyond itself as a mere symbol. Against this assertion we may make certain affirmations. The black Christ participates in the black experience. In some sense Christ makes contact with what the black Christian is aware of in his unique history and personal experience. He *encounters* Christ *in* that experience and is *confronted* by the claims of Christ also in his black experience. [17]

While Cone and Roberts could have taken a stand for the literal-historical Black Messiah, they elected not to do so. However, their mythological and symbolical uses of the term "Black Messiah" or "Black Christ" are very meaningful approaches to the understanding of who Jesus was, is, and who he will be in Black theology. Blacks have come to know Jesus Christ because of his work. Black theology does not deny that it was because Jesus was who he was that he did what he did. However, in the New Testament it was the other way around. So it is in the Black community; it is the other way around. It is through what Jesus has done and is doing in the Black community that Blacks have come to understand who he is. And thus, any Christology emerging out of Black religion is essentially emerging out of the Black response to the redemptive events of Jesus in Black history.

The Jesus of Black religion is not a theoretical concept. He is the One who is encountered in the Black historical situation of oppression. He is the One who takes the oppressed by the hand and leads them on. Swinging back to the New Testament for support of this idea, Bonino writes that the Johannine epistle is working out of the theme relating the knowledge of God to the love of the brother. So God is unknown unless humankind participates in his concrete life through love. There is no minimizing of the historical revelation of

Jesus Christ; yet, "this revelation is not an abstract theoretical knowledge but a concrete existence: the existence in love." [18] Any theoretical understanding of Jesus must be related to the practical application of his personal presence in the social context of history.

To be sure, the Jesus of history whose redemptive activities included involvement in the political emancipation of the oppressed, according to Scriptures, is the Jesus of the Black Christians. He is the Black Messiah. The creeds and doctrines which have been handed to Blacks by the white denominations had to be reinterpreted; this is reflected in Black religious expressions. The Latin Americans, just as the Black North Americans, also found the interpretation of biblical texts from the colonizers unacceptable. This led Bonino to write:

> Every interpretation of the texts which is offered to us (whether as exegesis or as systematic or as ethical interpretation) must be investigated in relation to the praxis out of which it comes. At this point the instruments created by the two modern masters in the art of "suspecting," namely, Freud and Marx, are of great significance. Very concretely, we cannot receive the theological interpretation coming from the rich world without suspecting it and, therefore, asking what kind of praxis it supports, reflects, or legitimizes. Why is it, for instance, that the obvious political motifs and undertones in the life of Jesus have remained so hidden to liberal interpreters until very recently? [19]

The answer to Bonino's question obviously rests in the need of the interpreters to protect their vested interest. But from the backwoods of the obscure plantations in the deep South to the spreading Black ghettos of the North, in settings spanning from massive church structures down to the flourishing storefront churches, there is a unity in the understanding of Jesus: He is a friend, a real and personal friend of the disinherited. One gospel song which expresses this fact follows:

Jesus Is a Friend of Mine

1

When my enemies are on my trail,
    And the host of hell assail,
I know Jesus, that Friend of mine;
One day He paid that awful fine,
    He is with me all the time,
I'm talking about Jesus, that Friend of mine.

Chorus
I'm talking about Jesus, that Friend of mine,
I'm talking about Jesus that is so kind;

> He is ever walking beside me,
>   Never more the tempest shall bind me,
>   I'm talking about Jesus, that Friend of mine.[20]

The author and the singers, here, know who the enemies are; they are a part of the host of hell who are on their trail. But in this sociopolitical situation the Jesus who has already paid an awful fine is with them all the time. He is ever walking beside them. For those who are pressed on every side, Jesus becomes flesh; he becomes the friend who walks beside them. It is important that the reader understand that this Friend, Jesus, spoken of in this gospel song, is a reality for the masses of Black Christians today. He is not a creation from the days of slavery who is no longer needed. Jesus was, is, and always will be the Redeemer of the disinherited. His mission in the world is to bring the dispossessed into a this-worldly confederation as well as into an eternal inheritance.

There are persistent questions as to why the Black and Latin theologians put so much stress on the social and political liberation in doing Christology. We are aware of the fact that there must be a balance between the Jesus of history and the Christ of faith. We are aware of the fact that there must be a balance between the understanding of redemption as salvation from oppression and salvation from sin and guilt. This is what Black theology is all about. In Black religious thought both dimensions have always had their rightful place as per the Black religious expressions. The problem lies in the fact that Black theology, until recently, has been an oral theology, and the white Christian community has not been aware of this fuller meaning of redemption as understood in the Black community. This problem is further magnified by the fact that some white theologians have deliberately overlooked the obvious salvation from oppression in the person and works of Christ.

Like the quest for the historical Jesus, the quest for a Black theology—a theology of redemption—is a struggle against the tyranny of the overriding Euro-American creeds, doctrines, and theologies. These creeds, doctrines, and theologies have been formulated by the oppressor class, by the wealthy, and by the socially and politically powerful rulers of the Western world. Consciously or unconsciously they were also formulated for the oppressors and power brokers of the West. There was no need for an interpretation which would promote the idea of Jesus as Redeemer from human-caused oppressions. Through military, economic, and political might, they were their own redeemers from threatening nations. This is particularly true of America. This was the position, philosophy, and the theology emerging out of Germany. It is the culture and ideals of the ruling class which shape the attitudes and acts of a nation. And it is the culture of the nation which shapes the theology of those who participate in the benefits derived from national policies.

It must be understood, too, that national policies which shape national theologies are not only directed toward other nations, but they are also designed to deprive those who have been marked for nonacceptance into the national mainstream of any socio-eco-political structure. The liberation dimension of redemption will not be developed by those who have no need for social, economic, and political liberation. That Jesus was, is, and will be the Redeemer who liberates humankind's bondage must be amplified by those who stand in need of liberation and who have encountered him in incidents of liberation. This is a vital truth in the concepts of redemption. Liberating humankind from human-caused suffering is not all that Jesus is doing, but neither is redeeming humankind from sin and guilt all that he is doing. Yet this seems to be the limit of the understanding of redemption in the bulk of Euro-American theologies.

The liberation from oppression aspect of redemption is a vital force in Black theology and in Latin American liberation theology. But as Schweitzer puts it:

> There is no historical task which so reveals a man's true self as the writing of a Life of Jesus. No vital force comes into the figure unless a man breathes into it all the hate or all the love of which he is capable. The stronger the love, or the stronger the hate, the more life-like is the figure which is produced.[21]

The idea has great significance for Black theology. Black theology is not writing a life of Christ, but it is reflecting upon a religious experience, an encounter with the risen Christ who in person, in works, and in spirit is a Redeemer of the oppressed. That vital force which makes him come to life grows out of the Black love for him who has been a Friend in the situation of racism in America.

Jesus Christ was, is, and will be an historical reality in Black religion and life. He is Redeemer in the fullest meaning of the concept. Only the oppressed who have had the experience of his walking with them through the valleys of death and bringing them out victoriously can express the full meaning of such an experience in theological terms.

Jesus As Redeemer of the Oppressed

Jesus is Redeemer of the oppressed because he is the One who cares. This assurance is expressed in a song regularly sung in the Black churches.

Does Jesus Care?

I

Does Jesus care when I'm oppressed
I know my Jesus sees and cares.
Does Jesus care when I'm distressed,
I know my Jesus cares.

Chorus

Oh yes, Jesus cares, Oh, yes I know my Jesus cares,
Oh yes I know He cares, I know my Jesus cares.

II

Does Jesus care when I'm laden down,
I know my Jesus sees and cares,
When my burdens press me to the ground,
I know my Jesus cares.

III

Does Jesus care when I'm filled with dread,
I know my Jesus sees and cares,
.When my pillow's wet from tears I've shed,
I know my Jesus cares.[22]

Blacks knew that Jesus was against oppression. There is a certainty: "I know He cares." They knew this from Scriptures and from his intervention in their social history. At all of the major turning points in the history of the Black pilgrimage in this country, there was Jesus redeeming the oppressed. They felt that it was Jesus who saved them from genocide and extinction during slavery. It was he who saved them from extinction and brought them into confederation after the Emancipation. They were provided neither a mule nor forty acres—no means for economic, physical, social, or spiritual survival. It was the redeeming love and presence of Jesus which brought them up from the plantations to the Promised Land— the North—and sustained them in the ghettos, when the Promised Land turned out to be not so promising after all.

The Black church credits the coming of Martin Luther King, Jr., and the concomitant extension of social opportunities and social justice to divine providence mediated through Jesus Christ. Bonino reports that not long ago a group of young people from a shantytown in Uruguay performed a play. A conversation between the actors and the congregation followed, and somebody asked the question, "What, then, is Jesus Christ?" What shot back immediately and spontaneously from one of the group members was, "For us, Jesus Christ is Ché Guevara." [23] Once getting over the initial shock of the first impression of such an answer, says Bonino, it then begins to dawn upon us that in the course of history, "the face of Jesus Christ has frequently taken on the features of the man—ideal or historical— who best represented what at that moment men linked most closely with the Christian religion or with the fullness of humanity." [24] Obviously, to say that Jesus Christ is Ché Guevara is an overstatement of the matter, but the essence of the statement is clear. The statement was designed to shock this well-to-do congregation into reality, but its undergirding truth was no less damaging to the theoretical Christian view of Jesus Christ as Redeemer.

We have not heard Blacks say that Jesus Christ is Martin Luther King, Jr., but there is an abiding understanding that Christ was in him liberating Blacks from oppression. What he was doing was what Jesus did to bring fullness to humanity. Not only does Jesus Christ carry out his continuous redeeming activity through leaders such as Martin Luther King, Jr., but also the Black religionists see the coming and function of the various human rights organizations as redeeming instruments brought into being and sustained through Jesus Christ. Jesus, as Redeemer of the oppressed, is also at work in other ways. It is not uncommon to hear members of the mass Black congregations saying that "it was the hand of the Lord" which guided Frank Wills to the Watergate burglars which eventually led to the ousting of Richard M. Nixon and his cohorts from the White House. God is active in our midst through his Son Jesus Christ who is active in the history of the oppressed.

Jesus As Resurrected Lord

The historicity of the resurrection of Jesus has not been a preoccupation of oral Black theology. Blacks have not only accepted the reports of the witnesses of the Gospels, but also they have had the experience of Paul, as reported in their testimonies. When Paul had to speak to the matter of the resurrection of Jesus, this is what he had to say:

> For I delivered unto you first of all that which I also received, how that Christ died for our sins according to the scriptures; And that he was

buried, and that he rose again the third day according to the scriptures: And that he was seen of Cephas, then of the twelve.. . . . And last of all he was seen of me also, as of one born out of due time (1 Corinthians 15:3-8, KJV).

Paul's belief in the resurrection rested upon two facts: First of all, it was true according to the report of the witnesses in the Scriptures. According to Scriptures Christ died and was buried and, according to Scriptures, he rose again on the third day. Secondly, Paul believed in the resurrection because the resurrected Lord had been seen by a number of witnesses (some of whom were alive at the time of Paul's writing) and the resurrected Lord had been seen by Paul himself. It is quite clear that Paul means that he did not see the risen Lord at the time in which he appeared to the apostles and to the others. His statement about being as one born out of due time shows that he considered himself as coming after the time when Jesus appeared and conversed with the disciples. Therefore, to see him at all meant to see him in an extraordinary way.

It is precisely this understanding of resurrection which is at the heart of Black theology. First, Jesus is the One who died for their redemption, according to Scriptures. He is also their risen Lord, according to the Scriptures. But their knowledge of the risen Lord does not stop here. Like Paul, they too have seen the risen Lord, not in the way in which he was seen by the apostles, but in an extraordinary way. Throughout the Black sojourn in this land and in the midst of their afflictions, the risen Lord has appeared time and time again according to the witnesses. He appeared as Redeemer. He redeems the oppressed from sin and from afflictions. A common testimony in the Black churches concerning the resurrection goes something like this: "I know that my Jesus died on Calvary for my sins. I know that he was buried, and I know that on the third day he rose from the grave; how do I know? Because he rose in my soul."

This testimony has far-reaching implications from Black theology. It affirms the crucifixion of Jesus. It affirms that the death of Jesus was for their sins and for their justification. It affirms that God raised Jesus from the dead. It affirms that Jesus has appeared unto them and lives within their souls. By the enthusiasm which usually accompanies this testimony, it is evident that the resurrected Jesus who lives in one's soul is constantly at work effecting the resurrection of the individual. He is being resurrected from death and the state of sin and guilt. He is also being resurrected from the circumstances of human oppression. This resurrection testimony also means that Jesus rose in the body of the church as well as in the body and experience of the individual; it means that he rose in the Black community. This resurrected Christ is constantly bringing about a resurrection among the members who make up the body of the Black church and the Black community. He is giving new life to the down-trodden who have been victimized on the crosses of dehumanization.

The resurrection of Jesus in Black theology is also a prototype of the future resurrection of the dead. This is usually attested to in the prayers which are on this order: "Lord, when time shall be no more, when the sun refuses to shine, and when the moon drifts away in blood; Lord, when the first trumpet sounds, I'm going to get up out of the ground. . . ." The hope of future resurrection of the dead saturates Black religious belief and faith. Blacks have fully identified themselves with the suffering, death, and victorious resurrection of Jesus. They put themselves back in time and stand with the crowd at the foot of the cross of Christ and they raise the question:

> Were you there when they crucified my Lord?
> Were you there when they crucified my Lord?
> O-o-o-o, sometimes it causes me to
>   tremble, tremble, tremble.

Then they sing:

> O see how they done my Lord,
> O see how they done my Lord,
> O see how they done my Lord,
> And He never said a mumbling word.

This Black identification with the suffering of Jesus, when turned around, brings Jesus into the suffering of Black people. And this is where the victorious resurrection becomes crucially important.

Jesus Walks with Me

The Jesus who walks with me in Black theology is the resurrected Lord. When Blacks sang "I Want Jesus to Walk with Me," the song had a double meaning for the participants. One meaning is that they needed Jesus to walk with them through the wilderness of oppression. The other meaning is that they needed Jesus to walk with them through a world of temptation and evil. In one way Jesus would walk with them as a political Redeemer; in another way Jesus would walk with them as a spiritual Redeemer.

The pilgrimage through the physical life in America for Blacks was and is difficult. Preoccupation with physical survival has always been the order of the day. And the task of survival at the level of being fully human under inhumane circumstances required the assistance of a force greater than one could muster from natural, physical, and mental strength. So, on the pilgrimage, Blacks invoked Jesus to walk with them. They knew that Jesus knew what it meant to be downtrodden because he was numbered with the downtrodden. They knew that he knew what it meant to be beaten without a cause because he, too, was beaten without a cause. So they appealed to Jesus: "Walk with me, Lord, do walk with me!" There was never any doubt as to whether Jesus would respond since Blacks knew the mission of Jesus was to the poor and to the dispossessed.

It was also a religious certainty that if Jesus walked with them through their sorrows, ultimately they would triumph victoriously over their human-caused troubles. This certainty is reflected in the song which is still heard in Black churches today:

> Victory, victory shall be mine,
> Victory, victory shall be mine,
> If I hold my peace
>   and let the Lord fight my battle,
> Victory, victory shall be mine.

The fulfillment of this victorious hope of freedom, equity, and justice in this "one nation, divided" has been thwarted and delayed by the powers that cause much of the unnecessary suffering. But consistent with the sojourn of the Black pilgrims has been that hope, kept alive by the Black church, that eventual victory is assured. "The Lord will fight our battle," "the Lord is with us," and "the Lord is on our side" are common expressions in Black religious circles.

Blacks also needed Jesus to walk with them to protect them from capitulating to the forces of sin and evil. The Black religionists were aware of the evil forces which tempted people. Persons are sinners when they attempt to be what they are not—when they attempt to play God—particularly in their relationships with other human beings and with natural resources. Persons are also sinners before God when they elect to settle for the lesser good in life when the greater good is both known and possible. Blacks must join Jesus in his work or redemption by using every means consistent with Christian principles to protest against injustice and to achieve full humanity. Martin Luther King, Jr., used love as his basic principle in his work of nonviolent protest. But protest by any means necessary is not absolutely alien to Black religion. Nonviolence has been the general method of protest by the Black church during the Black sojourn in this racist country.

In chapter 4 we mentioned that Blacks were taught that wine, women, whiskey, and such social involvements as card playing and theatergoing were sinful engagements. In some Black church quarters there is still a propensity to point to these involvements as the major sins of humankind. But Black people in general know that racism and oppression constitute the major threat to their being and fulfillment. The oppressors use their power and act as God in their relationships with other human beings. Again this does not absolve Black people from the temptations of sin nor from the eternal consequences of sin simply because they are not a part of the oppressors' group in this country.

Being subject to sin, then, just as all others are, the Black religionists need a Jesus who will walk with them and who will continue to turn them away from sin. This position is affirmed in the first stanza of the gospel song, "Since I Met Jesus":

I
Since I met Jesus, there's a burning
O such a burning deep within
It holds me with an unseen power
And turns me away from all sin
It changes me from day to day
As I trod along this narrow way
Since I met Jesus, since he blest this
Old soul of mine makes me want to run
on Hallelujah to the end.[25]

It is Jesus who treads with Blacks along the narrow way and who also holds them with an unseen power and turns them away from the sins and the temptations that await them.

Therefore, the Jesus who walks with the Black Christians is their Savior and Deliverer—Redeemer—from the human-caused troubles in life leading them to an assured victory. He is also their Redeemer who turns them away from sins. This band of Christians has been molded into a kind of psychic-spiritual unity which, despite the difference in their geographical settings and the degree of differences in their worship style, could be referred to as the Black Church. (There will be further discussion of the Black Church as a psychic-spiritual unity in chapter 8). This Black Church has developed a view of Jesus as the One who walks with the oppressed. This confederation of Black Christians was brought into being by Jesus who is at present walking with them. So they call upon each other to walk together as children. This old spiritual expresses the call to confederation of those who were walking together and who knew that Jesus was walking with them. It expressed the theological meaning of confederation of the oppressed which has not changed to this day. It had its origin during the Formative Period of Black theology and became a fixed concept in Black religion.

One version of this religious folk song of the slaves is that which follows:

Walk Togedder, Children

Oh, walk togedder, children, don't you get weary,
  Walk togedder, children, don't you get weary,
Oh, walk togedder, children, don't you get weary,
  Dere's a great camp meetin' in de Promised Land.
Gwine to mourn, and nebber tire;
  Mourn an' nebber tire; mourn an' nebber tire;
Dere's a great camp meetin' in de Promised Land.

Oh, get you ready, children, don't you get weary;
  Get you ready, children, don't you get weary;
We'll enter dere, oh children, don't you get weary,
  Dere's a great camp meetin' in de Promised Land.
Goin' to pray and nebber tire;
  Pray and nebber tire; pray and nebber tire,
Dere's a great camp meetin' in de Promised Land.[26]

Owens says "the untutored slave singers always interpreted their lives as a sure pilgrimage." Although "the ugly and bitter realities of slavery" had the effect of draining "their everyday life of its joy, happiness, and true meaning. . . . They were sure that their whole life was only another Exodus under God."[27]

This assurance was based upon their abiding belief in the once historical Jesus who was and is the Redeemer of humanity. In his existence as resurrected and ascended Lord, he is also the invisible One who is ever present and walking with them on their pilgrimage. He has set them free through justification, and the pilgrims are experiencing a continuing process of sanctification which is our central concern in the following chapter.

7

Justification and Sanctification

So we have come to cash this check—a check that will give us upon demand the riches of freedom and the security of justice. We have also come to this hallowed spot to remind America of the fierce urgency of now. This is no time to engage in the luxury of cooling off or to take the tranquilizing drug of gradualism. Now is the time to make real the promises of Democracy. Now is the time to rise from the dark and desolate valley of segregation to the sunlit path of racial justice. Now is the time to open the doors of opportunity to all of God's children. Now is the time to lift our nation from the quicksands of racial injustice to the solid rock of brotherhood.[1]

Oppressed and himself afflicted with the burden of injustices, Dr. Martin Luther King, Jr., presented this argument for social justice. The secret to the understanding of the power of this speech lies in the fact that while King was standing there before the world as a victim of social injustices, he was also standing there before his Maker as a free being because the justice which developed him came from above and not from below. This is an example of the existential absurdity which permeates the lives and experience of Black Christians in this country.

God in his self-disclosure through love and mercy justifies people. He sets them free from sin and from guilt. He gives to them the undeserved freedom to be. At the same time, other human beings, for selfish gains, prestige, and power attempt to negate the justice of God and to reduce other human beings to nonbeings. So the Black Christians have had to live in a state of existential absurdity. They are stretched between the poles of being and nonbeing, between the justice of God imputed to them on the one hand and the injustices of man forced upon them by other people.

As Martin Luther King, Jr., made this profound speech on that hot twenty-eighth day of August in 1962 before 200,000 persons and millions of television viewers, it was evident that he knew and felt the justice of God. The justice of God was the undergirding of his stamina. The justice of God in that moment superseded the injustices of man. This justice which kept King on his feet is the justice of God; it is the justice which is known throughout the Black religious community.

Justice, then, in Black theology has a meaning which extends its meaning in classical theology. Justice in classical theology clings to the love motif as foundation. The justice of God in Black theology is intertwined with Black redemption. The justice of God liberates Black people and brings them into confederation with God and with fellow pilgrims. God's justice sets Black people free so that they are able to stand upright before God and in the world. The Black religionists know the full meaning of being justified by the "precious blood of the Lamb." They know the full meaning of justification.

During their pilgrimage Black Americans have developed clear ideas about the justice of God. In their oral theology they talk about justice and the wrath of God and the relationship between justice and revolution. It is out of their understanding of the justice of God that they have perceived the need for sanctification which is the basis for their ethical orientation.

Justification in Black Theology

Justification in Black theology evolves out of the Black understanding of the reality of the justice of God in the history of Black people's sojourn in America. Justification from above contradicts the setting in which Black folks live. Justification sets the person in bondage free in such a way that one is free while still in bondage. This is exemplified in the excerpt from the speech of King cited above. Justification in Black theology is Black folks coming to know the impact of the justice of God in an unjust world—life situation.

This justice comes from above while there is no justice below. In light of the vast gross injustices Blacks have come to know, the transcendent meaning of justice has implications and meaning for time and for eternity. The justice in time which comes from above is that which makes sense out of a situation of existential absurdity. It gives ontological meaning to the pilgrims in earthly bondage. It assures being in a situation of nonbeing. Justice from above says "you do exist" to a people whose full existence is rejected by the majority culture. So the shouts of the 1960s—"I am somebody!"; "I'm Black and I'm beautiful!"; and "I'm Black and I'm proud!"—were not new ideas. They came out of the Black religious tradition. These are theological statements uttered in nondirect church-related settings. God has made us somebody through justification. We pointed out in chapter 3 that the Black church influenced all of Black life, and even nonchurch expressions and aspirations generally had their genesis in the Black church.

The shouts of "I am somebody!" were in response to the social situation of Blacks in relationship to the majority culture. James Baldwin has critical indictments against the oppressors who created the devastating social situation of Black people. He charges the so-called innocent white people with the crime. He wrote to his nephew, his namesake:

> . . . these innocent and well-meaning people, your countrymen, have caused you to be born under conditions not very far removed from those described for us by Charles Dickens in the London of more than a hundred years ago. (I hear the chorus of the innocents screaming, "No! This is not true! How *bitter* you are!"—but I am writing this letter to *you* to try to tell you something about how to handle *them,* for most of them do not yet fully know that you exist. . . .)[2]

His countrymen did not know the conditions under which James was born because they were not there, according to Baldwin. But Baldwin asserts that both he and his grandmother were there, and no one has ever accused his grandmother of being bitter. The innocent could discuss that statement with grandmother since she was not hard to find. Even though grandmother was not hard to find, there was one problem involved: "Your countrymen don't know that *she* exists, either, though she has been working for them all their lives."[3]

Baldwin might have further added the fact that grandmother also was the midwife who assisted in bringing them into the world and nurturing them through infancy and into maturity despite her nonexistence—her state of nonbeing—in the eyes of her countrymen. He does remind James: "You were born where you were born and faced the future that you faced because you were black and *for no other reason.*"[4] There was not much hope of whites changing their attitudes toward Blacks because the "black man has functioned in the white man's world as a fixed star, as an immovable pillar"; and if he moves out of place, "heaven and earth are shaken to their foundations."[5] This whole devastating situation in the history of the Blacks does not testify to the inferiority of Black people, Baldwin counsels; it testifies to white inhumanity and fear.[6] This brings us to the main point of this discussion. In the end of Baldwin's letter to James, he counsels him against despair. He tells James that "we, with love shall force our brothers to see themselves as they are. . . ." Then, he says:

> For this is your home . . . do not be driven from it; great men have done great things here, and will again, and we can make America what America must become. It will be hard, James, but you come from sturdy, peasant stock, men who picked cotton and dammed rivers and built railroads, and, in the teeth of the most terrifying odds, achieved an unassailable and monumental dignity. You come from a long line of great poets, some of the greatest poets since Homer. One of them said, *The very time I thought I was lost, My dungeon shook and my chains fell off.*[7]

This quote from a Black poet, "My dungeon shook and my chains fell off," comes directly out of the folk expressions in the Black church. It is not an expression that has fallen into oblivion with the passing of time; it might be heard in the prayer or testimony of a communicant in one of the mass Black churches next Sunday morning. This expression is used primarily to depict the previous unrighteous state of the person coming into the spiritual presence of God in that state; one is penitent, and God justifies one. God sets one free although one is undeserving. This was and still is a very real religious experience in the life of Black people. This experience of being justified—set free from the dungeons of unrighteousness and having the chains of the propensity to be disobedient to the will of God fall off—give one a sense of dignity and worth in the sight of God and in the world. The person is somebody despite the fact that the person does not exist in the sight of the oppressor. The same spiritual theme, "My dungeon shook and my chains fell off," is carried over mythologically into the social life of Blacks. When God justifies a person, that person is not only accepted by God into the community of the saved, but he or she is also fully human to somebody in the world. One does exist. One knows that whites will go on to deny one's full existence, one's full being; but one also knows that when Christ makes a person free, that one is free indeed—free to be. And to be means to be fully human.

Again Baldwin makes a cogent point when he writes: "In the same way that we, for white people, were the descendants of Ham, and were cursed forever, white people were, for us, the descendants of Cain."[8] He did not elaborate further on the subject of Cain. It is evident that we know who Cain is: he is the one who murderously deprived his brother of the life which was given to him by the heavenly Father to live out in its fulfillment in relationship with the heavenly Father and in community with his brother. To identify the oppressors with Cain is an honest and just comparison. C. T. Vivian quotes John F. Kennedy as saying: "A Negro baby born in America today, regardless of the section or state in which he is born, has about one-half as much chance of completing high school as a white baby born in the same place, on the same day. . . ."[9] This is all because of human lust which negates the social justice which ought to be available to every human creature.

Augustine saw the carrying out of such lust as a violation of the will of God which would eventually receive its just reward. J. Sherrell Hendricks points out in *Christian Word Book* that Augustine follows Paul in the conviction that the love of God calls people to be concerned about their neighbors. But people wrongly desire to possess others and to hurt them. They lust for power over others. They insult others in order to make themselves feel big.[10] It is under these conditions and circumstances that the Black folks must live and at the same time try to make sense out of the meaning of justification or the justice of God.

Carl Michalson correctly states that "we live between the time of the theology which no longer makes sense to us and the time of a theology which has not yet clearly dawned."[11] Of course, Michalson was not talking about the dawning of a Black theology. Yet what he said is apropos for Black theology which is dawning because, among many other things, the development of the concept of justice in Western, colonial theologies is not very helpful; it makes very little sense where justice speaks only or primarily to freedom from sin and guilt and not from social injustices.

The biblical concept of justice, says Hendricks, is built upon the conviction that God is righteous and just. He uses Amos 9 and Jeremiah 23:6 as biblical references. Amos 9 depicts God as One who will "shake the house of Israel among all the nations as one shakes with a sieve. . . . All the sinners of my people shall die by the sword" (Amos 9:9). Yet, in the next few verses God tells Amos:

> "In that day I will raise up
> the booth of David that is fallen
> and repair its breaches,
> and raise up its ruins,
> and rebuild it as in the days of old
> that they may possess the remnant of Edom
> and all the nations who are called
> by my name." . . .
>
> —Amos 9:11-12

The Jeremiah passage reads: "In his days Judah will be saved, and Israel will dwell securely. And this is the name by which he will be called: 'The Lord is our righteousness'" (Jeremiah 23:6). These passages are referred to in order to support Hendricks' belief that God treats man fairly and that the judgment of God on human life is never in error.[12] The wicked may prosper while the righteous suffer at present, but in the end this will not be the case. Psalm 72 also supports this view. It says in part:

> Give the king thy justice, O God
> and thy righteousness to the royal son!
> May he judge thy people with righteousness,
> and thy poor with justice!
> Let the mountains bear prosperity
> for the people
> and the hills, in righteousness!
> May he defend the cause of the
> poor of the people
> give deliverance to the needy,
> and crush the oppressor!
>
> —Psalm 72:1-4

> For he delivers the needy when he calls,
> the poor and him who has no helper.
> He has pity on the weak and the needy,

and saves the lives of the needy.
From oppression and violence he redeems their life;
and precious is their blood in his sight.
—Psalm 72:12-14

It is interesting to note how white scholars can point to those biblical passages which show that the writers understood God to be a God of righteousness and justice, and yet this fact is obscured in Western, colonial theologies and almost nonexistent in white preaching. The psalmist here is very clear; God is expected to judge the people with righteousness and the poor with justice. The righteousness and justice of God are tied up with his plan and program of redemption. The needy cry, and God delivers the needy when they cry. Then, from oppression and violence He redeems their lives. It is in this sense that Black theology understands the full meaning of the justice of God. God's justice gives validity to both the spiritual and the physio-social life of the oppressed. Blacks become strong upstanding beings through God's redeeming processes, despite the injustices which are designed to make Blacks weak and to rob them of the power of self-fulfillment and self-maintenance.

Roberts correctly sees justice rooted in the moral integrity of God. "In God's nature," he declares, "justice and mercy greet each other." He seems to accept the classical view of justice which means rendering to one his due. Then he asserts that the biblical meaning of the justice of God also includes an expression of righteousness. He goes beyond the discussion of Hendricks and brings in the love motif: "God is loving, but he is also just." The love which he talks about is that which, in the Christian sense, is always related to just and equal treatment of human beings. He charges that "just as, in the state, whites seek 'law and order' without justice, even so, in the church, they seek love without justice." Love, for him, requires compassion, "but justice requires that the institutions of society be altered so as to make the expression of love possible."[13]

James Cone talks about the justice of God using the terms "love" and "righteousness." For him Black theology

asks not whether love is an essential element of the Christian interpretation of God, but whether the love of God itself can be properly understood without focusing equally on the biblical view of God's righteousness. Is it possible to understand what God's love means for the oppressed without making *wrath* an essential ingredient of that love? What could love possibly mean in a racist society except the righteous condemnation of everything white?[14]

He is correct in suggesting that justice, through his use of the terms "love" and "righteousness," includes wrath—revolution—in the institutions and social systems in America. This full understanding of justice is a part of the very fiber of Black folk theology. White theologians, such as Paul Tillich, also recognized that any understanding of love without righteousness which makes demands leaves something to be desired.

He writes:

> Justice is that side of love which affirms the independent right of object and subject within the love relation. Love does not destroy the freedom of the beloved and does not violate the structures of the beloved's individual and social existence. Neither does love surrender the freedom of him who loves, and it does not violate the structures of his individual and social existence. Love as the reunion of those who are separated does not distort or destroy in its union. There is a love, however, which is chaotic self-surrender or chaotic self-imposition; it is not a real love but a "symbiotic" love. . . . Much romantic love has this character.[15]

He borrows the term "symbiotic" from Eric Fromm. It is the adjective from the noun "symbiosis," meaning the living together of two dissimilar organisms in close association or union, especially where this arrangement is advantageous to both of the organisms. Tillich presses his point further by restating the fact that divine love includes that justice which does both, acknowledges and preserves the freedom as well as the unique character of the beloved. Divine love does justice to persons while at the same time it drives them toward fulfillment. Neither does it force one or leave one. It does attract one and lure one toward reunion.[16]

Tillich makes the correct assessment as far as Black theology is concerned. The problem is, first, is anybody listening? Secondly, if there is someone listening, where is the application of this understanding of love and justice in the white Christian churches? "He that hath ears to hear" evidently has not heard.

The Black folk theology emerging out of the historical Formative and Maturative periods has always asserted that love unites into confederation with the divine and with others those who are experiencing the redemptive revelation of God. Black theology always knows that when the individual and when the community are justified by God, God sets the individual or the community free and preserves that freedom as well as the unique character of the beloved who is justified. It is this knowledge of being justified from above and the assurance that being does not require self-debasement of the beloved that impel the beloved toward self-fulfillment in every day and in every generation. The knowledge of justification and the awareness of worth as a justified being move the oppressed of this land to assert their being while experiencing the contradictions of injustices in their life settings.

Justification by faith is an ontological reality which gives meaning to Black religionists who dangle in a state of existential absurdity. But time and time again, in the historical sojourn of these pilgrims, God discloses himself as the One who justifies them and whose resurrected Son walks with them and who is bringing them toward victory over their social debilitating situations just as he has shaken their spiritual dungeons and has caused their chains of sins to fall off. The Black folks' trust or faith in God's acceptance of them provides for them a state of freedom which makes it possible for them to concern themselves with the work which is encumbered upon them as members of the Christian faith—that is, to be about their Father's business in the world.

Justice and the Wrath of God

There is a Black song which contains these lines:

> You better mind, mind, mind.
> O you better mind, mind, mind.
> You got an account to give in the judgment
> You better mind.

This song recognizes that justice of God includes wrath—retribution as well as mercy. People as free beings are held accountable for their acts, and here there is a recognition that there will be an end time—an otherworldly—accounting for their acts and deeds in this world. But whether otherworldly or not, the fact is established that people are accountable and the justice of God includes wrath and retribution as well as undeserved forgiveness for sins. God's justice which is expressed in terms of his righteousness is understood to mean that people must pay for their deeds which are considered as elements of unrighteousness. And in Black thought, this meant the oppression and humiliation of Blacks by whites whose objective was and is self-aggrandizement. In the end time, they (the white oppressors) would have to give an account. It must be pointed out that the accountability in the end applies equally to Blacks as well as to white oppressors. Blacks, too, had better mind how they behave in this world for they, too, have to give an account before the just Judge—the Creator and source of being—at the end of human history.

But it was not only in the end time that the justice of God would reveal his wrath as well as his love and mercy. This would take place in this world as well. A song which expresses that theological factor is evident in the following lines:

> You shall reap jes what you sow,
> You shall reap jes what you sow,
> On the mountain, in the valley,
> You shall reap jes what you sow.[17]

This reaping of what you sow was this-worldly and applied equally to the Blacks who might sow evil as well as to the oppressors who they knew sowed evil in that they oppressed the beloved who were justified by God in situations and circumstances which were in direct contradiction to the will of God. Here, it is clearly understood that the justice which sets the bondslaves free is also the justice which says "Cut them down!" when they refuse to behave in a manner which is consistent with the understood will of God. In Black prayers and testimonies in the Black church today there is a statement which comes out of the Maturative Black theological era. It goes something like this: "When justice said cut him down, mercy pleaded my case and bid my golden moments to roll on a little while longer."

When people choose to disobey the will of God, particularly in relationship with other beings, divine love ceases and divine wrath becomes operative as an expression of the justice—the righteousness of God. Tillich is helpful at this point when he suggests: "Where the divine love ends, being ends; condemnation can only mean that the creature is left to the nonbeing it has chosen. The symbol 'eternal death' is even more expressive, where interpreted as self-exclusion from eternal life and consequently from being."[18] According to Tillich's position here, and the position or stance of many white folks in America, it is they who are victims of nonbeing because it is they who have chosen to violate the will of God by using their powers to subjugate Blacks for their own personal and group advantages. So it is they who make themselves the sons of Cain while attempting to effect the condition of the so-called sons of Ham, who are misinterpreted to be condemned to everlasting subjugation. They who are the agents of evil, who would use their social and political powers to deprive others of their being, become themselves the real exhibits of nonbeings according to scriptural understandings. Not only that, but they also make themselves objects of the wrath of God, according to Psalm 72, cited earlier in this chapter.

God's justice is expressed through his mercy and love, but that element of righteousness which is also a part of his justice is also expressed in his wrath and judgment. The wrath and judgment of God are sometimes seen in his taking the initiative in bringing an end to injustices and in breaking the perpetrators of injustices. Blacks find biblical backing for this idea in Moses' song:

> Then Moses and the people of Israel sang this song to
> the Lord, saying, . . .
> "The Lord is a man of war;
>   the Lord is his name.
> "Pharaoh's chariots and his host
>   he cast into the sea;
> and his picked officers are sunk in
>   the Red Sea. . . .
> Thy right hand, O Lord, glorious in power,
>   thy right hand, O Lord, shatters the enemy."
> —Exodus 25:1-6

In Moses' song, God takes the initiative to institute wrath and judgment—destruction—upon the oppressors. It is the Lord who has cast Pharaoh and his chariots into the sea. It is he who shatters the enemies in his wrath. Amos says to Israel:

> Thus says the Lord:
> "For three transgressions of Israel,
>   and for four, I will not revoke the punishment;
> because they sell the righteous for silver,
>   and the needy for a pair of shoes—
> they that trample the head of the poor
>   into the dust of the earth,
> and turn aside the way of the afflicted."
> —Amos 2:6-7b

Again Amos says: "Hear this word, you cows of Bashan, who are in the mountain of Samaria, who oppress the poor, who crush the needy" (Amos 4:1a). Then in a kind of summary statement Amos quotes the Lord, saying, "But let justice roll down like waters, and righteousness like an everflowing stream" (Amos 5:24). From both Moses and Amos we must conclude that the justice of God included his wrath directed against those who were disobedient to the will of God. And further, at least in the passages cited above, the wrath of

God is directed against those who have been unjust in their relationships with others. The wrath of God was directed against those who had used their powers to oppress the poor and the needy.

Amos's call to "let justice roll down like waters, and righteousness like an everflowing stream" further suggests that the wrath of God is not an afterthought in the scheme of God's justice. It is a natural fallout of the justice of God. What Amos is calling for is simply to let justice run its full course, and God's wrath will bring down the oppressors as the waters of an everflowing stream bring down the towering banks of the rivers.

Black theology is built upon this understanding of justice. God's justice has a built-in wrathful element which is self-destructing to oppressors and to all those who choose to conduct themselves in a manner which is contrary to the will of the Creator. This self-destruction arises out of the condemnation of the unjust. Tillich declares that "condemnation can only mean that creature is left to the nonbeing it has chosen," as he said in an earlier quote. Tillich also writes:

> The wrath of God is neither a divine affect alongside his love nor a motive for action alongside providence; it is the emotional symbol for the work of love which rejects and leaves to self-destruction what resists it. The experience of the wrath of God is the awareness of the self-destructive nature of evil, namely, of those acts and attitudes in which the finite creature keeps itself separated from the ground of being and resists God's reuniting love. Such an experience is real, and the metaphorical symbol "the wrath of God" is unavoidable.[19]

Tillich is right, but his reference to wrath as an emotional or metaphorical symbol does not go far enough for Black theology. It is true that the work of love leaves to self-destruction that which resists it. But the experience of the wrath of God is more than an awareness of the self-destructive nature of evil. It is an element in the ground of Black ontology. That which gives meaning to life in the Black religious community in relationship to the justice of God is the assurance that God will bring down the oppressors and set the captives free not symbolically and metaphorically but in reality. Again, the experience of the wrath of God as an awareness of the self-destructive nature of evil (meaning those acts and attitudes in which the finite creature keeps itself separated from the ground of being and resists the uniting love of God) either must not have been revealed to the white power group in America; or if this self-destructive nature of evil has been revealed to the white power group, it has had no corrective effects. The acts and attitudes of the power class in this country show no signs of their having encountered the full meaning of justice which includes the wrath of God. For the white power class the justice of God is seen only from the perspective of his love being extended to those who are unworthy.

James Cone raises a cogent question: "Is it possible to understand what God's love means for the oppressed without making *wrath* an essential ingredient of that love?"[20] He also asserts: "A God minus wrath seems to be a God who is basically not against anybody."[21] Black theology has no room for such a God. God is our Redeemer in Black folk thought. He is for us, since we are his children; we have said "yes" to his bidding, and he has declared, through his Son, that he has come to justify us, to set us free from sin and from oppression. We are God's chosen people. To be chosen is to say "yes" to the calling and will of God as Redeemer. And to say "yes" is not merely an intellectual articulate assent of the mind formulated into theological concepts and jargons; to say "yes" means the organization and reorganization of one's life and thus the life of the chosen community in light of what is understood to be the will of the Redeemer. This includes conducting one's self in relationship with all other human beings in such a way as to affirm their humanity. It is at this point that the oppressors in this country fall short in meeting this criterion for membership in the community of the chosen. Since the Redeemer is for us, it must follow that he is against those who would and do afflict us. Black suffering continues primarily because of the misuse of white power. Therefore Cone is right when he argues that "Black Theology says that God's love is God's liberation of black people as expressed in Black Power."[22] This brings us to the point that God's justice also means revolution. In Black thought, justice and revolution are inseparable.

Justice and Revolution

In the prayers and testimonies of the Blacks, there is a statement which proclaims "God is going to set this world on fire!" The speaker might be referring to an apocalyptic catastrophe expected at the end of human history, but he is more likely to be talking about some intervening act of God which is to correct the course of white captains in charge of the ship of the state of affairs in America who have purposely deviated from the course of humanity which was charted in creation. "God is going to set this world on fire" is a statement (sometimes arranged into a song) growing out of the feeling of helplessness and frustrations emanating from the experiences of white brutality. The lynchings and assassinations of Blacks and the bombing and burning of Black churches and properties gave rise to this hope of a God-inspired and God-led revolution. God is going to bring about a revolution.

And after the assassination of Dr. Martin Luther King, Jr., in 1968, it seemed that the Redeemer had delayed his coming; so Blacks took to the streets and aided God in setting this world on fire. They literally stood back and watched their neighborhoods burn to the ground while shouts from the crowd rang out: "Burn, baby, burn!" There have been many questions as to why Black people burned their own neighborhoods. Why did they burn their own places of abode? Those who question the judgment of Blacks in this matter are probably not aware of the fact that Blacks did not own those dwellings. They were owned in large proportion by white suburbanites who came into those ghettos once a week or once a month to collect rent. Even where Blacks were buying their homes in these ghetto areas, in most instances they had already paid more than the true market value for the houses, did not have title to the properties, and were still paying. The furnishings in these homes were much overpriced when they were secured for a dollar down and a dollar a week. What, then, did the Black folks in the ghetto have to lose in burning down their own neighborhood? Nothing!

Another factor is that Blacks have never had the attachment to material things (never had that much to become attached to) that seems to possess the oppressors to the extent that they have acted and do act in a demonic way in their relationship with the oppressed. Again, if Blacks were to strike out and express their disenchantment against the white powers by hitting them where it hurts most, by attacking their coveted possesssion—property—it is obvious that Blacks had to start where they were. With all the security and protective instruments elsewhere, to start anywhere else would have meant suicide, and Blacks are not fools. They started where they were before the "man" could bring in his police and National Guard forces. Then they shouted with a sense of relief, "Burn, baby, burn!"

What does all this mean theologically? First, it must be understood that the idea of the wrath of God being expressed in a physical way against the oppressors in human history came out of the

Black church. The Black church did not support the "Burn, baby, burn" method of Black reprisals against the forces of white power, but the teachings and preachings of the Black church had prepared the background for those modern-day Zealots. Even the non-churched Blacks looked forward to the day when God would "set this world on fire" in human history and correct some of the evils which had demonic and devastating effects upon their physical, social, and spiritual well-being. The righteous element of God's judgment would break into the history of suffering. God, "The Old Repair Man," mentioned in chapter 5, would some day step in and repair this damaged nation. And with his strong hands he would mold a more enduring and humane society.

Who knew during the riots of the late nineteen sixties whether or not this was the time of his major redemptive intervention? Well, no one could then be sure that it was not the time that God was bringing to an end this unjust system. Blacks were aware of the Moses story in which God sent many plagues upon Pharaoh and his oppressive henchmen (the plague of flies, the plague of pestilence, the plague of boils, etc.), but the oppressors' hearts became harder and harder. In the Tillichian sense, they were left to the nonbeing that they had chosen. They continued to afflict the children of God. But when God, in his wrath, sent the tenth plague, he struck the oppressors where it did the greatest damage: he struck the firstborn. "Then the Lord said to Moses, 'I will send only one more punishment on the king of Egypt and his people. After that he will let you leave. In fact, he will drive all of you out of here'" (Exodus 11:1, TEV). Blacks did not know whether the riots constituted the tenth plague of God upon the modern-day Pharaoh and Egyptians of this nation or not, but the modern-day Zealots of the ghettos across this nation were ready to participate in bringing on that plague. In retrospect, we now know that the white power structure refused and still refuses to be humanized. Certainly, their dungeons were shaken, but their chains of racism did not completely fall off. Their hearts were and are still hard. But, many Black religionists still hold, today, that the riots were incidents of the work of the righteousness and justice of God in human history. God's righteousness says he will not withhold the punishment of them who reject the law of the Lord and have not kept his statutes (see Amos. 2:4).

We have suggested that the righteousness element of justice means revolution. But although we have just discussed the riots of the late nineteen sixties, we need to recognize that revolution and violence are not synonymous in Black thought. Deotis Roberts puts it this way:

> Freedom sums up *what is.* Liberation is revolutionary—for blacks it points to *what ought to be.* Black Christians desire radical and rapid social change in America as a matter of survival. Black Theology is a theology of *liberation.* We believe that the Christian faith is avowedly revolutionary and, therefore, it may speak to this need with great force.[23]

While the modern-day Zealots in the Black ghettos have not eliminated the "by any means necessary" approach to making the American society a humane place in which to live for all of her citizens, Black folk theology does hold somewhat tenaciously to the idea of nonviolent revolutions. While I was talking with a parishioner recently about the problems of the Black struggle, she said to me: "Well, Reverend, the Lord says, 'If I'm for you, I'm more than the whole world against you.'" What she meant was that which is often expressed in Black folk worship experiences: "If I hold my peace, the Lord will fight my battle." But we should not overemphasize the matter of nonviolence and humility for Black folks amid oppressive social situations. While Black folk theology holds up nonviolent revolution as the ideal, it does not eliminate violence as a means to that end. This is evident in a poem by Claude McKay, which says in part: "If we must die, let it not be like hogs, hunted and penned in an inglorious spot, . . . Like men we'll face the murderous, cowardly pack, pressed to the wall, dying, but fighting back!"[24] This sounds very much like a counsel to violence if necessary.

But Roberts seems to have his finger on the pulse of Black theology when he says liberation is revolution and then follows with the statement that Black Christians desire radical and rapid social change. Revolution in Black theology means radical and rapid change. Revolution—radical and rapid change—is a necessary step in the course of the justice of God in Black religious history both from the Christian, spiritual point of view and in the social order in which Blacks find themselves in this one nation divided, First, humanity in its fallen state—as a good thing spoiled—tends to bow to the lesser good in life when the greater good is both known and possible. There are numerous biblical incidents supporting Black theology's point of view that justification by the Redeemer has taken the form of radical and rapid change.

Isaiah's encounter with God in the year that King Uzziah died was a kind of revolutionary experience. It was radical and rapid in that, by his own confession, Isaiah was a man of unclean lips and praxis made him a part of people with unclean lips; yet he immediately said "yes" to the justifying experience and left the temple as a new creation. He had been justified, and that justification was revolutionary in proportion (Isaiah 6). When Paul was justified on the Damascus Road, his experience was no less dramatic and revolutionary than that of Isaiah. So we see that there are religious (spiritual) experiences on record which support my contention that justification, even spiritual justification, has its revolutionary ingredients. On the other hand, however, social justice for Blacks in North America is definitely a religious phenomenon. It is the other side of the coin of redemption from sin and guilt. It is a definite aspect of the faith and hope of Black folks.

No social justice has come to Blacks in America without revolution. It is somewhat akin to the statement ". . . and without the shedding of blood there is no forgiveness of sins" (Hebrews 9:22b). The benefits of white power have so warped the minds of some white Americans that nothing short of revolutionary actions on the part of the oppressed brought any semblance of social justice for Blacks. This is what led Dr. Martin Luther King, Jr., to declare on that August day in the nation's capital: "We have also come to this hallowed spot to remind America of the fierce urgency of *now*. This is no time to engage in the luxury of cooling off or to take the tranquilizing drug of gradualism." [25]

He had already reminded his listeners that one hundred years after the Emancipation Proclamation went into effect, Blacks were still not free. Thus, he came to the conclusion that neither a cooling-off period nor the tranquilizing drugs of gradualism would ever permit social justice for Blacks to become a reality in this country. The other alternative? Revolution—radical demands which, hopefully, might result in moving Blacks another notch up the scale of social justice—redemption from human-caused sufferings.

As a result of the fall, many Euro-American whites suffer from the sin of the need to possess and to dominate other human beings. In order that they might *be* socially, economically, and politically, they are addicted to the drug of possessing other people and treating them as nonbeings. The only social justice which they will permit is that which evolves in the process of revolution. Blacks are aware of this grim reality. Thus, social justification in Black theology is tied up with revolution. A long list of historical events attests to this truism. It took bloody revolutions to rid African nations from colonial domination. It took a national Civil War to bring about the legal emancipation of Blacks in this country. It took a Supreme Court edict to make it legal for Blacks to attend integrated schools in America. It took revolution, a confrontation with National Guardsmen and a state governor, Orval Faubus, before Daisy Gaston Bates could get nine Black students into the previously all-white Little Rock Central High School in 1957, three years after the Supreme Court edict. It took a massive bus boycott and an extended court battle in order to secure the rights of Blacks to sit anywhere that any other fare-paying white passengers could sit on buses in Montgomery, Alabama. It took confrontations and physical abuses with fire hoses, cattle prods, dogs, and vicious white people in order that Blacks might enjoy equal accommodations across this country. And it took a federal takeover of the way-up-north, Boston high schools in order to bring about integration in that northern city, twenty-one years after the Supreme Court desegregation order. The list goes on and on. But it is very evident that Blacks can expect very little social justice in America without some revolution. Revolution is inseparable from redemption in Black theology.

Social justification in Black theology is tied up with revolution. Social justice and revolution are inseparable in America. Revolution need not include violence. Just men and women in this racist society can become engaged in a program of rapid and radical social change which will negate the need and possibility of violent revolution. Of course America cannot look back to any point in her history for such directions; she can only look to the so-called American ideal, the realization of which is still future for Black folks.

Robert McAfee Brown gives us two pointed quotes. The first is from the late President John F. Kennedy who said: "Those who make peaceful revolution impossible will make violent revolution inevitable." The second quote from Reinhold Niebuhr who said: "Neutrality in a social struggle between entrenched and advancing social classes means alliance with the entrenched position. In the social struggle we are either on the side of privilege or need."[26] Here Kennedy predicts the inevitability of violent revolution when peaceful revolution is made impossible, and Niebuhr holds that one who does not participate in revolutionary struggles is siding with those who perpetrate structural social violence.

We have some problems with Major Jones when he writes:

Too many black people talk about a revolution void of hope. A man makes revolution because he has no other options; a boy makes revolution because he has no other thoughts. [I am not sure whether Blacks are men or boys in Jones' mind.] If revolution is the goal of black people, nothing other than revolution will do. If a changed and a just society are the goals, there may be several ways to achieve such changes. However, if one is honest, it must be admitted that there are those who have come to the point of thinking revolution because they see no other reasonable way to achieve reforms.[27]

One might respond to Jones in this way: In the first place, no one has suggested that violent revolution is the goal of Black people, unless it was the oppressors who made the charge. In the second place, a changed and a just society are the goals, and Blacks have made the ultimate sacrifices of giving up physical life in order to achieve a just society through nonviolent means. The assassination of the late Dr. Martin Luther King, Jr., is a case in point. In the third place, we do admit that there are those who have come to the point of thinking revolution, with some violence if necessary, because every nonviolent means which has been tried by Black folks in this country since August 20, 1619, has somehow not achieved its ultimate goal—a just society wherein Blacks have the freedom to *be*.

Jones has opted for what Paul Ricoeur describes as an "ethic of distress." This he says "is a time when the Christian recognizes that his action in general or the violent moment in particular can no longer be called Christian, that there can be no possible theological or ethical justification." He states further that, "In adopting an ethic of distress, the Christian seeks no ethical justification for what he feels he must do within the context of the movement, because he knows that there can be no such justification for what he is about."[28] One must object to the idea of adopting Ricoeur's ethic of distress for Black theology. It must be pointed out that Ricoeur arrived at his position, it seems, after reflecting upon revolution expressed in war and killing. War and killing are not central to the Black revolution for liberation in this country. Blacks never had and never will have in the foreseeable future the means to conduct a physical war against their oppressors in this country.

Paul Ramsey does not follow Ricoeur in his ethic of distress, but he raises the question as to whether it is possible to speak of justifiable violations of moral principles. He defines principles as directions for action based upon *agape*. In contrast to principles which govern or regulate conduct, "rules would be particular *directives* of an action, prescribing or proscribing a *definite* action."[29] He believes that principles which stand behind the rules and give direction to the rules are changeless. But the rules which prescribe definite action fall into the category of exceptionism. He puts it this way:

> ... while there may well be exceptionless *principles* there cannot be any exceptionless moral *rules* because, so far as human moral judgment alone is concerned, we cannot know and we cannot formulate rules of conduct that are *both* certain in their determination of wrongfulness or praiseworthiness and certain as to the description of the actions to which these verdicts apply.[30]

Ramsey seems to conclude that moral actions and behaviors based on principles are rules, and these rules might change with time, place, and circumstances. So while there cannot be any justifiable violation of moral principles, there is justification for adjustments of moral rules growing out of moral principles. Ramsey does not say so, but it seems that his view does provide room for a just revolution.

There must be in Black theology a place for just revolution. Robert McAfee Brown is helpful at this point. His book, *Religion and Violence,* is recommended to the readers as a very thought-provoking and informative treatise. First, Brown advances the fact that one of the Latin roots from which we get our English word "violence" comes from the Latin word *violare* which means "to violate." He concludes:

> Whatever "violates" another, in the sense of infringing upon or disregarding or abusing or denying that other, whether physical harm is involved or not, can be understood as an act of violence. The basic overall definition of violence would then become *violation of personhood.* While such a denial or violation can involve the physical destruction of personhood in ways that are obvious, personhood can also be violated or denied in subtle ways that are not obvious at all, except to the victim. There can be "violation of personhood" quite apart from the doing of physical harm.[31]

This is the kind of violence that the oppressors have directed against the Black pilgrims in this country for centuries. It is from this overt and subtle violation of Black personhood that Blacks must be redeemed. Blacks must be redeemed from those states and circumstances which destroy the values of human existence or human existence itself. This redemption might come about only through revolution. Brown outlines three types of violence, a description which he borrows from Dom Helder. The first, as we have mentioned before, is the violence of *injustice;* it leads to the second which is the violence of *revolt*. This happens when those who have been victims of the first type of violence decide to throw off the shackles of this oppression. And this leads to the third type of violence which he calls *repression*. Blacks know what this means without any further explanations.

The question now is whether or not there is justification for the second type of violence—revolt—from a Black theological and ethical point of view. The answer must be in the affirmative, and one need not be ready to join Ricoeur and Jones in calling this type of revolution an ethic of distress, putting it outside of Christian theological or ethical justification. Thus, a second point made by Brown is apropos to the argument. Brown gives us a list of six criteria for a just war.[32] Then he applies the same criteria in support of his idea of a just revolution. In summary they are as follows. The first says a just war must be *declared by a legitimate authority*. This criterion is difficult to transpose to the just revolution. But he points out that there are times when "normality" for a constituted government may mean oppression and repression. This is tantamount to a declaration of war by a legitimate authority. The second point is that the revolution must be *carried out with a right intention*. The impetus to the revolution must arise out of a profound sense of moral outrage because injustice is being perpetrated on a wide scale. The third criterion is that the revolution is undertaken *only as a last resort*. The fourth point says that the revolution must be waged on the basis of *the principles of proportionality*. This means that the good which is gained must far outweigh any evil that might result in gaining the good. The fifth criterion is that the revolution must have *a reasonable chance of success*. Blacks have always known the difference between martyrdom and suicide. The sixth point is that the revolution must be conducted *with all the moderation possible*. This idea of moderation is crucial in its application to the use of violence which must be kept to a minimum as far as possible within the particular situation.[33]

Brown makes a persuasive point when he argues that structural violence—that which violates the personhood of others—can become so deep-seated, so powerful, so entrenched, and so destructive and despotic that there remains no way to overthrow it short of physical violence. He continues:

The need to overthrow it by such means is not only permissible, but it is *demanded* in the name of justice, equality, and love. To shrink from the use of violence on the relatively small scale of the quick overthrow of a despotic government is to give tacit approval to the continuing use of structural violence on a massive scale by the same government.[34]

Black folk's religious thought supports this view. There comes a time in Black social situations when revolution is a necessary element in the divine process of redemption and those who would refuse to participate in such revolution would be committing a sin. Black Christians need not be afraid to admit an ethic of just revolution. Although taken somewhat out of context, a statement offered by Bishop John Robinson might well be transferred to this argument. He says: "My plea is that Christians must not fear flux or be alarmed at the relativity of all ethics to the ethos of their day. We assume too readily that God is in the rocks but not in the rapids."[35] It is going too far to suppose that God is in harmony with the rocks of the status quo in the American social system and not in the rapids of the Black revolution.

The Niebuhrian ethic of responsibility might also have something to say to the theological and ethical argument for a just revolution. One must struggle, says H. Richard Niebuhr, with what is the highest good to which one must subordinate the right. "But for the ethics of responsibility the *fitting* action, the one that fits into a total interaction as response and as anticipation of further response, is alone conducive to the good and is alone right."[36]

Responsibility is not synonymous with doing what some rule might say is good or right at any given time or in every situation. Responsibility in Niebuhr's term means doing what is fitting out of which must come the good and the right in that place and situation. For example, Rosa Parks was not doing what was good or right (according to rules of the oppressors in Montgomery, Alabama) when she refused to move to the rear of the bus. But she was acting responsibly and courageously, based on a matter of conscience, feeling, and intuition. What she did was not seen as good or right for that time and situation in history. But her interpretation of the force acting upon her was correct, and her fitting action brought about a reaction which had a positive effect upon Black life all across this country. The fitting action brought with it both the good and the right. A responsible act or set of acts in the Black revolution must be the fitting act related to the time, place, and situation which results in the good and the right for the majority of those whom the revolution is designed to help in the light of the agape taught in the Scriptures and which was exhibited in Jesus Christ.

Blacks who have been justified by their Creator know that Christ has made them free, and therefore they stand upright in stature and in spirit before God and before the oppressors whose abiding aim is to deny and to delay the fulfillment of social justice. But all along their pilgrims' journey they have been responsive to what they understood to be the will of the Creator. Their justification led naturally to the process of sanctification.

"Been Saved and Sanctified"

When the Black folks testify that "I've been saved and sanctified; I'm on my way to heaven, and I wouldn't take 'nothing' for my journey," such a statement has far-reaching implications for Black theology. "Been saved" means that one has had an experience or assurance that one has been justified by the Creator. "Been sanctified" means that through Christ one has organized this life and is in the continual process of reorganizing one's life in ways which are in accordance with the will of him who has seen fit to justify one. "On my way to heaven and wouldn't take 'nothing' for my journey" means that both justification and the process of sanctification are understood in the light of the eschatological hope. Justification and sanctification have eschatological meanings.

Sanctification, according to Van Harvey, is based upon the Latin word *sanctus*. This means holy. The term "sanctification" has been used traditionally "to describe the process in which new life is imparted to the believer by the Holy Spirit." The believer is now released from the compulsive power of sin and guilt and is enabled to love God and to serve one's neighbor.[37] If we accept Harvey's definition which says sanctification means that the believers are enabled to serve their neighbors, then white Americans either are not believers or are not sanctified, or they do not consider Black people to be their neighbors.

Harvey sees no sharp distinction between justification and sanctification in Roman Catholic doctrines. For the Roman Catholic, the "entire life of a believer should be a growth from 'grace to grace.'" There must be faith leading to both hope and charity. Superficially, he says, the views of the Protestant reformers are similar to those of Roman Catholics. Luther and Calvin did not draw any sharp line between justification and sanctification; both tended to interpret the new life as one aspect of justification. While justification by faith has a different interpretation in these two Christian bodies, justification and sanctification are tied together in the doctrines of both Roman Catholics and reformers.

Calvin and the reformers held the general view that while the compulsion to sin has been broken in the true person of faith, one's life is still subject to a day-to-day struggle with egotism and pride. Therefore, no perfection is final and complete in this life, and no action, no matter how exalted it might be, is without the taint of sin. Subsequently, the Pietist group in the Protestant faith made sanctification their main concern, and John Wesley, the founder of Methodism, fathomed the doctrine of Christian perfection. This led to the view of a kind of complete sanctification in this life.[38]

Hendricks believes that "sanctification presupposes justification and indicates what takes place in the Christian life between justification and death." He supports this view by pointing out that "in the New Testament a Christian is not a perfect man. He still has problems and struggles. Difficulties continue in his life after he professes faith in Jesus as the Christ. The Christian is in the process of being made whole."[39] Sanctification in Black theology tends to adopt the view articulated by Hendricks. While the Pentecostal groups today tend to press the thought of perfection in this life in the Wesleyan sense, this does not represent the view of the vast majority in the mass Black church. The oral theology and the practice in the life of Black Methodists do not support the idea of sanctification meaning perfection in this life. Sanctification in Black theology is a lifelong process in the faith experiences and expressions of the Black Christians. It is evident in the testimony of the old Black Baptist deacon who declares: "I know that I ain't what I ought to be, but thank God I ain't what I used to be."

It is quite clear that Black Christians, having been justified by the Creator, now set out to respond in faith and love. They recognize their previous state of nothingness in the eyes of the Divine. But since they have been redeemed, a whole new horizon of new possibilities opens up to them and they set out to organize and to reorganize their lives and behavior in such a way as to achieve their maximum humanity. They recognize that the grace of God—God's unmerited favor—justified them. Therefore, they move from the experience of unhappy consciousness and develop affirmative thoughts about self, humanity, and the future. They are not deluded into thinking that justification which leads directly to sanctification makes them perfect. They realize that sanctification is a continuing process. They are no longer "hooked" on the compulsion to sin and to do evil, but they also know that they are not perfect. So they are conscientiously, through faith, moving toward what they know that they ought to be. At each step along the pilgrim journey, they thank God that they "ain't what [they] used to be."

Sanctification and Ethical Orientation

"Etymologically," says James Sellers, "'ethics' and 'morality' meant the same thing, the former coming from the Greek . . . the latter from the Latin. . . . Both originals meant 'custom,' 'conventional conduct,' 'habitual way of action.' Perhaps because the Greeks are to have been more philosophical, the Romans more practical, a difference in level of abstraction has crept in. Morality now has to do with day-to-day, actual conduct, human activity as it is guided and gauged by the most direct working rules of proper behavior."[40] Ethics, according to Sellers, "consists in considered reflection about human actions from the point of view of some critical standard of excellence."[41] This analysis of the terms "morality" and "ethics" seems to be adequate for my reflection upon the deportment of Black folks. Morality in this work shall mean the conduct and behavior of the individuals, while ethics shall mean the standard of excellence which gives rise to conduct and behavior. And further, it is Black religion which provided the norm for Black ethics.

A word must be said in passing that Black folk religion is very practical in application. In the praxis of Black religion there is no clear distinction between morality and ethics. The communicant moves directly from religious conviction and faith to conduct and behavior. Blacks do not go to conduct and behavior by way of philosophical abstractions and explanations on the subject of ethics. While we in the academic arena do use philosophical abstractions at times for convenience, the dichotomy between morality and ethics is a Western approach evolving out of Greek philosophy. Africans, on the other hand, have a holistic world view; and because of the influence of African survivals in Black religion, there is no clear line of demarcation between morality and ethics. Again, in practice, the impetus for Black deportment flows directly from religion to conduct and behavior.

On a visit to three countries in Africa in 1972, I observed an extraordinary degree of expressions of kindness, hospitality, and respect on the part of the Africans. This expression of human respect and cordiality was shown in the relationship of the Africans with our party, but more importantly, it was also seen in their interactions with each other. This caused me to raise a question with one of the citizens of Nigeria. I asked: "How would you account for the kindness and respect which we have observed existing among the African people?" He responded without hesitation: "The milk of human kindness flows in the African veins!" This statement undergirds my contention that Black propensity toward humanity is an element of African survival mingled with and expressed through the Christian faith.

Mbiti makes an interesting observation. He says a visitor to an African village "will immediately be struck by African readiness to externalize the spontaneous feelings of joy, love, friendship, and generosity." He cautions that this expression must be balanced by the fact that Africans are human. "There are . . . occasions," he says, "when [the Africans'] feelings of hatred, strain, fear, jealousy and suspicion also become readily externalized. He makes this comparison:

> By nature, Africans are neither angels nor demons; they possess and exercise the potentialities of both angels and demons. They can be as kind as the Germans, but they can be as murderous as the Germans; Africans can be as generous as the Americans, but they can be as greedy as the Americans; they can be as friendly as the Russians, but they can be as cruel as the Russians; they can be as honest as the English, but they can also be as equally hypocritical. In their human nature Africans are Germans, Swiss, Chinese, Indians or English—they are men.[42]

With this kind of comparison by a person who is African himself, we would not dare to argue. We agree that by *nature* all people are human. However, when it comes to religion, the ethics and morality of one people may differ greatly from those of another people. In religion people do not behave purely from human nature; their behavior is influenced by their responses to God's justice and continuous sanctifying presence. It is a well-known fact that Africans are a very religious people; it should follow, then, that they would have developed a meaningful ethic.

Mbiti reports that the "African notions of morality, ethics, and justice have not been fully studied." But he does point to the work of E. Bolaji Idowu, *Olódùmarè: God in Yoruba Belief.*[43] Idowu gives a whole chapter to the subject of God and moral values among the Yoruba. "For the Yoruba," he contends, "moral values derive from the nature of God Himself, Whom they consider to be the 'Pure King,' 'Perfect King.' . . . Character *(Iwa)* is the essence of Yoruba ethics" and the life of a person depends upon the character of the person. Idowu draws a quote from the Yoruba people which says: "Gentle character it is which enables the rope of life to stay unbroken in one's hand." Another quote says: "It is good character that is man's guard."[44] Mbiti draws this conclusion from Idowu's study:

> Good character shows itself in the following ways: chastity before marriage and faithfulness during marriage; hospitality; generosity, the opposite of selfishness; kindness; justice; truth and rectitude as essential virtues; avoiding stealing; keeping a covenant and avoiding falsehood; protecting the poor and weak, especially women; giving honour and respect to older people; and avoiding hypocrisy. This can be applied, with additions to the list of what constitutes good character, to many African societies.[45]

This is the kind of ethical doctrine which saturated the lives and the conduct of the people who were stolen from the continent of Africa. One is still in a quandary when one tries to figure out who were the real "pagans" in those encounters—those who were stolen or those who did the stealing of human beings?

From what we have learned about African religions we may conclude that Black ethics and morality, to a large degree, are derived from African survivals. Black people brought their ethics with them from Africa. When they were introduced to Christianity and were redeemed through the blood of the Lamb, the ethical responses which they traditionally made to the "Pure King" were translated and transmitted into their reoriented religious life and expressions.

For Black theology, the ethical dimension of justification and sanctification is the call to work out one's soul salvation with fear and trembling. It is a call to obedience. It is a call to faithfulness. The individual works out soul salvation in the community of the justified. Redemption which liberates the individual in the process of justification also brings the justified into confederation through the process of sanctification. The response of obedience and faithfulness is expressed individually in that it takes the individual to make up the confederation. But the Black church community—that confederation of Black believers—is the sanctified community working together with God and with each other, moving as pilgrims toward the eschatological fulfillment of justification and sanctification, the fulfillment of that perfect union of being—individually and collectively—with the eternal Being. (Again one must keep in mind that there are Black sinners as well as there are sinners in other racial groups. All Blacks have not been responsive to the justice and mercy of God.)

In the Black church there are songs, prayers, and testimonies which seem to stress individual salvation, and indeed they do. But a close examination of the matter discloses that individual salvation is important in the Black church only to the extent that it is expressed in community; thus salvation is expressed in human encounters and relationship. Black religionists take seriously Jesus' statement: "Truly I say to you, as you did it not to one of the least of these, you did it not to me" (Matthew 25:45*b*). Obedience and faithfulness are worked out in confederation. And just as the individuals are called together to form a unity of one body in the here and now, it is this one body of the redeemed which will become one in unity with the Eternal "in the sweet by and by." Blacks could sing with assurance:

> When we all get to heaven,
> What a day of rejoicing that will be!
> When we all get to heaven,
> We will sing and shout the victory.

This "we" theme saturates Black religious expressions. By the power and love of God we have been formed into a community. Our sanctification is understood in the Tillichian sense. Tillich suggests: "'Sanctification' *can* mean 'being received into the community of the *sancti*,' namely, into the community of those who are grasped by the power of the New Being."[46] It is this understanding of being grasped by the power of God and drawn into the Canaan of human experience—a religious life that is replete with spiritual milk and honey—that shapes the obedient expressions of faith by Black people.

Obedience in the Black religious community is not a response to human laws, and it is not something passed to Blacks from white Christians. Blacks had developed a system of ethical responses to the will of the "Pure King" as a religious way of life before they were captured and brought to these shores by the imperialist oppressors. In the expression of obedience to God, Blacks were not merely imitating white Christian expressions. In the minds of white folks, obedience has a different connotation than it has for Black religionists.

Obedience for the oppressor means Blacks being obedient to the dehumanizing whims of the masters. This led Charles Long to talk about the master/slave dichotomy. From the master's perspective there is the call or expectation of imitation and obedience on the part of the slaves. But from the slave's perspective there is the notion of faithfulness and trust. This faithfulness and trust did not arise out of what the slaves thought to be their relationship with the masters; it arose out of what the slaves knew ought to be their relationship between themselves and their God. Long says this was a tradition which the slaves brought from Africa. It was a tradition which they gleaned as human beings in relationship to Being. Black slaves did some rebelling, says Long, but they did more than that; they did some living too. Blacks brought with them a humanity, and they continued to develop that humanity under the most inhumane conditions.[47] This humanity was expressed in obedience and implicit trust in the Redeemer who would redeem them from the state of suffering just as he had redeemed them from the state of compulsion to sin and evil through justification. Black religious obedience was not an imitation of white religious expressions; it was part and parcel of the fiber of their very existence which transcended the master-defined concept of obedience. It was sanctification in process in the Black religious community in a way that it was not understood in the white religious community.

"Love your enemies" could never mean the same thing for both master and slave. This is clearly evident in Black religion from two vantage points: The first point is that there has never been any question as to who the enemies of Black folks were and are in America. The second point is that historically Black folks have been guided by their Afro-American Christian ethics in their relationship with their enemies in this land. We are aware of the violent rebellions carried out by Blacks; but, on the one hand, they were of little significance when compared to the violence done to Black folks by white Christians. On the other hand, in many instances the rebellions might well be viewed as acts of the divine will to get Pharaoh to let his people go.

Surely the Reverend Nat Turner felt that he was acting as an agent of the Divine when he went on his rebellious rampage resulting in the deaths of more than fifty whites in Southampton County, Virginia, in October, 1831. In his confession the Reverend Mr. Turner makes an interesting report. At a point in his own life experience, he ran away from his slave master. After remaining in the woods for thirty days, he returned to the plantation to the astonishment of the other slaves who thought that he had escaped to another part of the country as his father had done. The reason for his return, he says, was that the Spirit appeared to him and told him that his wishes were directed to the things of this world and not to the things of heaven; so he should return to the service of his earthly master. When he told this to the Blacks

> . . . the negroes found fault, and murmered against me, saying that if they had my sense they would not serve any master in the world. And about this time I had a vision—and I saw white spirits and black spirits engaged in battle, and the sun was darkened—the thunder rolled in the Heavens, and blood flowed in streams—and I heard a voice saying, "Such is your luck, such you are called to see, and let it come rough or smooth, you must surely bare [sic] it."[48]

This vision, he says, took place in the year of 1825; it was later reinforced by other visions. It is clear that Nat Turner felt that he was being obedient to the will of God which conflicted with the will of his master when he led the bloody insurrection in 1831. Of course, this raises the question of whether obedience which leads to such actions is really the will of God or whether it is merely the whim of man who finds himself in a situation of oppression. Whatever we might think, Nat Turner was assured that his violent expressions against the oppressors evolved out of the will of God. Black religionists and Black people in general do make room in their thought for violent retaliations against oppression as obedience to the will of God. And the Old Testament is filled with incidents in which rebellions by the oppressed were seen as fulfilling the will of God; and in the New Testament, in a moment of disgust in the synagogue, Jesus himself used a whip to teach a lesson.

Now we return to the idea that obedience in the Black religious community is not a response to human laws. What the South American theologian, Míguez Bonino, says on this subject expresses the view of Black folks on this matter. He writes: "It is therefore decisive for an obedience that claims to be Christian obedience, the discipleship of that Christ, and not a new law or man-made ordinance."[49] He writes further: "Obedience is not found as a conclusion of a syllogism but in the prophetic word of discernment received in faith."[50] Black people's obedience and faithfulness grow out of their discipleship to Christ who continues to make them what they ought to be through the sanctifying grace of the Holy Spirit. Obedience and faithfulness grow out of the unraveling of the prophetic message of the Eternal through the faith and trust which are a part of Black being.

In his book *Black Power and Christian Responsibility*, C. Freeman Sleeper puts it this way: "This faithfulness, which involves both accountability and loyalty, is the presupposition of responsible action. It is the element of promise-keeping which is central in the structure of biblical ethics."[51] Even the enemies of Blacks will have to concede that the conduct of the folk in the mass Black church in this country has been characterized by accountability and loyalty in the sense of Sleeper's statement above and is in keeping with the central structure of biblical ethics.

Justification and sanctification are central concepts in Black theology. Justification comes out of the persistent grace of God. Justification is the setting free of one who is bound. It is standing the rejected on their feet upright before God and in the world among other human beings. Justification brings Black people into confederation with the justified and with the Justifier.

Sanctification is inseparable from justification in that it is the continuing work of the Holy Spirit in the individual and in the community—the confederation of the just—moving both the individual and the community of the redeemed toward the eschatological future. Eschatological hope says that complete sanctification will take place at the end of history, and the complete union of human creature with the Creator, and of being with Being, will come to fruition.

Because of God's gracious gifts of justification and sanctification, the masses of Black folks cashing in on their African traditions have developed an ethical stance and moral behavior in their human relationships which are unparalleled on the American scene. In the Bible there are incidents after incidents in which those who were the recipients of the justice, love, and mercy of God responded by way of ethical and moral self-discipline. At some points they would stop and build an altar to the Lord in response to his redemptive acts; at other points they would stop and sing a song to the Lord for his goodness. Like those biblical characters and groups, Black folks in this country in response to God's goodness have built altars, offered prayers, sung songs, and have also developed a conscious human Christian attitude and practice in their relationships with other human beings in this world. The cult of materialism which pervades the American culture is having its adverse effects on traditional Black morality and ethics.

The Black church does not wish to get into the so-called mythical mainstream of American Christianity. It is polluted. There is a lack of sensitivity to the needs of human beings who happen to be Black and who are bearing a disproportionate share of the suffering in this country caused by those who worship in white churches. There is not only a lack of sensitivity to human suffering on the part of many white Christians, but also they are leading this nation into an unprecedented flow of crime and corruption. In the yesteryears, the mobsters and the underworld figures promulgated crimes and corruption, even though they did influence and involve officials of all levels of government. But today, according to indictments, convictions, and resignations, the major crimes and corruptions are conspired and promulgated by the so-called "fathers" who occupy the city halls, the state houses, the house of the United States Congress, and the White House.

These people who are breeders of grafts and greed are people, in most cases, who hold membership in the American white religious communities. There is no question about it, the mainstream of the white religious community is polluted. The ethics of the Black religious community, if accepted and lived out in the American religious community as a whole, can prove to be the needed redeeming factor which will save America from self-destruction. While Blacks stood in the existential absurdity of a state of justification before God which gave them full being, and at the same time experienced the burden of the injustices of the oppressors, which said they were not fully being, they developed an ethic which is summed up in the word "soul." The Judeo-Christian religion might do well to consider the value of soul. Cobbs and Grier offer the following definition of soul:

> Soul is the toughness born of hard times and the compassion oppressed people develop after centuries of sharing a loaf that is never enough. It is a special brotherhood of those set apart from their fellows, made visible by physical appearance, and different customs. Soul is the *graceful* survival under impossible circumstance.[52]

The Black church is the place in which soul was nurtured and developed. As Black folks moved through the dark and desolate valleys of segregation and dehumanization, they developed a clear understanding of the concepts "justification" and "sanctification."

Justification might be seen as a kind of existential absurdity in that, for Black folks, it meant to be set free by God while at the same time they experienced bondage by the oppressors. Sanctification is the continuing process of organizing and reorganizing the life of the individual and community through the mercy of God in accordance with the will of him who has seen fit to justify that individual and community.

Justification and sanctification are refined and transmitted primarily through the Household of Faith—the Black church.

8

The Household of Faith

Moving on, moving on
Oh, the Church is moving on,
Moving on, moving on,
Oh, the Church is moving on.

I
With the heav'nly armor shining bright,
Moving on, moving on, moving on,
We are waging war for truth and right,
Moving on, moving on, moving on.
With the pow'r and might of Christ, our Lord
Moving on, moving on,
Guided by the ever blessed Word
Oh, the Church is moving on.

II
We will cheer our hearts with happy song,
Moving on, moving on, moving on,
In the Lord of hosts our hope is strong,
Moving on, moving on, moving on.
Soon we'll reach the land of endless day,
Moving on, moving on,

> *We must conquer Satan all the way,*
> *Oh, the Church is moving on.*

> *III*
> *On ev'ry mount the banner waves,*
> *Moving on, moving on, moving on,*
> *In Jesus' name it has been raised,*
> *Moving on, moving on, to victory.*
> *Let us all stand by the grand old chart.*
> *Moving on, moving on,*
> *Let ev'ry soldier bear his part*
> *Oh, the Church is moving on.*[1]

The Black Church and Black Theology

There has been no adequate treatment of the Black church from a Black theological perspective. Black theologians, to this point, have given only quick glances at the Black church as a theological concept. There are a few works by Black scholars on Black church history, but they do not claim to be theological treatises. Certainly the subject cannot be exhausted or even fully developed in one chapter. I intend to make some assertions about the Black church from a theological point of departure which have not been made to my knowledge. I will give attention to such ideas as the Black church being understood as a place of communion with the Eternal, a place of fellowship among pilgrim people, and a place of celebration in anticipation of a future celebration in the kingdom of God.

Church in Black religious thought is not merely a doctrine to be debated with regard to its authority or relationship to the world. Church in Black religious thought is a psychic-spiritual unity and union of a pilgrim people in the process of redemption.

The confederation of the redeemed who comprised the members of the Household of Faith met as the visible church to cheer their hearts with happy songs. In the song above several elements which are important to the understanding of redemption in Black theology stand out prominently. First, there is a definite understanding of the church—*ecclesia* and *koinonia*—which could be epistemologically articulated. This is not to imply that the masses of Black folks used such terms as *"ecclesia," "koinonia,"* or "epistemology." These terms were not used in the mass Black churches. But their full meanings plus an extension of these meanings are evident in the praxis of the Black religious faith. This is precisely why there must be a Black "hermeneutic" for the interpretation of Black oral theology. The Black hermeneutic is a comprehensive theory of understanding which is not limited to dealing with textual exegesis; it includes an analysis of the ontological realities which stand behind the words and expressions in a given historical situation or setting.

We can grasp a sense of the ontological realities which gave meanings to the existence of the Black folks who composed the song above and those who transmitted it from generation to generation if we examine not only the words but also the mood and aspirations of those who uttered the words. The "Church" which is moving on is clearly composed of a group of pilgrims. They are poor pilgrims of sorrow. The Creator has made himself known unto them through revelation—the unfolding of his grace. Although they are just poor pilgrims, they have been justified through the blood of the Lamb. The Lamb is Jesus Christ, the One who walks with them through the daily struggles which would bring them to ultimate defeat had it not been for the companionship of Jesus. It is this confederation of pilgrims who have been justified that makes up the church—the *ecclesia* and the *koinonia*—moving on.

The word "church," according to Gene E. Sease, is the English form of the word *kirk* in Scottish, which is derived from the Greek *kuriakon*. It designates a building for worship which may be translated "The Lord's House." He says even though this word does not appear in this context in the Bible, it came into use after the Christians began to have church buildings. This idea is akin to the Black understanding of the church buildings which are sometimes aptly described and referred to as "Redemption Headquarters" or "Redemption Station." It is the Household of Faith. Sease suggests that the word which is translated "church" in the New Testament is derived from the Greek word *ekklesia* "which does not mean a building but an assembly (Acts 19:32), a local congregation (Matthew 18:17), or the church universal (16:18)."[2] In Black thought the *ecclesia* is the invisible union of the poor pilgrims of sorrow who are united through the justifying and redeeming mercy of God.

The other word which is used for church, *koinonia,* "which means 'fellowship' or 'sharing' . . . employs the idea of Christians sharing together with Christ." Sease points to the following references as those which reflect this Christian togetherness and sharing:[3] "And they devoted themselves to the apostles' teaching and fellowship, to the breaking of bread and prayer" (Acts 2:42). "For Macedonia and Achaia have been pleased to make some contributions for the poor among the saints at Jerusalem" (Romans 15:26). "The cup of blessing which we bless, is it not a participation in the blood of Christ? The bread which we break, is it not a participation in the body of Christ?" (1 Corinthians 10:16). "Under the test of this service, you will glorify God by your obedience in acknowledging the gospel of Christ, and by the generosity of your contribution from them and for all others" (2 Corinthians 9:13).

It is this expression of togetherness and sharing which makes the Black church the *koinonia* in New Testament understanding. The Black church is not only a doctrinal concept, but it is also a practice in daily life. It is a way of living in relationship with fellow pilgrims and in relationship with Jesus Christ and the ideals which he has established in his historical, earthly existence and through his teachings. So while not using these specific terms, the Black church has always seen itself and conducted itself as the *ecclesia*—the called-out unity of Christian pilgrims, local and universal. The Black church has always conducted itself as the *koinonia*. It is an institution of fellowship and sharing of a pilgrim people participating in the process of redemption based upon the Christian faith and the gospel of Christ.

The second point which stands out in the song at the opening of this chapter is that the church is in a state of struggle. Stanza 1 talks about a confederation, a group of people who have been liberated by the justice of God and who are moving on. While moving, they must don the heavenly armor because they are waging an ethical and moral battle. The war that they are waging is one of truth and right. They are also fighting against their oppressors who deny them their full humanity. They know that Christ is on their side which is expressed thusly: "With the pow'r and might of Christ, our Lord," the church is "guided by the ever-blessed Word." And the church is moving on. Stanza 2 asserts the *koinonia* theme of fellowship and sharing. They commit themselves to cheer the hearts of each other by singing happy songs because in the Lord of hosts—the Redeemer—their hope is strong. The eschatological hope is brought into focus when they assert, "Soon we'll reach the land of endless day." And all along the way they face the stern reality of confrontations with Satan who desires to diminish them into nonbeings. So they sing and encourage each other, "We must conquer Satan all the way." Satan is evil, any force which would destroy the value of their human existence or their human existence itself. In stanza 3 there is an understanding of redemption in process. As they move through the valleys of oppression and evil, they also move from one mountain of victory to another. And on every mountain they wave a banner which they raise in Jesus' name; and they stand by the grand old chart—the Bible— and are moving on to final victory with every soldier bearing his part. This is descriptive of the Black *ecclesia* and the Black *koinonia*.

If we can speak of the Catholic Church or the Protestant Church, then we can speak of the Black Church. From observation and from findings in research we have found that the masses of Black churches across this country are bound together in a kind of psychic-spiritual unity which is evident in expressions, style, and mode. This bond is not predicated upon creeds, rituals, and doctrines which would distinguish the Catholic or the Protestant Church. Again the Black hermeneutic says that it is not only the written creeds and doctrines which must be analyzed in order to formulate a theology, but the manner of expressions, the style, and the mode are also part of the evidence which go into the making of a Black theology. We have already pointed out that the creeds, doctrines, and rituals of Black denominations are not different from those of their white counterparts. But when it comes to expressions, style, and mode, the situation of racism and the reality of segregated sabbaths had so shaped Black thought that a psychic-spiritual unity developed which transcended all denominational ties and lines.

The Black Church is that group of people—segment of our population—bound together by a kind of psychic-spiritual unity resulting as a consequence and growing out of a long history of segregated sabbaths. Even to this day, Sunday is the most segregated day in America. The Black Church is a psychic-spiritual unity which is an outgrowth of the Black folk's cultural development in a segregated social system.

All Blacks do not admit membership into the unique group which we know to be the Black Church, neither do all Black congregations admit membership into the same. Some Black congregations have become so efficient in imitating white Euro-American rituals and styles of expressions that on the surface they seem not to belong to the community of the Black Church. There are a few Blacks today who say that there is no difference between the Black Church and White Church because "we are all Christians." But when one hears such a statement, one must be aware of the fact that the speaker is usually trying to escape from something which is the authentic Black Church. If the speaker means that we as Christians ought to minimize the differences between the Black Church and the White Church and to promote those things which we have in common, that is a noble ideal. But if the speaker is really claiming that there are no differences between the Black Church and the White Church, that person is fooling himself or herself and trying to hide something. He or she is trying to hide the reality of the results of a century of segregated sabbaths. He or she is trying to escape the degrading stereotypes which white folks placed upon the Black Church. Generally the worship experience in the mass Black churches are meaningful for daily living as well as inspirational in expressions.[4]

When I speak of the psychic-spiritual unity which is my basis for speaking of the Black Church, I mean that unity which is constituted partly of psychic and partly of spiritual phenomena. The psychic phenomena include the social sensation, perception, imagination, memory, thought, judgment, behavior, beliefs, and attitudes which were shaped by the situation of social injustices in America. The spiritual phenomena include the Black folk's faith in the Redeemer, the historical experiences of redeeming events, and the need for the community response to God through sanctification, Christian ethics, and moral discipline.

An incident which supports my contention that there is a unique identity of the Black Church is reported by an Air Force chaplain, Richard D. Miller. In an article entitled "Any Soul in Your Chapel Service?" he relates an experience he had with a Black officer.[5] Miller said a Black officer and his family attended chapel every other Sunday. So when he felt himself friendly enough to do so, he asked the Black officer where he worshiped on the Sundays that he did not come to the chapel. The officer replied: "At chapel I still feel as if I'm in a white folks' church." Upon reflection, the chaplain recalled another officer who attended the Zion AME Church every other Sunday. That officer had spoken of the "wonderful spirit at the Zion church." This is an example of the psychic-spiritual unity which exists in the Black religious community.

As he worshiped with the Zion congregation, this Black officer felt a spirit of unity which he did not feel in the chapel. This psychic-spiritual unity is a feeling and not necessarily a visible expression which can be observed by onlookers. It is soul-force released and experienced. It is a feeling of unity with God and with others which comes out of a common experience of suffering and redemption. In many Black churches this psychic-spiritual unity is expressed in audible and visible forms. But whether audible and visible or not, it is a feeling of unity typical among Black Christians which justifies my reference to the conglomerate of Black congregations as the Black Church.

We know Black people of all socioeconomic class levels who do appreciate the authentic Black Church and do feel themselves as a part of that Church. There is a healing effect which is present and needed in the "wonderful spirit at the [Black] Zion church" which was spoken of by the Black officer. If, for convenience, here, we would divide the Black community into an artificial socioeconomically secure group and a socioeconomically insecure group, the former would admit in private what the latter would express openly—that there is a Black Church which transcends class, caste, and geography. I know this from personal experience because I have had the rare fortune of living in and experiencing both worlds—the backwoods of the rural South and the Empire City of the nation. I have had the rare fortune of associating with Black folks in both worlds, the world of the Black ghetto and the world of the Black bourgeois or elite. The echo from all areas of Black existence attests to the existence of a Black Church and a Black theology. Because of the lack of educational opportunities for Black clergypersons and because of the erroneous belief promoted by white Christians and even some Black church leaders who did get an education, there existed the idea that where there was a lack of education on the part of the clergy, there was a lack of theology. During the Maturation Period of the Black Church, in 1894 the Presiding Elder of the Selma, Alabama, District of the African Methodist Episcopal Church lamented for an educated ministry. He is quoted as saying, "Oh, for a studying ministry." Elder H. Edward Bryant went on to say: "I have visited many preachers, and have seldom found one with a single word on systematic theology, a dictionary, commentary or work on ethics." Benjamin Quarles' report shows Bryant holding that "without formal training in theology or the arts and sciences, many Negro ministers were, in the words of another contemporary churchman, 'all sound and no sense, depending upon stentorian lungs, and long-drawn mourn, for their success.'" "Under such pastors," continued Quarles, "church services tended to become intensely emotional, with trances and weird singing."[6] This does support my thesis on two points: (1) The Black Church did mature on its own, and (2) the Black Church did develop its own theology apart from whites.

The very fact that Bryant seldom found one single work on systematic theology and no dictionaries or commentaries on the works of theology among the pastors under his charge around the turn of the century supports our contention that the Black Church developed its own oral theology during the Formative and Maturative Periods. Bryant declares that the Black pastors were without formal training in theology, the arts, and the sciences. What is clearly revealed here is that the Black pastors had no formal training in the white man's theology, arts, and sciences. But Black folks did have a Black theology. They had a clear concept of God—"the Pure King"—and the relationships which ought to exist between King and subjects before they were snatched from the shores of Black Africa. Blacks also brought with them a well-entrenched ethics, the spiritual attunement to God which determined their deeds and their acts. Of course this is not the case with the Euro-American Christian ethics which taught love for neighbor but practiced lynching of neighbor if that neighbor happened to be nonwhite.

Evidently Bryant and a few others had somehow traversed their way through the white educative and theological systems. This now removes the clouds of enigma from our eyes as we try to understand why a Black person would say that many Negro ministers were "all sound and no sense." It does not take a wise person to understand why a person who had been indoctrinated in white thought would make such a statement. The criterion for measuring what made sense was fashioned by white thought. But the expressions in the Black Church grew out of the Black redemption experiences. They were not learned in classroom settings. The communicants of the mass Black church today still worship God through the mourn and other nonverbal expressions which have deep and abiding theological meaning but make no sense to the outsider. C. Eric Lincoln is right when he says: "Black religion is essentially an attempt on the part of certain Black theologians and others to shape the faith in such a way as to make it more relevant to Black needs."[7] Carter G. Woodson, speaking of that same group of Black uneducated preachers, says they were a "walking encyclopedia, the counselor of the unwise, the friend of the unfortunate, the social welfare organizer, and the interpreter of the signs of the times."[8] While these leaders were indeed persons who have had no formal training in white theology, arts, and the sciences, the critics of the Black Church and Black theology should give an account and a reason for the acumen and the astuteness of these walking encyclopedias, counselors, and inter-preters of the story of redemption in their time. The explanation lies outside of traditional white assumptions.

These Black folks brought with them from Africa a theology and an ethic. They were introduced to Christianity, adopted the Christian religion, and reinterpreted the Christian faith in the light of African survival. And they fashioned an authentic Black Church and a Black theology which are more akin to the early Christian church than any institution which existed or does exist on the North American continent. The Black Household of Faith is the *ecclesia;* it is the psychic-spiritual unity of a pilgrim people. The Black Household of Faith is the *koinonia* in its praxis—practice rather than theory—of fellowship and sharing.

The confederation of the redeemed into the community is seen in the organization of the visible Black Church which had its own preached theology all along. Preston Williams speaks of the uniqueness of Black religion: "It was born in slavery, weaned in segregation, and reared in discrimination. It ties Black people together in times of stress by a racial bond which cuts across all other variables such as denomination, status, and morality."[9] Whatever the theology might be coming out of this Black religious experience and practice of Black folks, it is thoroughly Afro-American. The theology of the Black Church has its own built-in strengths, too, which are summed up by G. Clarke Chapman, Jr., who writes: "The strength of Black Theology is both its realism, grounded firmly in the daily experience of a people sojourning in a strange land, and its 'soul,' the ability to enact joy and celebration in the face of demonic powers."[10] The Black Church was and is the redemption center where the poor pilgrims of sorrow met to try to make sense out of the existential absurdities and realities of the freedom which comes through justification from above and the bondage which is inflicted by the injustices which come from below. The stuff we call soul, which is both African survival and divine grace extended from the Redeemer, has kept ·us in confederation as a church under impossible circumstances. It is those meetings in the redemption centers where communal encounter with the Eternal is renewed over and over again and again.

A Place of Communion with the Eternal

It is little wonder that as one travels across this country and rides through the Black sections, North or South, East or West, one will soon find names of churches with theological implications. These churches cover the spectrum from the storefront variety to the cathedral type in size and structure. These names with theological implications include: "Refuge Deliverance Center . . . Church," "Redemption Headquarters . . . Church," "Refuge Temple . . . Church" and "Highway . . . Church." These names have theological implications. Redemption is implicit in each of them. These names were not adopted from the white church community; they evolved out of the Black *sitz im leben* (situation in life). The church was the place where Blacks gathered to commune with the One who was bringing about their social and physical redemption as well as their spiritual redemption. A few white churches do employ the terms "Refuge," "Deliverance," "Redemption," and "Highway" in their names, but as a general rule these white churches are of the Pentecostal and Holiness denominations and their general use of the terms means salvation from sin and guilt. On the practical side, they mean salvation from alcohol, tobacco, and this-worldly pleasures. They could not mean, for them, salvation from oppression in the same sense as they are understood by Blacks since whites do not consider themselves, and are indeed not, in bondage as are the Black people. It is reasonable to believe the report that many white Christians are members of the Ku Klux Klan.

It is not possible to explore the full theological and redemption implications of the names used for Black churches in this single work, but before leaving the discussion I would like to go a step further. A cursory review of the section under the heading Churches, Baptist, in the Yellow Pages of the Baltimore Telephone Directory reveals that twice as many Black Baptist churches take their names from biblical mountains as take their names from biblical saints. This is because in Black religious thought the mountains have the double meaning of being places of refuge from cruel enemies who impose physical afflictions and also being places of communion with the Eternal. It was on Mount Sinai that Moses had his communion with the Eternal (the receiving of the Ten Commandments) which has affected the entire Judeo-Christian religion. It was on Mount Carmel that Elijah experienced the redemptive and vindicating act of God and was able to confound and to triumph over the prophets of Baal. It was on the Mount of Olives that Jesus and his confederation frequently retired for the double purpose of getting away from the cruel enemies and to commune with the Father in prayer.

Then there is the eschatological outlook which is also implicit in the names of the churches. In every Black section of this country where there are churches, one does not need to look long before one finds a "Mount Zion . . . Church." Mount Zion is the theological symbol of the eschatological state of human redemption. The Mount Zions in the here and now are the prolepses of the future and eternal Mount Zion. They are the anticipation of the fulfillment of redemption—liberation from the evils and oppressions which tend to destroy the value of human existence and human existence itself and confederation into full communion with the Eternal. Black folks still sing:

> If you miss me
> from singing down here,
> And you can't find me no where,
> Come on up to Mount Zion,
> And I'll be waiting up there.

One Black denomination even employs the term "Zion" in its denominational title, namely the African Methodist Episcopal Zion (AMEZ). We have not been able to ascertain why Peter Williams, Sr., employed the term "Zion" when he organized this denomination in 1796. But there are some things we do know about the coming of this Black denomination.

Peter Williams, Sr., was a sexton in the John Street Methodist Church (white) in New York where he also held membership. He came to realize that his people were unwelcome in the John Street Church. And just as Richard Allen, Absalom Jones, and William White were rejected by the parishioners of the St. George Methodist Episcopal Church in Philadelphia and were ushered out when they attempted to join other parishioners at prayer at the altar, so Peter Williams and James Varick were refused communion with white worshipers in Manhattan's John Street Methodist Church.[11] So Peter Williams led a group of Blacks in founding the AME Zion Church in 1796. From his earnings as a tobacco merchant he is reported to have financed the building of its first temple.[12] (His son Peter Williams, Jr., became the first Black priest to be ordained by the Protestant Episcopal Church.) Other leaders in the group included George Collins and Christopher Rush. John Hope Franklin tells us that these Black men "could find no one either in the Episcopal or the Methodist church who would ordain and consecrate their elders, and finally they had to do it themselves." They overcame their problems of schisms within and oppositions from without and the church had sufficient stability by 1822 to elect James Varick as its first bishop.[13]

The "Zion" in the name of this new Black denomination might have been added to distinguish it from the African Methodist Episcopal Church started by Richard Allen in Philadelphia in 1794, but the fact remains that the idea of Zion was more than just a name; it is a theological and transcendent metaphor which describes the visible redemption center. The term "Zion" has also had a prominent place in reference to that psychic-spiritual unity of the American population which we call the Black Church.

Black folks see the Church as a kind of center of earthly life. It is the place where the pilgrims meet to commune with the Eternal. "Black people are religious people," says C. T. Vivian. "For many, the church is their life."[14] And when Black people gather to commune with the Eternal, they tell him of all their struggles; they pour their hearts out to their Redeemer—to hear his word of redemption.

It is not the sacraments which are central in the total worship experience; it is the sermon—the *kerygma,* the message and its eternal content. For this message of redemption Black folks depend upon the Black preacher. Black religion asserts that the Redeemer is on the side of the oppressed which is to say, according to Lincoln, that he is on the side of Black people. This also means that Black people need not ally themselves with white institutions which humiliate and demean them.[15] The Black preachers of old, though illiterate or nearly so, could recite the biblical stories of redemption with amazing consistency and accuracy. So when Black folks came to the redemption center, they found themselves in an existential state of a cornucopia of spiritual richness.

The Acts of the Black Preachers in the Black Church

While the Black Church is the center of Black religious life, the preacher is the central figure in the Black Church. In light of the African social organization it is easy to understand why the Black preacher became the central figure in the Black Church. He replaced the tribal chief back home in his role in the Black Church's social structure. He became the head of the church family and indeed the head of the community including the nonchurchgoers. Black theology must take seriously the theological tradition which was fashioned and transmitted by the Black tribal chiefs—the Black oral preachers.

"The Negro clergyman," says Quarles, "was a natural leader because his support came from the mass of people; he was therefore in a position to speak more frankly on their behalf than a Negro leader whose job required that he have the good will of the white community."[16] Again, the famous Black scholar W. E. B. Du Bois wrote in the Maturation Period, in 1903:

> The [Black] preacher is the most unique personality developed by the Negro on American soil. A leader, a politician, an orator, a "boss," an intriguer, an idealist—all these he is, and even, too, the centre of a group of men, now twenty, now a thousand in number.[17]

There is no doubt about it, his message was from another world; but his message was a message of redemption—liberation and confederation. The Black preacher was the center of focus in the Black Church. William E. Hatcher, a white Virginian, who by his own admission "claims no exemption from Southern prejudices and feels no call to sound the praises of the negro race,"[18] says of John Jasper, a Black ante-bellum and post-bellum preacher:

> He was the last of his type, and we shall not look upon his like again. It has been my cherished purpose for some time to embalm the memory of this extraordinary genius in some form that would preserve it from oblivion. I would give to the American people a picture of the God-made preacher who was great in his bondage and became immortal in his freedom.[19]

Hatcher was wrong in his opinion that Jasper was the last of his type. One can understand why a white preacher of that day who was so much influenced by formal training would conclude that whatever was not reduced to writing would vanish into oblivion. However, God made some more John Jaspers who have maintained the Black preaching tradition of the John Jasper of bondage. When this John Jasper of bondage (who maintained his style after Emancipation) died, the leading morning paper in Richmond, *The Richmond Dispatch,* stated:

> It is a sad coincidence that the destruction of the Jefferson Hotel and the death of the Rev. John Jasper should have fallen upon the same day. John Jasper was a Richmond Institution, as surely so as was Major Gintner's fine hotel. He was a national character, and he and his philosophy were known from one end of the land to the other. Some people have the impression that John Jasper was famous simply because he flew in the face of the scientists and declared that the sun moved. In one sense, that is true, but it is also true that his fame was due, in great measure, to a strong personality, to a deep, earnest conviction, as well as to a devout Christian character.[20]

The personality, the character, and the conviction of the preacher—the preacher himself—cannot be separated from the preaching. C. D. Coleman, in his introduction to Bishop Joseph A. Johnson's *Soul of the Black Preacher,* describes the Black preacher:

> In pursuit of his call he was frequently without the necessities of life, but never without the dignity of his office. He was often without honor, but never without integrity. He was a poet—his sermons compare with the finest prose and poetry. The wonderful creativity behind his preaching created the scene out of which spirituals were born. . . . He was an orator—his words held his audiences spellbound. He was a prophet—always declaring "a better day is coming." This rare breed remains unheralded in the annals of history, but their names are written in the book of life.[21]

Out of the bosom of the Black preacher came a redemption hope that kept Black people alive physically and spiritually while everything around them wooed them to an untimely death. The Black preacher was the cultural hero. He possessed a reversed quality of character, a sense of commitment, and a charisma that was saturated with the Holy Spirit. Thus he spoke with the voice of a prophet and the authority of a king. The Black preacher has been the hub around which the Black Church and the Black community revolved.

The Black preacher is a kind of mediator and facilitator in bringing about communion with the Eternal on the part of Black Church folks and fellowship with one another in the process of redemption.

A Place of Fellowship with Others

The church is the center of worship; it is the center of redemption, but this has never been the limit of the function of the Black Church. The Black Church has never made that sharp distinction between church and world which seems to be present in Euro-American theologies. The church is the center for all of life in the here and in the hereafter. In his book, *Say Amen, Brother!* Pipes makes the following assertion, a portion of which he quotes from *After Freedom* by Hortense Powdermaker (1939):

> It is not a difficult matter to explain this popularity of the church among Negroes when one realizes that "the Negro church is the one institution where the colored people of the community are in full control. It is their own." Also, in addition to the profoundly important religious urge, Negroes cling to the church because it serves a social purpose by being a center where friends meet.[22]

The Black folks found themselves in a meaningful confederation as they gathered in the church setting. The Black Church was and is the institution which gave meaning to and provided the basic ingredient for family stability. It must be pointed out that in the African tradition the institution of the family is a sacred and social requirement. There is an overabundance of evidence which reveals the wholesomeness of the family structure. Whatever has gone wrong to mar that African family tradition among American Blacks can definitely be laid to the white oppressors. The Black slaves were separated from their relatives upon being dumped upon these shores. Marriage was not permitted among the slaves; and where Black men and women were thrown together for breeding purposes, they were later separated at the whim of the white masters and mistresses. But the Black Church served as the redemption center for broken family circles.

Moving through Black history, in the Period of the Great Migration and the Harlem Renaissance, we find northern labor agents going South to recruit able-bodied Black men to come North to the so-called Promised Land. Henry Ford and other northern industrialists promised Black men a guaranteed job at five dollars ($5.00) a day. LeRoi Jones quotes Paul Oliver as follows:

> . . . The cessation of the influx of European immigrants coincided with Henry Ford's announcement, in 1914, that none of his workers would earn less than five dollars per day, and it was in that year also that he commenced to employ Negroes on his assembly lines.[23]

Jones also points out that many blues songs were written about the Ford company and Ford products. One such song follows:

> Say, I'm goin' to get me a job now, workin' in Mr. Ford's place
> Say, I'm goin' to get me a job now, workin' in Mr. Ford's place,
> Say, that woman tol' me last night, "Say, you cannot even stand Mr. Ford's ways."[24]

This is a folk song which reflected the socio-religious condition and thought of Blacks of that period. The North was not the kind of refuge that the Negroes had been led to believe that it was. Although there were no signs indicating "White Only" or "Colored," Blacks soon became aware of segregated churches and social clubs. The color line became visible in sections of the cities "characterized by rat-infested houses, poor health and sanitation facilities, high incidence of crime and juvenile delinquency, and policemen too quick with nightsticks or guns."[25] Then came the worsening of the labor market when World War I ended and government contracts with industries dwindled rapidly. Many of the Negroes who had left the South in droves were laid off or fired, and those who retained jobs were placed in the hot and heavy operations in the industries. Quarles points out that

> the Negro who had left the South was not disposed to return. But faced with unemployment, job ceilings, and ghetto-like living conditions, he might sometimes have wondered whether the city to which he had come was less a frontier of escape than a new imprisonment.[26]

So many of the Black husbands and fathers could not and did not go back South to their families. The reason these Black husbands and fathers could not send for their families as they intended to do nor return to them was not due to lack of family concern or immorality on the part of these men. These families were not reunited because of the devastating blows of an unjust, oppressive, white-controlled system—the color line, the ghetto, the brutality, and finally, unemployment. But again the Black Church provided the needed stimuli and guidance which kept the mothers and children who were trapped on the southern plantations from ultimate despair. Mothers became the heads of the families. The African survival of the extended family arrangement was reinterpreted in Black family patterns. The Black pastors continued their roles as tribal chiefs for the extended families and church family life. Without the Black Church the Black families in America could not have survived the cruelties of the white masters. Theologically, the Black Church was a divine institution of redemption.

It is disturbing to hear white folks indict Black people for family disorganization based on white Euro-American standards. It was they who stole Blacks from their native land and disrupted their family customs and traditions. Although not based on the European model, African family customs were well organized, and they worked for the Africans. It was the whites who prevented the establishment of a Black family pattern during slavery. It was they who used economic manipulations to separate Black families after the era of Reconstruction and particularly during the Great Migration.

It was they who used the welfare system to force husbands out of the homes beginning in the period of Passive Protest and continuing during the period of Radical Reassertion—generally from the mid 1940s to 1970s. During this era, white folk who controlled the welfare system and who also controlled the job market kept the percentage of Black unemployment from two to four times that of whites. At the same time, the welfare system denied aid to dependent wives and children when unemployed and, in many instances, unemployable fathers were living in the home. The unemployables mentioned here are not fathers who had physical handicaps. The real handicap evolved out of racism resulting in the "grandfather clauses" in union-management contracts in the crafts (that is, only those persons who had relatives in the crafts were considered eligible for apprenticeship). Black fathers were unemployable because of the educational and previous experience clauses in job applications. So again, the Black fathers had to muster every bit of their innate ingenuity for physical survival over these dehumanizing schemes. In the Black ghettos across this nation, Black unemployed men had to separate from their families in order that the wife and children could be eligible for welfare assistance. They camped with their peers by day and slept with their families by night. This was simply a survival technique. But the "man" (the white oppressors) found out about this forced arrangement, and I can vividly recall that in my community the welfare system had a cadre of night agents whose function it was to spy out and to get into these Black homes (break in if necessary) and catch these fathers living with their families. I remember the raids, and I also remember the screaming newspaper headlines reporting the results of these raids in both the Black and white newspapers. For example, there were headlines, such as "Negro Father Found in Home of Welfare Family" or "Negro Father Goes to Jail for Welfare Cheating."

The many devious ways that the oppressors have used to disorganize Black families in this one nation, divided, lead one to reject the verdict of the self-styled white jurors who indict Blacks for family disorganization which does not meet the oppressors' standards.

In chapter 4 we have pointed out that there are Black sinners as well as white sinners. But any family disorganization which exists in the Black community is far more the result of the sickening system of racism in America than it is a result of the lack of righteousness on the part of Black people.

It is the Black Church which has picked up the pieces of the fragmented Black families and has given meaning and direction to family life. The Black preacher was always aware of the pressures which caused Black family disorganization. The Black preacher was aware of the system which caused the away-by-day and the at-home-at-night arrangement on the part of Black fathers. Frequently, members of the separated families were members of the same church. And in any case the church always provided that extra ingredient, that family cohesiveness which might have been missing as a result of forced Black family disorganization. The Household of Faith was and still is the place of fellowship among the Black pilgrim people who meet to cheer their hearts with happy songs.

The Black Church has stood and does stand, theologically speaking, as the redemption center for those who labor and are heavy-laden. As a place of fellowship among the Blacks dispossessed of this land, the Black Church has given life and support to unnumbered institutions of social justice. We have heard the voices on campuses of some youthful Black critics who were not really aware of the social contributions of the Black Church complaining about the lack of Black Church leadership and involvements in the Radical Reassertion Period. When they lived in Black churches, were fed by the Black churches, and were bailed out of southern jails by the Black churches during their civil rights involvements in the South during the stormy events of the 1960s, they changed their minds about the value of the Black Church. Roy Wilkins, Executive Secretary of the National Association for the Advancement of Colored People (NAACP), acknowledged the redeeming work of the Black church in a speech before the 93rd Annual Session of the National Baptist Convention, U.S.A., Inc., meeting in Los Angeles on September 7, 1973. He said:

> We have been partners—the church and the National Association for the Advancement of Colored People—for six-and-a-half decades of our life as an organization. Together we have seen the marching ahead, the stalemates, the marking time, the joyous times when the Lord was compassionate and the people were prayerful and righteous. We have muddled together through periods of dark despair, but never gave up, never abandoned the faith that one day it would be all right.

> The church took us under its wings. It nurtured us, gave us, in our local units, the service and guidance of its ministers of all denominations and faiths. When the inns of our nation turned their flinty faces against us and we had no place to meet, it was the church which threw open its doors and ministered to our needs, both spiritual and physical. . . . We have a partnership not made with hands, but with the instant and mutual recognition of the rights of men, whatever their color or station in life. . . .

The story never changes. Man's need never changes. In this hurly-burly world, so prone to brush aside man's rights here on earth and his salvation in the time to come, the church and the NAACP have a mission.[27]

This statement is consistent with the Black Church tradition which, by divine appointment, is the institution of redemption—liberation from sin and from oppression and confederation into a community of fellowship and mutual support. The physical gathering is a visible expression of the underlying psychic-spiritual unity of the Black Church.

A Place of Celebration

The visible Black Church is not only a place for communion with the Eternal and a place of fellowship among the poor pilgrims of sorrow, but it is also a center for celebration. Three factors undergird celebration in the Black Church. First, Blacks celebrate the ontological reality of a state of freedom in Jesus Christ. They celebrate the reality of being justified and thus being members of the community of the redeemed moving toward the completion of the state of the Eternal redemptive process. Secondly, Blacks celebrate the reality of their survival under the impossible circumstances of racism which is designed to reduce them into nonbeing. Thirdly, Blacks celebrate the hope of future redemptive interventions on the part of the One who is effectuating their full and final redemption from oppression in the here and now and in the hereafter.

One need not argue the point; it is too well known that when Blacks meet for worship on Sunday, they all bring one thing in common to the center, differing only in degree. That is, the masses of folks come from a week's experience of unfulfilled dreams and aspirations which are the general result of the pressures which are directed toward quashing them into nonbeing. This force is operative at every level of the American class system; thus, no Blacks can completely escape the fallout, even when educational achievements and economic stability serve to shelter them from the immediate and overt blasts of unconscious and undisciplined white power. All Blacks, therefore, come with a degree of pent-up frustrations which give rise to an immediate psychic unity.

Celebration means the "doxological expressions" on the part of Black communicants. The term "emotional expressions" can be misleading, because white folks have cast a negative and stereotyped halo around this term when it is used to express events which take place in Black worship situations. This was not meant to be in its original usage. The following quote from *Social Psychology* supports my conviction that emotion or emotional expressions are not inherently negative. Here Otto Klineberg speaks for himself:

> Emotional behavior is accompanied by a series of physiological changes which presumably occur in all individuals. Social factors may, however, affect the emotions in various ways. There are, for example, differences in the situations which will arouse the various emotions in different societies. . . . There are differences also in the amount of overt emotional behavior, as well as in the specific emotions which are permitted expression. Although it has been suggested that anatomical characteristics may play a part, it is certain that cultural influences are much more important. . . .
>
> Emotional expressions, apparently common to all societies are the occurrences of tears in pain or sorrow, of laughter as a sign of joy or well-being. . . . On the other hand, the great difficulty experienced by untrained human observers in recognizing the emotions of chimpanzees from their facial expressions strengthens the hypothesis of cultural or social determination of the expression of the emotions in man. Emotional expression is analogous to language in that it functions as a means of communication, and that it must be learned, at least in part.[28]

From Klineberg's statement it is clear that there is nothing negative inherent in emotional expressions. Indeed such an expression could mean the affirmative way to show appreciation for a state of well-being. Klineberg also affirms what Black scholars and religionists have been saying all along, that is, (1) emotional behaviors differ with different societies and in different cultures; (2) there are great difficulties in untrained human observers recognizing the emotions of chimpanzees from their facial expressions; and (3) emotional expression is analogous to a language in that it functions as a means of communication.

To go a step further in discussing the three points above—first, because of forced segregation and separation in this one nation, divided, Black culture differs from white culture and therefore the emotional expression of Black people would be different from that of whites. Secondly, since white folk have not shared in the Black experience of oppression and repression, as outside observers they cannot make an objective analysis of emotional expressions any more than an untrained human being can recognize the emotions of chimpanzees from their facial expressions. And thirdly, Black emotional expressions do serve as a language—as a means of communication—in the Black Church. Emotional expressions in Black worship are a means of communicating with God. Black emotional expression in Black Church worship is a means of highest praise to the Redeemer.

While there may be apparent an exaggeration of doxological expressions in some Black churches, generally the doxological expressions which are practiced in the mass Black churches are authentic and theologically meaningful. They are expressions of soul responses and soul fulfillment of an oppressed people. Blacks do literally worship—celebrate—with their mind, soul, and body, with thoughts, voices, hands, feet, and with their entire being. Black religious celebration is not merely an exercise of the mind and a so-called assent of the heart. It is an involvement of the entire being. This total involvement leads to the state of ecstasy. Johannes Pedersen in attempting to explain the ecstasy of the prophets puts it this way: "What happens in the ecstatic state is that the soul bursts its frame." [29] This is precisely what happens when Blacks reach a state of ecstasy in celebration. Celebrating brings healing. And more healing takes place in the Black Church on Sundays than takes place in hospitals during the week. Throughout the congregation there are incidents of "soul burst." Their souls simply burst out of their frames. A "soul burst" is the result of a kind of theogonic experience—an adjective derived from the Greek noun *theogonia,* meaning an account of the origin and descent of the Gods—in which God comes down and gets into the individual in the situation of celebration. The evidence of this "soul burst" might be visible to an observer through physical movement or an audible shout of praise, or it might be unobservable in that it is nonphysical and nonverbal. It is a feeling of soul satisfaction and soul fulfillment which transcends objective instruments of observation. [30]

The "amens" which often punctuate the various elements of worship in the Black Church are generally incidents of "soul burst." In the context of worship, "amen" means a simple affirmation of faith or an approval of what is being said. "Amen" means much more in Black religious celebration. The following is a case in point: On the evening of May 13, 1970, Dr. Thomas Kilgore, Jr., the first Black president of the American Baptist Churches (predominantly white) was delivering his presidential address before the delegates to the Sixty-third Annual Session of the organization. After he spent a considerable amount of time giving statistics in a very intellectual and pleasing manner, the delegates—Black and white—were caught up in a quiet and attentive atmosphere. There were frequent applauses but seldom were there any expression of "amens."

Nearing the end of his address, which was entitled "There Is No Escape," he shifted his style and moved into the sphere of his Black heritage of preaching. He said:

> When the slaves looked at the evil system, some of them created a spiritual that was prophetic: "God's goin' to set this world on fire."

Then he said there is another Negro spiritual which says:

> Time, Oh, time is winding up
> Corruption in the land
> People take your stand
> Time, Oh, time is winding up.

By this time a Black brother sitting two seats away from me was steadily and quietly crying out, "Amen." "Amen." The president continued:

> Time ran out on Jonah . . .
> Time ran out on a fig tree . . .
> Time ran out on five maidens
>   who had no oil in reserve. . . .

By now this Black brother was struggling to control the outburst of his "amens." Then Dr. Kilgore recited from Psalm 139:1, 7-10. The brother could not contain himself any longer. Despite his being surrounded by a predominantly white audience of nearly five thousand, out came the responses: "Amen!" "Yes!" "Go ahead." "Amen!" This is a praising God for the Good News and for the experience of his redeeming events in the lives of the oppressed. The fallout of a "soul burst" is a feeling of transcendence with the Eternal and a humanity—at-oneness—with fellow travelers.

Celebration of God's redeeming love takes many forms and shapes in the Black Church. There is rhyme, rhythm, repetition, rhetoric, and cadence in the finest meaning of these terms which make up the ingredients of Black Church celebrations. There is a high degree of antiphony among the various segments of the congregation. There is a high degree of *responsory*—alternation in leading and responding in worship expressions—in Black celebration. In the Black idiom this activity might be called "call and response," "feedback," "audience participation," or "collective participation."

A fine example of the rhythm, repetition, call and response, and cadence which are part of the ingredients of Black Church celebration is drawn from a "collective participation," led by the late Dr. Martin Luther King, Jr. According to Louis E. Lomax, a church in a little Alabama town had been packed to capacity since five o'clock one afternoon, and there were three thousand people standing outside to hear what was to be a call for an all-out bus boycott in Montgomery, Alabama. When the meeting began and other speakers had completed their statements, then Martin Luther King, Jr., came to the podium and this is how things went:

> *King* (K)—"There comes a time when people get tired."
> *Audience* (A)—"Yes, Lord."
> (K)—"We are here this evening to say to those who have mistreated us for so long that we are tired—"
> (A)—"Help him, Jesus!"
> (K)—"—we are tired of being segregated and humiliated."
> (A)—"Amen."
> (K)—". . . *tired!* . . . did you hear me when I said *'tired'?'*"
> (A)—"Yes, Lord!"
> (K)—". . . tired of being kicked about by the brutal feet of oppression. Now we have no alternative but to protest. For many years we have shown amazing patience. We have sometimes given our white brothers the feeling that we like the way we are being treated. But we come here tonight to be saved from the patience that makes us patient with anything less than freedom and justice."[31]

While this was not a meeting specifically called for regular worship and celebration, there is little difference between the style and method of worship and celebration and the activities of the meeting mentioned above. The cadence of the Black preacher and the response of that audience were the same as would have taken place at a regular Sunday worship. The Redemption theme was very much alive. "We have come tonight to be saved," said King, and it is clear that he was not talking about salvation from sin and guilt, but rather from the shackles of anything less than "freedom and justice." Black Church celebration has its otherwordly pull, but it never overlooks the gravity of dehumanization which keeps Blacks anchored also in the this-worldly need of redemption.

So Blacks celebrate the sovereignty of God and the blessing of being justified and therefore members of the redeemed community who are moving on to the state of eschatological redemption. This is revealed in excerpts from a Black prayer which, in varying versions, might be heard in any mass Black Church in this country.

"From everlasting to everlasting; from way back beyond back; before there was a when or a where, or a then or a there, you stepped out from nowhere and stood on nothing, and said, 'Let there be.' And worlds leaped from your presence like sparks from a blacksmith's anvil. Then you left word that whenever I needed you to call on you. Lord, I need you now because I have no one else to turn to." [32]

Such prayer is one of absolute faith; it is one of rejoicing and celebrating the fact of being a member of the redeemed community who may call upon the Redeemer who responds on the side of the oppressed. Black celebration is a fervent expression of a fervent commitment to authentic Christian ideals and an unflinching faith in the fatherhood of God and the brotherhood of pilgrim people.

The fact that Blacks celebrate the victories of survival under impossible circumstances is revealed in a mother's advice to her son in a poem by Langston Hughes:

Mother to Son

Well, son, I'll tell you:
Life for me ain't been no crystal stair.
It's had tacks in it,
And splinters,
And boards torn up,
And places with no carpet on the floor—
Bare.
But all the time
I'se been a-climbin' on.
And reachin' landin's,
And turnin' corners,
And sometimes goin' in the dark
Where there ain't been no light.
So boy, don't you turn back.
Don't you set down on the steps
'Cause you finds it's kinder hard.
Don't you fall now—
For I'se still goin', honey,
I'se still climbin',
And life for me ain't been no crystal stair. [33]

Celebration is seen here in the sense that the mother has quite a positive view and feeling about her victories in spite of her obstacles. While life "ain't" been no crystal stair, she still boasts about the fact that "I'se been a-climbin' on, And reachin' landin's, And turnin' corners." Despite her life-threatening encounters, she is moving on.

Evidence of this redemption hope is also proclaimed in a song which is regularly sung in the mass Black Churches and which has a very positive line: "I'm so glad, trouble don't last always."

Headstart Program for the Kingdom

As we shall discuss in the next chapter, the Black religionists do have a definite anticipation about a kingdom beyond the mundane existence which we now know. This kingdom is a "prepared place" for a "prepared people." So down here is "our dressing-up room," according to Black oral testimonies. It is the only place where they can make preparations to participate in that place of eternal bliss. The program of the Black Church is the headstart program for the future kingdom of God. It must also be noted that Black religion views the Black Church as the kingdom of God at hand.

The Black Church is on a mundane scale what the eternal Church will be on a cosmic scale at the end of human history. The Black Church is a paradigm of all that God is bringing about as his eternal kingdom in the future. The eschatological kingdom which is at hand is also understood to be "inbreaking" in that it is evident in crisis situations and it finds no precedent in the past. The negative experiences of the members of the Black Church create the crisis situation out of which an understanding of the eschatological kingdom can be anticipated and comprehended. Black religionists are members of the kingdom at hand which is the headstart program for the eschatological kingdom.

There must be full participation in the headstart program of the kingdom at hand on the part of everyone who wishes to participate in the eternal kingdom. In the utterances and oral confessions of Blacks there is a plethora of indications that the self-manifestation of God was and is an ongoing process. There is a tradition of response on the part of Blacks to the ethical demands of God. As a consequence, Blacks have experienced a degree of the inbreaking of the kingdom at hand. But since Blacks did not experience the fulfillment of love, peace, and justice, since there are always crises, and since there is room for new possibilities, the faith of Blacks has always had great affinities for the not yet. The golden days are not in the past but in the kingdom of the future. That faith is in a kingdom which has no precedent but which is anticipated in and available through the headstart program of the Black Church.

To participate in the Black Church is to participate in the only program which is designed to provide a passport into the eternal Church of the future. In the Household of Faith, the justified continue in the process of sanctification so that they will be eligible candidates to enter the "Sweet Beulah Land," "way by and by." Only those who are faithful members of the church now may expect to "make it into the kingdom." Somewhere in the eschatological future the *ecclesia* which is also the *koinonia* will be transformed into the eternal kingdom. In the oral testimonies of the Black masses, "One day the Church militant will join the Church triumphant and reign with God through ceaseless ages." Both dimensions of redemption are explicit in that statement. First, the church will be liberated from earthly encumbrances. One day the "Church militant," that is, the pilgrim people of God who are waging war for truth and right (stanza 1 of the opening song) will move on to final victory. Secondly, the pilgrim people of the "Church militant" will be brought into confederation with God the Father, God the Son, and God the Holy Ghost. There will be a confederation of all the righteous who have proceeded in death.

So the Household of Faith—the Black Church—has an oral theology. It is a place of communion with the Eternal through the leadership and acts of the Black preacher. It is a place of fellowship and celebration for a pilgrim people. The golden age for Blacks is not in the past but in the future; therefore, their participation in the Household of Faith is an anticipation on a mundane scale of that which will take place on a cosmic scale at the end of history.

9

Everybody's Talking About Heaven

All God's Chillun
Got a Song

I got a song, you got a song,
  All God's chillun got a song;
When I get to heab'n, goin' to sing a new song,
  Goin' to sing all over God's heab'n.

Heab'n, heab'n, ev'rybody talkin' 'bout heab'n ain't goin' dere,
Heab'n, heab'n, goin' to shout all over God's heab'n.

I got shoes, you got shoes,
  All God's chillun got shoes;
When I get to heab'n, goin' to put on my shoes,
  Goin' to walk all over God's heab'n.

I got a robe, you got a robe,
  All God's chillun got a robe;
When I get to heab'n, goin' to put on my robe,
  Goin' to shout all over God's heab'n.

I got a harp, you got a harp,
  All God's chillun got a harp
When I get to heab'n, goin' to take up my harp,
  Goin' to play all over God's heab'n.[1]

The Place of Heaven in Black Theology

The aim of this chapter is to remove the stigma arising out of the stereotype which has been perpetrated against the discussion of heaven or otherworldiness in Black literature and Black theology in recent times. The aim is to put the idea of heaven back into its proper pristine relationship with all other faith concepts in Black religion. Paul writes to the Romans: "For I am not ashamed of the gospel: it is the power of God for salvation to every one who has faith . . ." (Romans 1:16). To paraphrase Paul in regard to the discussion of heaven in Black theology, "For I am not ashamed of the concept of heaven in Black religion; it is the power of God, being the ultimate state of redemption, to every one who has faith."

Black folks have always expressed a clear concept of heaven in religious proclamations. In my experiences extending from the country churches in the South to city churches of the North spanning the spectrum in organizational structure and size, I have heard the preachers talking about heaven; I have observed the deacons praying about heaven; I have witnessed the choirs singing about heaven; and I have listened to the lay people testifying about heaven; in fact, everybody was talking about heaven. Black religionists have never centered their ultimate concern in the accumulation and the possession of the abundance of things in this world.

In the 1960s and the early 1970s I felt the strong pressures to minimize the otherworldiness of Black religion, concurrently on the campus of Howard University and in the various civil rights organizations with which I worked in Baltimore. This pressure to minimize the otherworldliness in Black religion had its rebirth and most effective results in the Black Power movement. (This reference to the Black Power movement must not be misconstrued to mean that I hold a negative outlook of that movement. Indeed, I was in the midst of it and an active part of it.) But as Cobbs and Grier put it: "Blackness sometimes has unwanted side effects, as do most miracle drugs." Then they concluded: "By far the most troubling is that under its powerful influence some men go mad."[2] At another point they argued that over-militancy and unstructured outlet of feelings are the fallout of this side effect of blackness. They wrote: "For the newly black, the rhetoric and the militant stance are a welcome outlet for new feelings. The sudden freedom from the oppressive fear of the white man vaults him into a new, unstructured relationship with his world."[3]

They are correct insofar as their argument is concerned. One of the side effects of the new burst of blackness during the Black Power movement was seen in vocal and physical expressions of "madness" on the part of some Blacks. (And maybe this was not so negative as the newspapers and televisions made it seem after all.)

One of the major side effects of the new Black thrust emerging out of the Black Power movement spilled over into the realm of Black theology. It was that of the rejection and negation of the other-worldly dimension of Black religion as if there were something inherently negative about such an idea. The words of James H. Cone in his first book, *Black Theology and Black Power,* are a telling example of this mood—this side effect of the miracle of Black Power. He wrote: "The idea of heaven is irrelevant for Black Theology. The Christian cannot waste time contemplating the next world (if there is a next)."[4] This was Cone's position in his first book written in 1969, but he has since modified his position which will be discussed later.

Black theology is a theology which centers in redemption, and the Judeo-Christian religion in its pristine and unspoiled form has as its ultimate goal of redemption the restoration of an uninterrupted union between the Redeemer and people. Final mending of the fission which exists between God and humankind is the ultimate end of Christian strivings. The Christian hope is that human beings will be eventually brought back to a relationship with the Eternal which is consistent with his will in creation. The idea of heaven, then, the term masses of Black folks used instead of the term "eschatology," is essential to Black theology. We in theology know that definitively, the term "heaven" refers to a place even though that place cannot be defined or located in time and space. We also know that eschatology (to be more fully defined later) has to do with the doctrine of last things at the end of the ages.

It is precisely the thought of last things which the masses of Black folks have in mind when they talk about heaven. Heaven is variously conceived to be a state of existence in which God, angels, and the blessed will share in an unbroken relationship after the death and resurrection of the people of God and when "time shall be no more." No Black theology can be adequate which does not give equal time to the concept of heaven or eschatology as that which is given to other theological concepts.

Generally, theologians are in agreement with the definition of eschatology advanced by Eric Lane Titus:

The term "eschatology" is derived from the Greek *eschatos,* meaning "last." Eschatology is, therefore, the doctrine of the last things. In connection with biblical thought it refers to the end of the present evil age. Both Jews and early Christians viewed time in linear fashion. Both looked forward to a consummation of history. Therefore eschatological . . . elements are to be found in the religion and literature of both groups.[5]

Roberts put it in Black perspective when he wrote:

Eschatology for blacks must be both *realized* and *unrealized.* Whereas the evangelical-pietistic version of eschatology is preoccupied with the *future,* Black Theology must *begin,* I believe, with the *present.* In other words, for black Christians realized eschatology, the manifestation of the will of God in the present, *abstractly* as social justice and *concretely* as goods and services to "humanize" life, must be a first consideration for a doctrine pointing to the eventual consummation of God's purposes in creation and history.[6]

Pannenberg advanced a similar view when he wrote:

. . . eschatological consciousness has a twofold political relevance: with regard to the difference between the eschatological destination and the present world, it drives toward altering present circumstances; and it nevertheless guards against identification of the consummation with the particular change being striven for.

. . . [it] becomes a power determining the present without thereby losing its futurity.[7]

It was the side effect of the newfound Black Power which played havoc with heaven or the future dimension of eschatology in Black scholarship and Black literature during the Black Power movement. The emphasis was upon "Freedom Now!" Despite this temporary loss of emphasis on the future dimension of eschatology in the vocal circles which had the ear of the press and the media, the mass Black church kept alive the otherworldly aspect of eschatology while actively supporting programs and ideas which promoted what Roberts calls *"realized* eschatology." Personally, I had to maintain a careful balance during the height of the Black Power era. The tension was maintained, on the one hand, by the pressures of students from other disciplines at Howard University, the pressures from the "Black United Front," and other liberation organizations with which I was involved. On the other hand, there was pressure to hold onto the traditional reality of heaven in the Black religious community—the mass Black church in which I was deeply involved.

The vocal element of the Black community was saying "away with pie in the sky; we want pie on our plates!" However, though less vocal at some points, the Black church has always had and maintained throughout the Black Power era the elasticity to hold on to its otherworldly view of eschatology and to participate in the high calling of bringing into being realized eschatology. This is evident in the theme song of the civil rights movement, "We Shall Overcome." The Black church members marched with the nonchurch members and with white liberals singing lines from the theme song:

> We shall overcome,
> we shall overcome,
> We shall overcome some day,
> Deep in my heart
> I do believe
> we shall overcome someday.

This stanza could and did express the hope of realized eschatology. There was the hope for redemption—liberation from human-caused suffering and confederation into a community based upon equity and social justice in the here and now. But the Black church folks who participated in those marches knew full well that there are other verses to that song which have future meanings which may be realized only "when time shall be no more." One stanza is:

> We shall see His face,
> we shall see His face,
> We shall see His face someday.
> Deep in my heart,
> I do believe,
> we shall see His face someday.

While this otherworldly verse was seldom heard during the civil rights marches, being a definite element of Black religious consciousness, it gave meaning to the struggle for realized eschatology. In other words, the efficacy of the transcendent hope was a sustaining factor in the struggle for mundane redemption. The Black church has always maintained a balance between redemption for the now and redemption reserved for the end-time. It is just that the visible emphasis placed upon either of the sides varied with the overt and covert degree of the infliction of racism. The degree of emphasis on redemption now or redemption hereafter which might have been expressed at any given time must be viewed in the light of Black folk's genius for survival.

The Black Power movement and the side effect of the burst of militant retaliation against the oppressors sent the pendulum of Black eschatology swinging intensely in the this-worldly direction for a season. The otherworldly dimension of eschatology has been used by the white masters in an attempt to delude the slaves into setting their hopes upon rewards in heaven in the after life. And at points in American history the Black folks had to harness their this-worldly ambitions and play ball with the white masters, because under the crushing anvils of the demonic white masters, any other activity would have meant instant suicide. Blacks were not fools; they have always known the difference between being a martyr and committing suicide. They also always knew that they were endowed with a divine right to share in the benefits of their toil and labor in the here and now. Thus in fact when whites thought that Blacks were satisfied with postponing earthly redemption and rewards for heavenly redemption and rewards, it was the deluders who were being deluded.

This position is sustained by the report of the Nat Turner episode related earlier in this work. The Travis family went to sleep, evidently with a degree of contentment on the night of August 21, 1831, knowing that the slaves were satisfied with the idea of forfeiting rewards now for rewards in heaven after this life is ended. Thirty-six hours after Turner and company went on the first successful, reported, and well-documented venture which, in retrospect, might be referred to as a "get whitey" campaign, the white masters, mistresses, and their offspring of that Southhampton, Virginia, community were awakened to the naked reality that fifty-five of their kind had lost their lives at the hands of Black folks who sang about heaven all the time. Evidently these brave martyrs had thoughts of rewards which were not to be postponed for some future time after this life.

Again evidence of Black ingenuity to delude the deluders is evident in this poem cited in chapter 3.

> Got one mind for white folks to see
> 'Nother for what I know is me;
> He don't know, he don't know my mind,
> When he see me laughing
> Just laughing to keep from crying.[8]

This makes it clear that white researchers can never be sure of making a correct analysis of Black thought or Black theology with white instruments of observation. What the investigator sees and hears in Black expressions is not the full story of Black thought. Like an iceberg, the largest portion of what is truth in the Black community is submerged in the sea of Black religion. The full meaning of any Black religious concept is not easily grasped by outside observers. While the master used the otherworldly point of reference to blind the eyes of Black folks to the this-worldly rewards, the Black church and the Black preachers have been the constantly busy ophthalmologists removing those cataracts designed to impair the this-worldly view of Black people.

Lack of success in sharing in the rewards resulting from Black toil in this one nation, divided, is not due to any lack of this-worldly concern on the part of Blacks, stemming from their religion and evidenced in their singing and praying about heaven. The lack of equitable sharing in this nation's goods and services on the part of Blacks is the result of the cruel and the unlimited use of white power.

Eschatology in Black thought is both earthly and eternal. And the time has come when those who are reflecting on Black theology in literary form must swing the pendulum back to the center where it belongs. This does not mean that for special emphasis it should not be swung from one side to the other. The mistake rests in the possibility that either the earthly or the eternal outlook of eschatology might be sacrificed at the altar of asserting the other side in Black theology.

For the moment, in Black theology, there is adequate treatment of the this-worldly side of redemption and the element of this-worldly side of eschatology. So a word more might be said here about the otherworldly side of eschatology since much of what has come forth in Black literature recently has shunned the idea of future eschatology in order to avoid the fallout of the stereotype which has characterized the idea of the otherworldly outlook. The idea of eschatology was not merely a creation of Black folks which had compensatory values. Eschatology was and is in Black religious thought a very real and divine promise revealed in Scriptures, taught by Jesus Christ, and believed by Blacks who have also experienced installments of realized eschatology in their pilgrimage in America. The element of redemption which we call future eschatology has had an ontological impact in the lives of Black folks. It has effectuated a state of being for an oppressed people which transcended what the oppressors would let them be. It has given meaning to the existential absurdities of the now in the Black experience. It is the bringing into confluence of the earthly and the eternal wings of eschatology which gives wholeness to the eschatological concern of Black theology. One might start from above or from below, but eschatology has two poles, both of which must be given full consideration.

In the preface to his book *The Future of God,* Carl Braaten makes a statement which is apropos to our work at this point. His challenge is this:

> Whether one cut his theological eyeteeth more on Barth, Bultmann, or Tillich, the feeling is quite general that we can hardly go on the way we have been going. But how do we begin again? Where do we go from here? . . . The new place to start in theology is at the end—eschatology.[9]

What Braaten saw in the development of theology was a tendency to "accept the past or the status quo as the picture of the 'homeland' and 'happy days' which all men seek in one way or another." It us understandable how the oppressors could make the happy days of the past, growing out of their religio-political position of superiority and security, their central concern in theology. But Black theology cannot afford such an expedition. For the faith of the fathers, Blacks look to the past, but for redemption, Blacks look to the future. Braaten says that those theologians who reject revolutionary theological thinking did not "realize—or did they—that in chucking utopianism altogether they lost their own eschatology which looks to the future of God's final and fulfilling coming."[10] Braaten's shift to the future might be too far for Black theology, which must never neglect the past Black religious experience. Today's Blacks must affirm the Black forefathers who charted the course of Black religious thought while at the same time affirming the future hope which they transmitted to them. Braaten's counsel is important for Black theological reflections, however, in that the end— eschatology—has been a major concept in the faith of our fathers.

What Black theologians must face squarely is the fact that, as stated by Roberts: "Eschatology can no longer be a mere addendum to black theology. It is at the center of any theology which endeavors to bring a meaningful hope to the weak and the powerless."[11] In *The Spirituals and the Blues* and in his latest book *God of the Oppressed,* James Cone had modified his views which were pronounced in his first book *Black Power and Black Theology.* We heard him say in the first book, "The idea of heaven is irrelevant for Black Theology." But in *God of the Oppressed,* he writes:

> While the meaning of liberation includes the historical determination of freedom in this world, it is not limited to what is possible in history.

There is a transcendent element in definition of liberation which affirms that the "realm of freedom is always more than the fragments of a free life which we may accomplish in history."[12]

Then he offers an interesting quote from a Black preacher which, he believes, expressed the truth that Blacks have a future not made with human hands. This truth is expressed with apocalyptic imagination. The lengthy quote is an eschatological dissertation coming fresh from the folks in Black religion:

> I know the way gets awful dark sometimes; it looks like everything is against us. Sometimes we wake up in the dark hours of midnight, briny tears flowing down our cheeks, crying and not knowing what we are crying about. But because God is our Captain and is on board now, we can sit still and hear the Word of the Lord. Away back before the wind ever blowed or before the earth was made, Our God had us in mind. He looked down through time one morning and saw you and me and ordained from the very beginning that we should be his children. You remember Old John the Revelator who claimed he saw a number that had come through hard trials and great tribulations and who had washed their robes in the blood of the lamb. Oh, brothers! Ain't you glad that you have already been in the dressing room, because it won't be long before we will take the wings of the morning and go where there will be no more sin and sorrow, no more weeping and mourning.[13]

At the conclusion of this quote, Cone says: "This sermon makes clear that liberation is also beyond history and not limited to the realities and limitations of this world." Cone is right. Heaven or eschatology must be given greater consideration in literary Black theology if it is to be a true reflection of oral Black theology.

This World Is Not My Home

Black religion has always been very clear about the idea of death. Heaven in the eschatological future would triumph over death. Thus death was not necessarily an event in life's experience which would deprive the individual of the good life in the here and now. It was often seen in Black folk's religious expressions as a welcome relief— redemptive event—from the suffering in this life. Out of this faith Black folks created eschatological songs, such as this one:

I'll Fly Away
1
Some glad morning when this life is o'er,
I'll fly away, fly away, fly away.
To a home on God's celestial shore,
I'll fly away, fly away, fly away.

Chorus
I'll fly away, fly away, oh glory,
I'll fly away, fly away in the morning,
When I die, hallelujah, by and by,
I'll fly away, fly away, fly away.

2

When the shadows of this life have grown,
I'll fly away, fly away, fly away,
Like a bird from prison bars has flown,
I'll fly away, fly away, fly away.[14]

When death comes, it will be a "glad" morning when the deceased will fly away like a bird from prison bars to a new home on God's celestial shore. Then we have this bit of counsel in an excerpt from "Go Down Death" (a Funeral Sermon) by James Weldon Johnson:

Weep not, weep not,
She is not dead;
She's resting in the bosom of Jesus.
Heart-broken husband—weep no more;
Grief-stricken son—weep no more;
She's only just gone home.

Day before yesterday morning,
God was looking down from his great, high heaven,
Looking down on all his children,
And his eye fell on Sister Caroline,
Tossing on her bed of pain.
And God's big heart was touched with pity,
With the everlasting pity.

And God sat back on his throne,
And he commanded that tall, bright angel
    standing at his right hand:
Call me Death!

. . . .

And God said: Go down, Death, go down,
Go down to Savannah, Georgia,
Down in Yamacraw,
And find Sister Caroline.
She's borne the burden and heat of the day,
She's labored long in my vineyard,
And she's tired—
She's weary—
Go down, Death, and bring her to me.

. . . .

And Death took her up like a baby,
And she lay in his icy arms,
But she didn't feel no chill.
And Death began to ride again—
Up beyond the evening star,
Out beyond the morning star,
Into the flittering light of glory,
On to the Great White Throne.
And there he laid Sister Caroline
On the loving breast of Jesus.[15]

The Black preacher in Johnson's poem clearly removes any remorse about the problem of death. Sister Caroline had borne her burden in the heat of the day, and despite the coldness, Sister Caroline felt no chill as she was conveyed in the icy arms of death to be laid in the loving breast of Jesus. In Black thought, human life was a sacred trust and was not to be trampled into nonbeing by the cruel whims of those who committed the sin of trying to be God and to possess other human beings. But despite this sacredness of human life in its earthly existence, Black religious teachings admitted the divine reality that life must pass through the gateway of death in order to arrive into the Promised Land. And this death was not the worst enemy of Black folks.

Dr. Kübler-Ross, in her book *On Death and Dying,* reports that in the fall of 1965, four theological students who were required to write a paper on "crisis in human life" approached her for directions because they had concluded that death was the biggest crisis people had to face. Dr. Ross points out that death has always been distasteful to people in most cultures and at all times. It probably always will be so. "Death . . . is associated with a bad act, a frightening happening, something that in itself calls for retribution and punishment." Death is accompanied by and associated with grief, shame, anxieties, guilt, none of which are far removed from feelings of anger and rage, according to Dr. Ross. "Death is still a fearful, frightening happening, and the fear of death is a universal fear even if we think we have mastered it on many levels."[16] She discusses the role religion has played in the encounter with death.

Then she charges that paradoxically "while society has contributed to our denial of death, religion has lost many of its believers in life after death . . . and has thus decreased the denial of death in that respect." This has been a poor exchange in terms of the patient.

While the religious denial, i.e., the belief in the meaning of suffering here on earth and reward in heaven after death, has offered hope and purpose, the denial of society has given neither hope nor purpose but has only increased our anxiety and contributed to our destructiveness and aggressiveness—to kill in order to avoid the reality of facing our own death.[17]

These are the findings of a white researcher in a white society. To examine Black thoughts on the idea of death and dying, I went to Howard Thurman's little book, *The Negro Spiritual Speaks of Life and Death.* Here we get a panoramic view of the thoughts of Black religionists on the subject of death and dying during slavery and during the Formative Period of Black religion immediately following slavery. This Black understanding of death has not changed radically. One reason is that the social situation of racism which influenced the shaping of such a view in the first place has not changed radically. Thurman says he chose to

. . . examine the Negro spirituals as a source of rich testimony concerning life and death, because in many ways they are the voice, sometimes strident, sometimes muted and weary, of a people for whom the cup of suffering overflowed in haunting overtones of the majesty, beauty and power![18]

"Life [for the Negroes]," says Thurman, "is regarded as an experience of evil, of frustration, of depair."[19] Such an outlook on life is evident in two moods: One has to do with the impersonal characteristic of life itself while the other mood "has to do with a personal reaction to the vindictiveness and cruelty of one's fellows." He makes the important point that "the mood is set in a definite moral and ethical frame of reference which becomes a screening device for evaluating one's day-by-day human relations."[20]

Thurman is correct when he suggests that the moral and ethical frame of reference of Black people evolves from the life situation of the community. He might have added "and the African survivals among the folk of African descent." Life's moral and ethical expressions in the Black community are shaped not only by the surroundings of social situations but also by the teachings and beliefs which the folks bring to the situation. Three sources of the spiritual which include the testimonies of Black people about death and dying, according to Thurman, are: "the world of nature, the stuff of experience, and the Bible."[21]

He also divides the attitude of Black folks toward death and dying into three parts: First, death was a fact which was inescapable and persistent. He offers the grim reminder that slaves were chattels, and the notion of personality, of human beings as ends, which was so basic to the Christian faith, had no authentic application when it came to relationships between slave and master. So, was death the worst thing that could happen to an individual? Obviously not, according to the following lines:

> Oh, Freedom! Oh, Freedom!
> Oh, Freedom, I love thee!
> An' before I'll be a slave
> I'll be buried in my grave
> And go home to my Lord and be free.

This is not mere counsel to suicide. It is an affirmation of the sense of alternatives; death is a private option.

The second attitude toward death as described by Thurman is one of recognition mixed with elements of fear and a manifestation of dread. He believes that all of us participate in a conspiracy to reduce our immediate contract with death to zero except under extraordinary circumstances. However, Blacks were able to cope with this resignation tendency through religion and the redemptive motif. In order to overcome the fear of the approach of death, Blacks created a spiritual which transcended the immediate reality of the end of the present life existence:

> I want to die easy when I die.
> I want to die easy when I die.
> I want to die easy when I die,
> Shout salvation when I fly.
> I want to die easy when I die.

Thurman does not go this far, but I want to assert that the request and longing to "die easy" brings with it a far-reaching and deep theological meaning. To "die easy" in Black thought has two important meanings: First, it means victory over the fear of death and the concomitant wrestling, writhing, and striving to get a stay of death. Secondly, to die easy means that the dying person has definitely been adjudged favored by God who alone can and does remove the fear of death from the life of the redeemed. When God removes the fear of death by the righteous, there is no need for a reprieve when death comes. There is no fighting and struggling to hold on to life; one just dies easy, simply slips away. This easy dying is evidence of the Eternal's satisfaction with the past life of the deceased.

From the time that I was just a small boy, I can remember listening to the elders discuss the dying and death of persons in my little hometown of Jamestown, South Carolina.

When a person in the community would die (and most of them died in the home, not in hospitals), there would always be some church people on hand. This was almost always the case when the person who passed had been sick for a time. As soon as the word spread concerning a death, those who were not present would inquire of those who were in attendance at the time of death, "How did he (she) die?" The answer almost always was "Brother (Sister) X died easy! And we know he (she) is at rest in heaven." So to die easy meant that the fear of death which leads to struggle against its imminent takeover had been overcome by faith in God on the part of the dying, and to die easy was also a mark of divine favor upon the dying and the assurance of his or her eternal salvation in heaven. The song "I Want to Die Easy When I Die" was more than a song of consolation to Black folks; it was a theological statement on death and dying. And this idea has held on with amazing tenacity in the Black church to this day. It traveled North with the Great Migration and was transmitted from one generation to another through the Black oral tradition. In December, 1975, a member of our fellowship passed away. Because she had no relatives, our church and its pastor had promised to assume responsibility for her funeral and burial. It was just past midnight when she went across her room to turn out a light and she collapsed and died immediately. I was promptly called to the scene by one of the deacons who had been called by the tenants in the home of the deceased. She had always expressed the hope that she would not linger when it came her time to die. Her prayers were answered. She did not linger. When word of her easy passing was made known among the members of the congregation, there was a kind of exuberance which came out in statements such as, "Reverend, we are so happy to know that she died easy when she died."

The fourth line in the verse above—"Shout salvation when I fly"—is of particular theological significance, too. There is the line which explicitly expresses the redemption theme. The deceased will celebrate the transition from this existence of life to the other. He or she will "Shout salvation when I fly." After dying easy, which is tantamount to eternal acceptance into the community of heaven, the deceased will not wait until arriving in the new situation before celebrating. Celebration will commence by shouting a redemption song—salvation—as one flys away like that "bird from prison bars has flown" in the song "I'll Fly Away," mentioned earlier in this chapter. As the angels sang in midair at the birth of Jesus, there seems to be a clear notion of a kind of similar activity on the part of the just in the resurrection. There will be singing in midair by the redeemed.

A third attitude of Blacks with regard to death was discussed by Thurman. He feels that Black folks regarded death as a release from the cares and anxieties of this life. He says this is to be distinguished from what is to come after death. The attitude toward death in this case is to be measured strictly against the background of the immediate experiences of this present life. Yet, it is not a renunciation of this life; it is rather an exulting sigh of release from a weary human-caused burden. Such an attitude is expressed in the following lines:

> Let us cheer the weary traveler,
> Let us cheer the weary traveler,
> Along the heavenly way.

Death is not an enemy in the religious sense in Black thought. Death is an agent of redemption which lifts the weary traveler right out of the troubles of this life. In the general resurrection those of the redeemed are united with God and with former fellow pilgrims. This is why in the Black church everybody is talking about heaven.

When the First Trumpet Sounds

From Scriptures, Blacks have come to the conclusion that there will be two resurrections, the first of which occurring when the dead in Christ will rise. One Scripture reference used in support of this view is 1 Thessalonians 4:16: "For the Lord himself will descend from heaven with a cry of command, with the archangel's call, and with the sound of the trumpet of God. And the dead in Christ will rise first." This understanding of the resurrection is captured and passed on to the faithful in the following song:

> Where shall I be
>   when the first trumpet sounds?
> Where shall I be
>   when it sounds so loud?
> It's going to sound so loud
>   that it's going to wake up the dead!
> Where shall I be when it sounds?

Hope in Black theology is and must be anchored ultimately in the other world. This is necessary because if Black history has anything to say to Black scholars and Black folks, it is that whatever the measure of realized eschatology might be at any given period in history or whatever the degree of lessening of the pains of oppression might be, white folks in America have no intentions of permitting Black folks to be full citizens of this country in the meaning of the term which applies to themselves. Another reason why ultimate hope in Black theology is anchored in the other world is that Black religionists are aware of the fact that "this world is not my home," and "I ain't got long to stay here." Blacks have experienced a step in the fulfillment of this wordly redemption in the Emancipation only to see that divine right thwarted at the end of Reconstruction. Blacks saw steps in this worldly redemption from oppression in the Great Migration, the Harlem Renaissance, and in the rise of the Black bourgeoisie, commencing during World War II. Blacks saw a ray of hope for redemption from this-worldly pains resulting from racism and segregation in the Supreme Court Desegregation edict of 1954, the civil rights movement, and the Black Power movement. All of these hopes for salvation from oppression turned out to be what Dr. Martin Luther King, Jr., referred to as a bad check which has come back marked "insufficient funds." Black folks know that they cannot set their ultimate hope for salvation from the pains of the oppressor and human-inflicted suffering on what might happen in this nation.

Then, even if the masses of Blacks could imagine a state of existence in this country which could be vaguely defined in terms such as equity and justice, they still know that this does not fit them for membership in the heavenly community. Ultimate hope is in the events promised in Scriptures, taught by Jesus, believed by the poor pilgrims, and expected after the "first trumpet sounds."

Blacks have been a people of hope, and that hope is inseparable from Black religion. Braaten is helpful at this point when he says: "Where there is life, there is hope, and where there is hope, there is religion." Again, he declares: "The utterances of hope are signals that send out messages concerning the human condition. They tell us that man is like a ship suffering distress at sea while on its way to some destination." [22] Black hope has always had two foci. One is set upon the destination of deliverance from human-made shackles in this world, and the other, like that ship at sea which may pass many islands, is set on the destination of the mainland of eternity after the first trumpet sounds.

Black people have always had to live in two worlds in America, and this duality is seen from two positions. First, there was the position of the world which was "the one for the white man to see," and the other is the one which "I know is me." From an eschatological position the duality is found in the contrast between the world of injustices and nonbeing, resulting from the cruelty of sinful folks, and the world which is being justified by the Redeemer. The hope of this world stands beyond the sounding of the first trumpet at the end of time which extends down into time in the form of the Black church— the kingdom of God at hand—which contradicts the absurdities of the now and gives meaning to Black existence. In Black religious thought faith in God's promise of a new heaven and a new earth opens up new possibilities amid the sufferings of the now for Black people. It is that hope in the unrealized which helps Black folks to participate in the redemptive struggle to effectuate what can be realized in the present.

America has been able to sustain herself in the world among other nations because of her gun power. White folks have been able to keep Blacks in servitude in this nation because of racial power. White folks across this nation almost went "mad" at the outbreak of Black Power. They realized how they had used white power to reduce Black people to a social and economic state of nonbeing. And the outburst of Black Power had threatening overtones. There was the fear that Black Power might have been a kind of reaping of the harvest of white power all over this nation. In order to quell this potential, the ruling race of this nation swung into police power, CIA power, and FBI power in unlimited fashion. The various private and governmental investigation committees are now revealing what columnist Jack Anderson, Dick Gregory, and others have been saying all the time. That is, the late J. Edgar Hoover and his FBI and other law-enforcement agencies were conducting illegal espionage designed to destroy the value of the existence, if not the existence itself, of the late Dr. Martin Luther King, Jr., and all civil rights leaders and organizations. It must be said, too, that they were quite successful. Many Black leaders and Black organizations fell, one after another, succumbing to the police power on the national and the local levels.

There is another power which has been more potent and encompassing than any of these powers; it is Black faith power which sees the redemption force at work in this world but takes its inception in redemption from another world—heaven. Despite the darkness of life situations, Blacks still sang, "I'm on my way to heaven anyhow!" Amid situations where Blacks did not experience the fulfillment of love, peace, and justice and where there was always crisis, Blacks still maintained the hope for new possibilities—faith power. Black faith was rooted not in the abundance of things and powers which they possessed, but in the not yet. The good old "golden days" are not in the past, but in the future. The experiences of the present unhappiness provided the basis for the development of a consciousness of new possibilities. The horizon of expectation has always been the becoming factor in the Black experience.

The Black hope theme is here cleverly put by Pauli Murray in

> Dark Testament
> Hope is a crushed stalk
> Between clenched fingers.
> Hope is a bird's wing
> Broken by a stone.
> Hope is a word in a tuneless ditty—
> A word whispered with the wind,
> A dream of forty acres and a mule,
> A cabin of one's own and rest days often,
> A name and place for one's children
> And children's children at last . . .
> Hope is a song in a weary throat.

> *O give me a song of hope*
> *And a world where I can sing it.*
> *Give me a song of faith*
> *And a people to believe in it.*
> *Give me a song of kindliness*
> *And a country where I can live it.*
> *O give me a song of hope and love*
> *And a brown girl's heart to hear it.*[23]

Blacks have experienced hope crushed between clenched fingers and as a bird's wing broken with the stone of racism, but the pull of heaven provided the undergirding for the continual song of hope. So they sang:

> In dat Great Gettin' up mornin'
> Fare you well, fare you well.

This attested to an apocalyptic cosmic expectation which would accompany the ending of this present age just preceding the sounding of the first trumpet. The event is seen as so personal and cosmic that the rocks, the mountains, the stars, and the seas are all involved:

My Lord, what a morning!
My Lord, what a morning!
When the stars begin to fall.

You will hear the trumpet sound
To wake the nations underground,
Standing at my God's right hand
When the stars begin to fall.[24]

At no point would the chosen people of God be affected by the calamities of the apocalypse, because when the first trumpet sounds, waking the nation underground, they will get up and take their place at the right hand of God.

James Cone shares an interesting folktale entitled "Swapping Dreams."

The master told Ike: "I dreamed I went to Nigger Heaven last night, and I saw there a lot of garbage, some torn-down houses, a few old broken down, rotten fences, the muddiest, sloppiest streets I ever saw, and a big bunch of ragged, dirty Negroes walking around." But rather than accept the master's perspective about himself and his community, Ike responded with a comment that was deceptive and full of humor but liberating in its rejection of the present white value system. "Umph, umph, Massa," said Ike, "yah sho' musta et de same t'ing Ah did las' night, 'cause Ah dreamed Ah went up ter de white man's paradise, an' de streets wuz all ob gol' an silvah, and dey was lots o' milk an' honey dere, an' putty pearly gates, but dey wuzn't uh soul in de whole place."[25]

We are struck with three facts as we read this tale. The first is the ingenuity and cleverness of the slave. He was able to respond to his master relating a transcendent truth and at the same time did not arouse the demonic power of his master. The second fact which stands out in the tale is that the slave retained his identification with heaven. And thirdly, the slave subtly asserted that no white person could expect to make it into heaven.

No Strangers and No Segregation

Again we turn to our opening song: "Everybody Is Talking About Heaven." But in the chorus of this spiritual it is made clear that everybody who is "talkin' 'bout heab'n ain't goin' dere." Now we can understand the thinking which molded the idea of the slave who made the quick and subtle response to his master on the subject of the dream about heaven. White folks talked about heaven, too, but Black folks learned in church that everybody talking about heaven was not going there. In Black sermons, testimonies, and prayers, the teaching is well-defined and distinct: "Heaven is a prepared place for a prepared people." Jesus' statement is recorded in the Gospel of John: "In my Father's house are many rooms; if it were not so, would I have told you that I go to prepare a place for you? And when I go and prepare a place for you, I will come again and will take you to myself, that where I am you may be also" (John 14:2-3).

Blacks took this literally; it was not merely an abstract idea of a state of eternal bliss. Heaven is a place with mansions, houses, and rooms. While modern theologians might interpret heaven as a state of existence beyond death, Black folks are not off base when they use the language of Jesus in talking about heaven. They fashioned a song about heaven based upon the report of John who wrote the Revelation out of his experience of the presence and directions of the Spirit while he was imprisoned on the Isle of Patmos. The song says:

> I've never been to heaven
> But I've been told,
> The streets are pearl
> And the gates are gold.

Having lived under conditions which made them unwelcome aliens in a strange land, as well as in the community and home of the oppressors, their faith taught them that there will be a place in the not yet where there will be no strangers and no segregation. There would be no signs saying "White Only" or "Colored" or "Negroes and dogs not allowed." There would be no racial or social atmosphere which would make poor pilgrims feel unwelcome. Thus, in Black testimonies we hear the assertions: "I'm on my way to a new Jerusalem; Jesus said he was goin' to prepare a place for me, and when I get there, I'm going to walk right in and make myself at home." Then they would sing:

> I got a robe
> You got a robe
> All God's children got robes.
> When we get to heaven,
> We're going to put on our robes
> We're going to shout all over God's heaven!

It goes without saying that no guest would make himself at home in the house of a neighbor unless there had been some prior communication between the parties which made the guest know that he or she would be unequivocally welcomed. Going a step further, no guest would walk through the home of a host unless invited to do so.

But Blacks say that upon arriving in heaven they were not only going to walk through the kingdom, but they were also going to put on their robes and shout *all over* God's heaven! It is important to understand the definition of the word "shout" here. It does not mean to call out or to speak loudly. In the Black religious idiom, "shout" means to bring to the fore the African survival method of expressing joy and happiness. The "shout" here means to "dance." But we must remember that when these spirituals were created, white folks had cast a sinful cloud on dance. To dance was a sinful act.

Again calling upon every ounce of ingenuity, Blacks had to create a new name for their traditional method of joyful expressions. They exchanged the term "dance" for the term "shout," a word which eluded the white religious critics. They changed the term but kept the practice. They found a new word, but they retained the old act which expressed their joys.

To welcome visitors and to express joy and happiness is not demonstrated by thunderous applause or exuberant hoorays in Africa! The Africans, in general, still hold to the beautiful tradition of expressing joy and happiness by dancing and singing, usually in beautiful and distinct antiphonal, responsive, and rhythmic patterns. While our party could not participate in singing the words with our African brothers in the many villages which we visited in Africa, we had no problem identifying with the antiphonal, responsive, and rhythmic patterns which were projected in their ceremonies, welcoming us. When Blacks sing about shouting all over God's heaven, they are really talking about having a "dancing good time." The shouting—"dancing"—which takes place on a large scale in many Black churches today is, on a microscale, that which is anticipated on a cosmic scale in the *eschaton*. Blacks sometime refer to the *eschaton* as the "way-by-and-by"; so they sing "We're going to have a good time way-by-and-by." And everybody in the Black religious community knows what is meant. It means that we are going to shout all over God's kingdom. It means that heaven is a place where there will be no strangers and no segregation.

There will be no strangers because Black folk's religious expressions have always identified Black folk with that innumerable multitude which was seen by John coming up through the common corridor of "great tribulation" having had their robes washed and made white in the blood of the Lamb. They will not be strangers one to another because the common sharing of the cup of tribulation in this world and the common sharing in the cup of faith will then have fashioned them into a common kinship of sons and daughters of one Father. Along with their long white robes they will also put on their heavenly crowns and golden slippers. And "when the saints go marching in," it is this tribulation community which will make up its number.

Aside from shouting all over God's kingdom, Blacks look forward to sitting down with Abraham, Isaac, and Jacob; they look forward to "chatting with the Father and talking with the Son, and telling them about the world that I've just come from." Blacks also expect to "sit at the welcome table, eat and never get hungry." These aspirations are repeated over and over again in Black oral sermons, songs, prayers, and testimonies. In this nation, during the creation of this spiritual, and until very recent times, Blacks knew what it was to be excluded from the tables of restaurants and other eating places. While there are still a few "unwelcome tables" in various corners of this nation, any of us who are ten years old or older can well remember this was the case on a national level in the not-too-distant past. We have not forgotten. But in his redemptive acts in time and in history, God has seen fit to redeem us from that national human-caused malfunction of his divine purpose with regard to human relationship.

Through the vision of faith Blacks saw God bringing them into a future state in which, when the table was prepared, it would be a "welcome table" in that no one would be excluded based on race, color, or previous condition of servitude. The table will be a "welcome table" because in that state "the wicked will cease from troubling." What this means in a prayer of hope is that the wicked— those who create tribulation by segregation and discrimination—will no longer be in control of things. These wicked troublemakers will have to cease from troubling while the "weary will be at rest."

The idea of sitting at the welcome table, eating and never getting hungry, grew out of the social situation of human-caused starvation and malnutrition. In this nation of affluence and abundance, Blacks have been a malnourished people. But the Bible speaks of and the preacher proclaims from biblical references that heaven is a place flowing with milk and honey. Blacks believed, therefore, that in his redemptive process, God was bringing them into that place in the "way-by-and-by." When that day comes, "we are going to eat and never get hungry."

The idea of heaven in Black religious expressions goes on and on, but we feel that enough has been said so that an open mind will begin to take note that there is something intrinsic and transcendent about heaven in Black religious thought which has ontological quotients and therefore must be brought into the sphere of theological investigation and reflection. The description of heaven coming out of Black religious expression is inerrantly biblical. Should there be any critics of the Black view of heaven, they must remember that their criticisms must be directed at the biblical writers before they begin to focus upon the Black church. They must remember to take on that one who was imprisoned on the Isle called Patmos to whom the Lord addressed himself while this prisoner was in the spirit on the Lord's Day.

It might be possible to describe heaven theologically in the abstract, meaning a state of existence which is not described in terms with concrete connotation. This does not mean a negation of the idea of heaven as a place as defined in Black religious expressions. Every theologian will have to admit that any epistemological deduction of a religious or transcendent concept does not exhaust the meaning inherent in the reality out of which the concept arose. In explaining theological concepts, the theologian must speak in symbols, similes, and metaphors. Thus, no matter what any theologian has said or will say, any conceptualization of heaven will not exhaust the meaning of the reality out of which the concept has come unless that person speaks from the other side of the *eschatos*. And obviously that is not where the speaker is.

Blacks have every right (and have exercised the same) to choose the symbols, similes, or metaphors which best describe the realities to which the symbols, similes, or metaphors point. The Black folks' view and description of the transcendent reality of heaven, one must remember, was developed and nurtured under conditions of segregated sabbaths and a discriminated society. Heaven for the masses of Black religionists is a prepared place for a prepared people. And even with its spatial connotations, we are not ready to scrap this symbol or metaphor—place—as a valid theological reflection upon the reality which gave rise to the concept.

The other word that we want to say about heaven from a Black theological perspective is from the more abstract epistemological mold. But we must hasten to say that Black folk have a strong tendency to see things in their concreteness and to speak in concrete terms. When they sing "I'm going to walk in Jerusalem just like John," this transcendent idea has very concrete meaning. In imagination and hope Blacks look forward to walking into a concrete place. This is why Blacks could say hallelujah, which is in a sense an expression of freedom while being bound by the shackles of human-inflicted tribulations.

> Oh! Nobody knows the trouble I've seen,
>   Nobody knows but Jesus;
> Nobody knows the trouble I've seen
>   Glory, hallelujah.
>
> Sometimes I'm up, sometimes I'm down;
>   Oh, yes, Lord!
> But still my soul is heavenly bound
>   Oh, yes, Lord!

It was that transcendent freedom imputed to the chosen people in the process and moment of justification which has eschatological ultimacy but is trajected back through time and in a very concrete way gives ontological meaning to the existential now. In the world surrounded by troubles there is still a feeling of hallelujah in the life of the pilgrim because his or her soul is heaven bound. There is a kind of abstract thought of heaven in Black theology which is also symbolized as a state of final redemption when the final confederation of the pilgrim people of God will be consummated. The ultimate at-one-ment with the Eternal and with fellow travelers which was anticipated in the Black church—the union of the chosen people—on earth will come to full fruition in a manner incomprehensible to human reason. This final redemptive act on the part of the Eternal will complete the purpose and plan of God in creation—that is to bring humankind back into an unbroken and unspoiled relationship with himself and with their peers.

The Black preachers of the Formative and Maturative Periods set the mold for all who followed them. They were masters in the art of storytelling (biblical storytelling) and image making. They made heaven so real in their sermons that at times earthly residents would feel that they were already in that heavenly community and state. Black tradition tells about a Black preacher who died and a fellow Black preacher who was called upon to give the eulogy. The deceased had lived a circumspect life. Certainly this was an occasion for the eulogist to speak of the deceased in the heavenly surrounding. Thus, at a point in the eulogy the preacher began to describe heaven and he said, "And I can now see Reverend X walking into heaven and taking his seat in the heavenly choir." One member of the choir in the congregation was so caught up in the beautiful imagery and the description portrayed by the eulogist that she began to slide over in her seat to make room for Reverend X who was taking his seat in the heavenly choir.

It is this idea of heaven which is basic to Black oral theology. It is in this heaven which stands beyond the *eschatos* that the chosen people of God will experience the final consummation of the redeeming act of God.

In spite of the attempts to minimize the idea of heaven—other-worldliness—in Black religion during the Black Power movement, heaven has always been and remains one of the central concepts in Black theology. Redemption in Black theology looks in two directions: one is salvation from the states and circumstances in this world, and the other is salvation from sin and guilt and the ultimate consequences thereof. Heaven is that place or state of existence at the end of time when the redeemed will be reunited with fellow pilgrims and with the Creator in an unspoiled relationship.

10

The Stone
Which the Builders
Rejected

Question and Answer

Groping, hoping,
Waiting—for what?

A world to gain.

Dreams kicked asunder,
Why not go under?

There's a world to gain.

But suppose I don't want it,
Why take it?

To remake it.[1]

The builders of theology in America have consistently rejected or ignored the religious thoughts of Black Christians. Therefore Black Christians developed their own theology. This Black theology was not put into literary form. But a new day has come. Black Christians have had a tremendous spiritualizing and moralizing effect upon the lives of Black people. Black theology is built upon the redeeming activity and love of God as revealed, experienced, and responded to by the people in the Black religious community.

Black religionists have been groping, hoping, and waiting—for what? A world to gain, a world which will take seriously the contributions which Black religion has to make to Christian theology. But this is the stone which the builders of American theology have rejected or ignored. It might well be that Black humanity, which is a direct result of Black religion, will become the cornerstone of a more humanized religious and social order. As Langston Hughes puts it, "There's a world to gain." And we believe that Black theology will play a major role as the scholars and theologians of this generation "take it" and "remake it."

Black theology is redemption theology. The pristine, Hebrew meaning of redemption was salvation from the states and circumstances which destroy the value of human existence or human existence itself. In reexamining the Christian use of the concept "redemption," we found that the traditional Christian theological use of this concept was far more limiting than its theological use by the Hebrews who first appropriated the commercial term to religious usage.

The use of redemption in Black theology suggests both liberation and confederation. Liberation in this context means salvation from sin and guilt and salvation from human-caused oppression. But most Western theologians who are products and beneficiaries of imperialism and colonialism have neglected the liberation-from-human-caused-oppression side of redemption because it condemns the social system of which they are members. However, redemption in Black thought is not limited to liberation *from* something. It also means coming *into* something. It means confederation among fellow pilgrims and confederation with the Eternal. As we examined the sermons, songs, prayers, and testimonies of Black folks and their usage of the concepts of human nature, revelation, Jesus, justification and sanctification, church, and heaven, we have discovered that redemption is the hub around which Black theology revolves.

In the remaking of theology, the following implications of this study of the theology of redemption will be pertinent.

First: The understanding of the concept "redemption" in the Black religious community extends beyond the classical usage of redemption in Christian theology. Also the redemption theme, which is central in Black religious thought, can be isolated and described through an examination of the historical expressions of the masses of Black folks.

Second: The term "redemption," when used in Christian theology, is borrowed from the Hebrew (Old Testament) tradition, and its usage in the Old Testament meant salvation from oppression as well as salvation from sin and guilt. Whether intentionally or by oversight, it is a fact that most Western theologians who are influenced by and beneficiaries of cultural imperialism and colonialism have neglected the salvation-from-oppression dimension of redemption. The vertical dimension of redemption in Western theology has overshadowed the horizontal dimension which is an integral aspect of the original meaning of the word in Hebrew thought.

Third: The theo-historical approach is an adequate method for doing Black theology.

Fourth: Since there is a relatively limited amount of literature which has been produced by the Black church and Black denominations, the best source for Black theological research is still in the oral songs, sermons, prayers, and testimonies of the folk in the mass Black church. Most of the Blacks who compose the elites in religious worship and style would not be an adequate group for study in doing Black theological research because their religious expressions will be typically white. Their definitions and explanations of theological concepts will also reflect their encounters with classical white Western theology.

Fifth: The program of Black theology must be carried out by those who are a part of the Black religious tradition. The modes, feelings, and the psychic-spiritual view of Black Christians are also a part of the evidence, and, thus, an outside observer can never get the same kind of indepth understanding of the Black religious expressions and thought as a person on the inside could get. The closer the researcher is to the marketplace—the masses of the Black Christians—the more likely he or she is able to grasp and to give a true report of what Black religious thought is all about. Whenever the investigator is not closely associated with those in the marketplace, he or she must be able to speak the language, communicate with, and interpret the expressions of those in the marketplace.

Just as this book has provided some new insights into the understanding of redemption from the Black theological perspective, other religious concepts ought to be examined from a Black theological perspective in order to determine whether their usage has the same theological meaning in both Black and white thought.

As the program of Black theology continues, the theologians of other cultures will have to recognize its legitimacy and become aware of its potential contribution to the total discipline of theology. This is already being done by some German theologians, particularly Jürgen Moltmann and Helmut Gollwitzer.

Some of the white American theologians who are giving some attention to Black theology include Frederick Herzog, Peter C. Hodgson, Rosemary Ruether, and Paul L. Lehmann.

White Christian theology was developed without any input from that body of Christians in America who are of African descent. Black theology might well be viewed as an antithesis to white theology by those outside of the Black tradition. But this is a positive sign. If the dialectical formula works and runs its full circle, then we might anticipate a day when there will be a synthesis. I do not foresee a complete synthesis of Black theology and white theology as long as the oppressors perpetuate the situation which gave birth and life to two cultures—one Black and one white in America. But a degree of theological synthesis can take place in those many areas where the Black-white cultural differences are minimal. When this happens, the whole Christian theological enterprise will be enriched and enhanced.

One of the prerequisites with which both Black and white theologians must come to grips is the awareness that no group has the ultimate theological truth for all peoples and for all eternity.

Christian theology is a big animal, and we must remember the advice to the six blind men in the folktale related in chapter 1. Christian theologians have touched only parts of theology, and there is a need to put all of the parts together in order to get a portrait of what might be called Christian theology.

The stone which the builders of white theology has rejected—Black theology—might well "become the head of the corner" (Mark 12:10b) for the restructuring of Christian theology.

Notes

CHAPTER 1

[1] J. Garfield Owens, *All God's Chillun: Meditations on Negro Spirituals* (Nashville: Abingdon Press, 1971), p. 55. Copyright © 1971 by Abingdon Press. Used by permission.

[2] James H. Cone, *The Spirituals and the Blues: An Interpretation* (New York: The Seabury Press, Inc., 1972), p. 120. Copyright © 1972 by James H. Cone. Used by permission of The Seabury Press, Inc.

[3] William L. Banks, *The Black Church in the U.S.* (Chicago: Moody Press, 1972), p. 49.

[4] James S. Tinney, "Black Origins of the Pentecostal Movement," *Christianity Today*, vol. 16, no. 1 (October 8, 1971), p. 4.

[5] Banks, *op. cit.*

[6] J. Deotis Roberts, Sr., "The Black Caucus and the Failure of Christian Theology," *The Journal of Religious Thought* (Washington, D.C.: Howard University Press, 1969), Summer Supplement, p. 15.

[7] Charles V. Hamilton, *The Black Preacher in America* (New York: William Morrow & Company, Inc., 1972), pp. 59-60.

[8] James D. Tyms, *The Rise of Religious Education Among Negro Baptists* (New York: Exposition Press, 1965), p. 178. Reprinted by permission of Exposition Press, Inc., Hicksville, N.Y.

[9] J. Deotis Roberts, Sr., "Black Consciousness in Theological Perspective, *Quest for a Black Theology*, ed. James J. Gardiner, SA, and J. Deotis Roberts, Sr. (Philadelphia: United Church Press, 1971), p. 65.

[10] Bernard Ramm, *A Handbook of Contemporary Theology* (Grand Rapids: William B. Eerdmans Publishing Company, 1966), p. 43.

[11] We first encountered this term in the opening line of Tom Wicker's

"Introduction" to the *Report of the National Advisory Commission on Civil Disorders* (New York: Bantam Books, 1968), p. v.

[12] Bruce Vawter, C.M., *The Conscience of Israel* (New York: Sheed & Ward, Inc., 1961), p. 1.

[13] August Derleth, *Emerson, Our Contemporary* (New York: Crowell-Collier Press, 1970), p. 82.

[14] Rosemary Ruether, *Liberation Theology* (New York: Paulist Press, 1972), p. 129.

[15] Frederick Herzog, "Theology at the Crossroads," *Union Seminary Quarterly Review*, vol. 31, no. 1 (Fall, 1975), p. 59.

[16] Jürgen Moltmann, "Introduction," *Union Seminary Quarterly Review*, vol. 31, no. 1 (Fall, 1975), pp. 3-4.

[17] J. Deotis Roberts, Sr., "Religio-Ethical Reflections upon the Experiential Components of a Philosophy of Black Liberation," *Journal of the Interdenominational Theological Center*, vol. 1, no. 1 (Fall, 1973), p. 81. Used with permission of the Board of Editors.

[18] E. Franklin Frazier, *The Negro Church in America* (New York: Schocken Books, 1964), pp. 9, 11-14.

[19] Melville J. Herskovits, *The Myth of the Negro Past* (Boston: Beacon Press, 1958), pp. 143-291.

[20] Henry H. Mitchell, *Black Belief: Folk Beliefs of Blacks in America and West Africa* (New York: Harper & Row, Publishers, 1975), p. 1.

[21] *Ibid.*, pp. 66.

[22] *Ibid.*, p. 37.

[23] James H. Cone, *A Black Theology of Liberation* (Philadelphia: J. B. Lippincott Company, 1970), pp. 30-31. Copyright © 1971 by James H. Cone. Reprinted by permission of J. B. Lippincott Company.

[24] James H. Cone, *God of the Oppressed* (New York: The Seabury Press, Inc., 1975), p. 51. Copyright © 1975 by The Seabury Press, Inc. Used by permission of the publishers.

[25] *Ibid.*

[26] *Ibid.*

[27] C. Eric Lincoln, "An Interview with C. Eric Lincoln," *Black Enterprises* (December, 1972), p. 52.

[28] Osmund Lewry, *The Theology of History* (Notre Dame, Ind.: Fides Publishers, Inc., 1969), pp. 9-10.

[29] William Leo Lucey, S. J., *History: Methods and Interpretation* (Chicago: Loyola University Press, 1958), p. 22.

[30] Bernard F. J. Lonergan, S. J., *Method in Theology* (New York: Herder and Herder, 1972), p. xi.

[31] Wolfhart Pannenberg, *Basic Questions in Theology: Collected Essays*, vol. 1., trans. George H. Kehm (Philadelphia: Fortress Press, 1970), fn. 1 on pp. 16-17. Copyright © 1970 by Fortress Press. Reprinted by permission of Fortress Press.

[32] Van A. Harvey, *A Handbook of Theological Terms* (New York: The Macmillan Company, 1964), p. 117.

[33] Pannenberg, *op. cit.*, p. xii.

[34] Johannes Pedersen, *Israel: Its Life and Culture* (London: Oxford University Press, 1926), pp. 25-26.

[35] *Ibid.*, p. 167.

[36] Gerhard Von Rad, *Old Testament Theology* (New York: Harper & Row, Publishers, 1962), vol. 1, pp. 105-106.

[37] Kenneth B. Clark, *Dark Ghetto: Dilemmas of Social Power* (New York: Harper & Row, Publishers, 1965), p. 79.

[38] *Ibid.*, pp. 79-80.

CHAPTER 2

[1] Tom Wicker, "Introduction," *Report of the National Advisory Commission on Civil Disorders* (New York: Bantam Books, 1968), p. v.

[2] Lawrence E. Toombs, *The Interpreter's One-Volume Commentary on the Bible,* ed. Charles M. Laymon (Nashville: Abingdon Press, 1971), p. 292.

[3] Donald Daniel Leslie, D.del'U (Fellow in Far Eastern History Australian National University Canberra), *Encyclopaedia Judaica,* vol. 14 (Jerusalem: The Macmillan Company, 1971), p. 1.

[4] Alexander Glennie, *Sermons Preached on Plantations to Congregations of Negroes* (New York: Books for Libraries Press, The Black Heritage Library, 1971, first published in 1844), p. iii.

[5] *Ibid.,* p. 30.

[6] Shannon made this assertion in an address before the Hampton Institute Ministers' Conference in Hampton, Virginia, June, 1975. The address is among this investigator's collection of tapes.

[7] William Muehl, *All the Damned Angels* (Philadelphia: Pilgrim Press, 1972), pp. 29-30.

[8] *Ibid.,* p. 30.

[9] Leslie, *op. cit.,* p. 1.

[10] *Ibid.*

[11] H. Wheeler Robinson, *Redemption and Revelation in the Actuality of History* (New York: Harper & Row, Publishers, 1942), p. 220. Used by permission of James Nisbet & Co., Ltd.

[12] Leslie, *op. cit.*

[13] *Ibid.*

[14] *Ibid.,* col. 2.

[15] David Flusser, Professor of Comparative Religions, the Hebrew University of Jerusalem, *Encyclopaedia Judaica,* vol. 14, p. 3.

[16] *Ibid.*

[17] *Ibid.,* pp. 3-4.

[18] *Ibid.,* p. 4.

[19] Alvin J. Reines, Rabbi, Professor of Philosophy, The Hebrew College—Jewish Institute of Religion, New York, *Encyclopaedia Judaica,* vol. 14, p. 4.

[20] *Ibid.*

[21] Soteriology is concerned with the doctrine of salvation. Gene E. Sease points out: "In the Old Testament, salvation meant 'made wide,' 'set in an open place,' or 'freedom in spacious places.' It became definitely related to victory and deliverance from oppression. In the New Testament it came to mean release from the captivity of sin to the freedom of a new life." "Soteriology," J. Sherrell Hendricks et al, *Christian Word Book* (Nashville: Graded Press, 1968), p. 285.

[22] Reines, *op. cit.*

[23] *Ibid.,* p. 5.

[24] *Ibid.*

[25] Gershom Scholem, Emeritus Professor of Jewish Mysticism, The Hebrew University of Jerusalem, *Encyclopaedia Judaica,* pp. 5-6.

[26] Michael J. Graetz, "Jerusalem," *Encyclopaedia Judaica,* p. 7.

[27] *Ibid.,* p. 8.

[28] *Ibid.*

[29] *Ibid.*

[30] *Ibid.,* p. 9.

[31] *Ibid.*

[32] *Ibid.*

[33] Albrecht Ritschl, *The Christian Doctrine of Justification and Reconciliation,* trans. H. R. Mackintosh and A. B. Macaulay (New York: Charles Scribner's Sons, n.d.), p. 4.

[34] *Ibid.,* p. 5.

[35] *Ibid.*

[36] *Ibid.*

[37] *Ibid.,* p. 6.

[38] *Ibid.,* pp. 9-10.

[39] *Ibid.,* p.10.

[40] *Ibid.,* p. 13.

[41] Robinson, *op. cit.,* p. ix.

[42] *Ibid.,* p. x.

[43] *Ibid.,* p. 219.

[44] *Ibid.,* pp. 219-220.

[45] *Ibid.,* p. 222.

[46] *Ibid.,* p. 223.

[47] *Ibid.,* p. 235.

[48] *Ibid.,* p. 243.

[49] J. Deotis Roberts, Sr., *Opening Closed Doors: Redemption and Reconciliation* (St. Louis: O. W. Wake, Christian Board of Publication, 1973), p. 10.

[50] *Ibid.*

[51] H. F. Davis, "The Atonement," *A Catholic Dictionary of Theology,* vol. 1. (Edinburgh: Thomas Nelson & Sons, Ltd., 1962); reprinted in *The Theology of the Atonement,* ed. John R. Sheets (Englewood Cliffs, N.J.: Prentice-Hall, Inc., 1967), pp. 11-21.

[52] Martin Luther King, Jr., *Strength to Love* (New York: Harper & Row, Publishers, 1963), p. 121. Copyright © by Martin Luther King, Jr. Used by permission of Joan Daves.

[53] *Ibid.,* pp. 121-122.

[54] Gayraud S. Wilmore, "Slaves Left Heritage of Liberty," *The Black Church,* vol. 2, no. 4 (Winter, 1974), p. 15.

[55] James D. Tyms, *The Rise of Religious Education Among Negro Baptists* (New York: Exposition Press, 1965), p. 8.

[56] *Ibid.,* p. 9.

[57] *Ibid.,* pp. 9-10.

[58] *Ibid.,* pp. 10-11.

[59] *Ibid.,* p. 179.

CHAPTER 3

[1] Ruby F. Johnston, *The Development of Negro Religion* (New York: Philosophical Library, 1945), pp. xix-xxi.

[2] Osadolor Imasogie, "African Traditional Religion and the Christian Faith," *Review and Expositor,* vol. 70, no. 3 (Summer, 1973), pp. 283-293.

[3] *Ibid.,* pp. 286-287.

[4] *Ibid.,* p. 288.

[5] *Ibid.,* p. 289.

[6] Ortiz M. Walton, *Music: Black, White and Blue* (New York: William Morrow & Company, Inc., 1972), pp. 21-22.

[7] E. Franklin Frazier, *The Negro Church in America* (New York: Schocken Books, 1964), p. 10.

[8] James H. Cone, *God of the Oppressed* (New York: The Seabury Press, Inc., 1975), p. 24.

[9] Frazier, *op. cit.,* p. 14.

[10] William L. Banks, *The Black Church in the U.S.* (Chicago: Moody Press, 1972), pp. 16-17.

[11] John Hope Franklin, *From Slavery to Freedom* (New York: Alfred A. Knopf, Inc., 1974), p. 35.

[12] Louis E. Lomax, *The Negro Revolt* (New York: Harper & Row, Publishers, 1962), p. 45.

[13] Frazier, *op. cit.,* pp. 35-37.

[14] Banks, *op. cit.,* pp. 19-21.

[15] Franklin, *op. cit.,* p. 141.

[16] Banks, *op. cit.,* p. 25.

[17] *Ibid.,* pp. 22-23.

[18] *Ibid.,* pp. 25-27.

[19] Chuck Stone, *Black Political Power in America* (New York: The Bobbs-Merrill Company, Inc., 1968), p. 37.

[20] Banks, *op. cit.,* pp. 35-37.

[21] Stone, *op. cit.,* p. 30.

[22] Quoted in *ibid.*

[23] Banks, *op. cit.,* p. 34.

[24] Paul Laurence Dunbar, "We Wear the Mask," *International Library of Afro-American Life and History: An Introduction to Black Literature in America,* ed. Lindsay Patterson (Cornwells Heights, Pa.: The Publishers Agency, Inc., 1976), p. 95.

[25] Benjamin Quarles, *The Negro in the Making of America* (New York: Collier Books, 1964), p. 161.

[26] W. E. B. Du Bois, *The Souls of Black Folk* (New York: Fawcett Publications, Inc., 1961), p. 143.

[27] *Ibid.,* pp. 144-145.

[28] August Meier and Elliott Rudwick, *From Plantation to Ghetto,* 3rd ed. (New York: Hill and Wang, 1976), p. 235.

[29] Gilbert Osofsky, *Harlem: The Making of a Ghetto* (New York: Harper & Row, Publishers, 1963), p. 128.

[30] *Ibid.,* pp. 128-129.

[31] *Ibid.,* p. 128.

[32] Joseph R. Washington, Jr., *Black Sects and Cults* (New York: Doubleday & Company, Inc., 1972), p. 59.

[33] *Ibid.,* p. 61.

[34] James S. Tinney, "Black Origins of the Pentecostal Movement," *Christianity Today,* vol. 16, no. 1 (October 8, 1971), p. 5.

[35] Wilemena S. Robinson, ed., *International Library of Afro-American Life and History: Historical Afro-American Biographies* (Cornwells Heights, Pa.: The Publishers Agency, Inc., 1976), pp. 193-194.

[36] Quarles, *op. cit.,* p. 196.

[37] Sterling Brown, *Negro Poetry and Drama and the Negro in American Fiction* (New York: Atheneum Publishers, 1972), p. 60.

[38] Quarles, *op. cit.,* p. 199.

[39] *Ibid.,* p. 201.

[40] Langston Hughes, "Feet o' Jesus," *International Library of Afro-American Life and History: An Introduction to Black Literature in America,* ed. Lindsay Patterson (Cornwells Heights, Pa.: The Publishers Agency, Inc., 1976), p. 159.

[41] Joseph R. Washington, Jr., *Black Religion* (Boston: Beacon Press, 1964), p. 33.

[42] Robert H. Brisbane, *The Black Vanguard* (Valley Forge: Judson Press, 1970), pp. 161, 166.

[43] *Ibid.,* p. 166.

[44] *Ibid.*

[45] Benjamin E. Mays, *The Negro's God* (Boston: Chapman & Grimes, Inc., 1938), p. 47.

[46] Lomax, *op. cit.,* p. 82.

[47] *Ibid.,* p. 83.

[48] Hymn #193, *Baptist Standard Hymnal,* ed. Mrs. A. M. Townsend (Nashville: Sunday School Publishing Board, National Baptist Convention, U.S.A., Inc., 1961), p. 147.

CHAPTER 4

[1] Benjamin E. Mays, *The Negro's God* (Boston: Chapman & Grimes, Inc., 1938), pp. 165-166.

[2] J. Deotis Roberts, Sr., *A Black Political Theology* (Philadelphia: The Westminster Press, 1974), p. 98.

[3] James H. Cone, *God of the Oppressed* (New York: The Seabury Press, Inc., 1975), p. 50.

[4] Nels F. S. Ferré, *Christ and the Christian* (New York: Harper & Row, Publishers, 1958), p. 72.

[5] Bernard Ramm, *A Handbook of Contemporary Theology* (Grand Rapids: William B. Eerdmans Publishing Company, 1966), p. 46.

[6] John S. Mbiti, *African Religions and Philosophy* (New York: Praeger Publishers, Inc., 1969), p. 92. Copyright © 1969 by John S. Mbiti. Reprinted by permission of Holt, Rinehart and Winston and John S. Mbiti.

[7] J. Deotis Roberts, Sr., "Religio-Ethical Reflections upon the Experiential Components of a Philosophy of Black Liberation," *The Journal of the Interdenominational Theological Center,* vol. 1, no. 1 (Fall, 1973), p. 81.

[8] *Ibid.,* p. 82.

[9] *Ibid.,* p. 85.

[10] *The New Gospel Song Book,* p. 45.

[11] Donald M. Baillie, *God Was in Christ* (New York: Charles Scribner's Sons, 1948), p. 203.

[12] Martin Luther King, Jr., *Strength to Love* (New York: Harper & Row, Publishers, 1963), p. 123.

[13] J. Deotis Roberts, Sr., *Liberation and Reconciliation: A Black Theology* (Philadelphia: The Westminster Press, 1971), p. 114.

[14] James H. Cone, *A Black Theology of Liberation* (Philadelphia: J. B. Lippincott Co., 1970), p. 189.

[15] *Ibid.,* 187.

[16] *Ibid.,* p. 191.

[17] Paul Ramsey, *Christian Ethics and the Sit-in* (New York: Association Press, 1961). Paul Ramsey declares that the "sit-in" was a proper method of expressing the grievances of segregation in accommodation as long as it was commensurate with law and order. He is sensitive to the sin of whites who did not understand that property is to be used for the benefit of humanity. Waldo Beach also discusses the issue in "A Theological Analysis of Race Relations," *Faith and Ethics,* ed. Paul Ramsey (New York: Harper & Row, Publishers, 1957), pp. 205-224.

[18] Cone, *A Black Theology of Liberation,* p. 193.

[19] *Ibid.,* p. 190.

[20] Albert B. Cleage, Jr., *The Black Messiah* (New York: Sheed & Ward, Inc., 1968), pp. 51-52.

[21] Joseph R. Washington, Jr., *The Politics of God* (Boston: Beacon Press, 1967), p. 156.

[22] Major J. Jones, *Black Awareness: A Theology of Hope* (Nashville: Abingdon Press, 1971), p. 107.

[23] Roberts, *Liberation and Reconciliation,* p. 49.

[24] *Ibid.,* p. 53.

[25] Cone, *A Black Theology of Liberation,* p. 181.

[26] Roberts, *op. cit.*

[27] Richard L. Rubenstein, *After Auschwitz: Radical Theology and Contemporary Judaism* (New York: The Bobbs-Merrill Company, Inc., 1966).

[28] William R. Jones, *Is God a White Racist?* (New York: Anchor Press/Doubleday & Company, Inc., 1973), Part II.

[29] J. Deotis Roberts, Sr., *The Journal of Religious Thought* (Washington, D.C.: Howard University Press, Summer Supplement, 1969), p. 15.

[30] William H. Pipes, *Say Amen, Brother!* (Westport, Conn.: Negro University Press, © 1951; reprinted, 1970), p. 48.

[31] Cone, *God of the Oppressed,* pp. 138-139.

[32] Paulo Freire, *Pedagogy of the Oppressed,* trans. Myra B. Ramos (New York: The Seabury Press, Inc., 1970), p. 33.

[33] James D. Tyms, *The Rise of Religious Education Among Negro Baptists* (New York: Exposition Press, 1965), p. 8.

[34] William H. Grier and Price M. Cobbs, *The Jesus Bag* (New York: McGraw-Hill Book Company, 1971), pp. 115-116. Used with permission of McGraw-Hill Book Company.

[35] Christopher Hill, *The World Turned Upside Down* (New York: The Viking Press, 1972), p. 312.

[36] Langston Hughes, "I, Too, Sing America," *International Library of Afro-American Life and History: An Introduction to Black Literature in America,* ed. Lindsay Patterson (Cornwells Heights, Pa.: The Publishers Agency, Inc., 1976), p. 160.

CHAPTER 5

[1] Benjamin Brawley in Benjamin E. Mays, *The Negro's God* (Boston: Chapman & Grimes, Inc., 1938), p. 153.

[2] James H. Cone, *A Black Theology of Liberation,* (Philadelphia: J. B. Lippincott Company, 1970), p. 91.

[3] J. Deotis Roberts, Sr. "Black Theology in the Making," *Review and Expositor,* vol. 70, no. 3 (Summer, 1973), p. 321.

[4] *The New Gospel Song Book,* p. 76.

[5] Paul Tillich, *Systematic Theology* (Chicago: The University of Chicago Press, 1951), vol. 1, p. 106.

[6] *Ibid.*

[7] *Ibid.*

[8] Fenton Johnson, "The Old Repair Man," *International Library of Afro-American Life and History: An Introduction to Black Literature in America,* ed. Lindsay Patterson (Cornwells Heights, Pa.: The Publishers Agency, Inc., 1976), p. 218.

[9] Bruce Vawter, *Conscience of Israel* (New York: Sheed & Ward, Inc., 1961), pp. 4-5.

[10] *Ibid.*

[11] Tillich, *op. cit.,* pp. 111-112.

[12] Cone, *op. cit.,* p. 85.

[13] James H. Cone, *The Spirituals and the Blues* (New York: The Seabury Press, Inc., 1972), p. 138.

[14] *Ibid.,* p. 141.

[15] *The New Gospel Song Book,* p. 2.

[16] Cone, *The Spirituals and the Blues,* p. 141.

[17] Tillich, *op. cit.,* p. 144.

[18] Rolf Rendtorff, "The Concept of Revelation in Ancient Israel," *Revelation As History,* ed. Wolfhart Pannenberg, trans. David Granskou (London: Collier-Macmillan Ltd., 1968), p. 32.

[19] Wolfhart Pannenberg, "Dogmatic Theses on the Doctrine of Revelation," in *ibid.,* p. 131.

[20] *Ibid.,* p. 132.

[21] Gershom Scholem, *Encyclopaedia Judaica,* vol. 14, p. 6.

[22] Cone, *A Black Theology of Liberation,* p. 116.

[23] *Ibid.,* p. 101.

[24] Mays, *op. cit.,* pp. 116-117.

[25] Wilemena S. Robinson, "Historical Afro-American Biographies," *International Afro-American Life and History,* pp. 137-138.

A brief resumé of Robinson's biography of David Walker ought to be helpful at this point. David Walker was born in Wilmington, North Carolina, of a free mother and a slave father. This entitled him to his freedom. By 1827 he lived in Boston and became the operator of a second-hand clothing store. The first edition of his book from which this excerpt came was published in 1829. The title of the book was *David Walker's Appeal: . . . with a Preamble to the Colored Citizens of the World, but in Particular, and Very Expressly to Those of the United States of America.* The third edition was published in 1830. Following shortly thereafter, the author died under mysterious circumstances. While abolitionist leaders rejected his appeal to violence, the South considered the circulation of his book a capital offense. The officials of Massachusetts refused to suppress the publication of his book; so a reward of $10,000 was offered for the deliverance of Walker alive, or $1,000 for his corpse, by a group of Georgia citizens. Walker's book, published at his own expense, became one of the most widely circulated books of the antislavery era. It is important to note that *Walker's Appeal* was republished by the Reverend Henry Highland Garnet, who was a leading light in the drive for liberation. The republication of the *Appeal* by Garnet indicates that what might have been said to be radical views by Walker were really an overflow of the religious views of the Black oppressed people in America. The call to participate in striking blows of liberation was understood to be in the revealed will of God.

[26] Henry H. Mitchell, *Black Belief* (New York: Harper & Row, Publishers, 1975), pp. 109-110.

[27] Josiah Henson, *An Autobiography of the Reverend Josiah Henson* (1881; reprint ed. Reading, Mass.: Addison Wesley, 1969), p. 84, quoted in *ibid.,* p. 132.

[28] Ulrich Wilkens, "The Understanding of Revelation Within the History of Primitive Christianity," Pannenberg, *op. cit.,* pp. 88-96.

[29] Cone, *A Black Theology of Liberation,* p. 95.

[30] Alain Locke, in *Black Literature in America,* by Houston A. Baker, Jr., (New York: McGraw-Hill Book Company, 1971), p. 146.

CHAPTER 6

[1] James H. Cone, *God of the Oppressed* (New York: The Seabury Press, Inc., 1975), p. 117.

[2] *Ibid.,* p. 121.

[3] William H. Lazareth, "Foreword," *Doing Theology in a Revolutionary Situation,* by José Míguez Bonino (Philadelphia: Fortress Press, 1975), p. xv. Copyright © 1975 by Fortress Press, reprinted with permission of Fortress Press.

[4] Lindsay Patterson, ed., *International Library of Afro-American Life and*

History: An Introduction to Black Literature in America (Cornwells Heights, Pa.: The Publishers Agency, Inc., 1976), p. 97.

[5] *New Gospel Song Book*, p. 35.

[6] Albert B. Cleage, Jr., *The Black Messiah* (New York: Sheed & Ward, Inc., 1968), p. 35.

[7] *Ibid.*, pp. 39-41.

[8] Olin P. Moyd, "The Ethnic Background of the People of Israel" (Unpublished term paper, Old Testament Theology, Howard University School of Religion, January, 1970).

[9] W. E. B. Du Bois, *The World and Africa* (New York: International Publishers, 1965), p. 86.

[10] *Ibid.*, p 88.

[11] Carter G. Woodson, *The African Background Outlined* (Washington, D.C.: The Association for the Study of Negro Life and History, Inc., 1936), p. 15.

[12] *Ibid.*, p. 12.

[13] Cone, *God of the Oppressed*, p. 119.

[14] James H. Cone, *A Black Theology of Liberation* (Philadelphia: J. B. Lippincott Company, 1970), pp. 214-216.

[15] J. Deotis Roberts, Sr., *Liberation and Reconciliation* (Philadelphia: The Westminster Press, 1971), p. 134.

[16] *Ibid.*, p. 132.

[17] *Ibid.*, p. 139.

[18] Jóse Míguez Bonino, *Doing Theology in a Revolutionary Situation*, p. 90.

[19] *Ibid.*, p. 91.

[20] *The New Gospel Song Book*, p. 58.

[21] Albert Schweitzer, *The Quest of the Historical Jesus* (New York: The Macmillan Company, 1948), p. 4.

[22] *The New Gospel Song Book*, p. 1.

[23] Bonino, *op. cit.*, p. 2.

[24] *Ibid.*

[25] *The New Gospel Song Book*, p. 11.

[26] J. Garfield Owens, *All God's Chillun: Meditations on Negro Spirituals* (Nashville: Abingdon Press, 1971), p. 43.

[27] *Ibid.*, p. 44.

CHAPTER 7

[1] Martin Luther King, Jr., "I Have a Dream," *Principles and Types of Speech* by Alan H. Monroe and Douglas Ehninger (Glenview, Ill.: Scott, Foresman and Company, 1967), p. 462. Used by permission of Joan Daves, copyright © 1963 by Martin Luther King, Jr.

[2] James Baldwin, *The Fire Next Time* (New York: The Dial Press, 1963), p. 20.

[3] *Ibid.*

[4] *Ibid.*, p. 21.

[5] *Ibid.*, p. 23.

[6] *Ibid.*, p. 22.

[7] *Ibid.*, p. 24.

[8] *Ibid.*, p. 62.

[9] C. T. Vivian, *Black Power and the American Myth* (Philadelphia: Fortress Press, 1970), p. 49.

[10] J. Sherrell Hendricks, "Justice," *Christian Word Book* (Nashville: Graded Press, 1968), pp. 160-161.

[11] Carl Michalson, *Worldly Theology: The Hermeneutical Focus of an Historical Faith* (New York: Charles Scribner's Sons, 1967), p. 19.

[12] Hendricks, *op. cit.,* p. 160.

[13] J. Deotis Roberts, Sr., *A Black Political Theology* (Philadelphia: The Westminster Press, 1974), p. 68.

[14] James H. Cone, *A Black Theology of Liberation* (Philadelphia: J. B. Lippincott Company, 1970), p. 130.

[15] Paul Tillich, *Systematic Theology* (Chicago: The University of Chicago Press, 1951), vol. 1, p. 282.

[16] *Ibid.,* pp. 282-283.

[17] James Cone, *The Spirituals and the Blues* (New York: The Seabury Press, Inc., 1972), p. 105.

[18] Tillich, *op. cit.,* p. 284.

[19] *Ibid.*

[20] Cone, *A Black Theology of Liberation,* p. 130.

[21] *Ibid.,* p. 131.

[22] *Ibid.,* p. 138.

[23] J. Deotis Roberts, Sr., *Liberation and Reconciliation: A Black Theology* (Philadelphia: The Westminster Press, 1971), p. 27.

[24] Quoted in Houston A. Baker, Jr., *Black Literature in America* (New York: McGraw-Hill Book Company, 1971), pp. 8-9.

[25] King, *op. cit.*

[26] Robert McAfee Brown, *Religion and Violence: A Primer for White Americans* (Philadelphia: The Westminster Press, 1973), p. 73.

[27] Major J. Jones, *Christian Ethics for Black Theology* (Nashville: Abingdon Press, 1974), pp. 180-181. Copyright © 1979 by Abingdon Press. Used by permission.

[28] *Ibid.,* pp. 175, 176.

[29] Paul Ramsey, "The Case of the Curious Exception," *Norm and Content in Christian Ethics,* ed. Gene H. Outka and Paul Ramsey (New York: Charles Scribner's Sons, 1968), pp. 73-74.

[30] *Ibid.,* p. 93.

[31] Brown, *op. cit.,* p. 7.

[32] *Ibid.,* pp. 19-20.

[33] *Ibid.,* pp. 58-61.

[34] *Ibid.,* pp. 56-57.

[35] John A. T. Robinson, *Christian Morals Today* (Philadelphia: The Westminster Press, 1964), p. 18.

[36] H. Richard Niebuhr, *The Responsible Self* (New York: Harper & Row, Publishers, 1963), p. 61.

[37] Van A. Harvey, *A Handbook of Theological Terms* (New York: The Macmillan Company, 1964), p. 214.

[38] *Ibid.,* p. 215.

[39] Hendricks, *op. cit.,* p. 271.

[40] James Sellers, *Theological Ethics* (New York: The Macmillan Company, 1966), pp. 3-4.

[41] *Ibid.,* p. 31.

[42] John S. Mbiti, *African Religions and Philosophy* (New York: Praeger Publishers, Inc., 1969), p. 210.

[43] E. Bolaji Idowu, *Olódùmarè: God in Yoruba Belief* (New York: Frederick A. Praeger, Inc., 1963).

[44] Mbiti, *op. cit.,* p. 212.

[45] *Ibid.,* pp. 212-213.

[46] Tillich, *op. cit.,* vol. 2, p. 179.

[47] Charles H. Long, "The Religious Experience of Black People in America," address before the Faculty Alumni, staff and friends of the School of Theology Virginia Union University, Richmond, Virginia, April 20, 1971.

[48] Patricia W. Romero, ed., *International Library of Afro-American Life and History: I Too Am America* (Cornwells Heights, Pa.: The Publishers Agency, Inc., 1976), p. 60.

[49] Jóse Míguez Bonino, *Doing Theology in a Revolutionary Situation* (Philadelphia: Fortress Press, 1975), p. 100.

[50] *Ibid.*, p. 103.

[51] C. Freeman Sleeper, *Black Power and Christian Responsibility* (Nashville: Abingdon Press, 1969), p. 174.

[52] William H. Grier and Price M. Cobbs, *The Jesus Bag* (New York: McGraw-Hill Book Company, 1971), p. 167.

CHAPTER 8

[1] Edward Boatner, ed., *Spirituals Triumphant Old and New* (Nashville: Sunday School Publishing Board, National Baptist Convention, U.S.A., 1927), p. 84.

[2] Gene E. Sease, "Church," *Christian Wordbook* (Nashville: Graded Press, 1968), p. 51.

[3] *Ibid.*

[4] We must point out that the Black churches do have charlatans among some of the leaders. There are worship practices which are empty and meaningless. But there are two reasons why we will give only passing attention to this matter in this examination of the Household of Faith—the Black Church—in Black thought. First, the percentage of charlatan leadership and meaningless emotional practices is comparably small, but it is those charlatans and/or those empty emotional practices which seem to get more time on radio and television, and space on billboards. This is not just a Black problem. The same is true in the white community. Secondly, the Black Church has experienced so many derogatory blows as a consequence of the empty emotionalism of the vocal, but vast minority of Black churches, we feel that the meaningful experiences which take place in the vast majority of the Black churches ought to be the center of our concern. Later in this chapter we shall give more attention to the positive aspect of emotional expressions—celebration—in Black worship.

[5] Richard D. Miller, "Any Soul in Your Chapel Service?" *The Chaplain* (March, 1969), p. 26.

[6] Benjamin Quarles, *The Negro in the Making of America* (New York: Collier Books, 1964), p. 161.

[7] C. Eric Lincoln, "An Interview with C. Eric Lincoln," *Black Enterprise* (December, 1972), p. 32.

[8] Quarles, *op. cit.*, p. 162.

[9] Preston N. Williams, "Black Church: Origin, History, Present Dilemma," *McCormick Quarterly*, vol. 22, no. 4 (May, 1969), p. 223.

[10] G. Clarke Chapman, Jr., "Black Theology and Theology of Hope: What Have They to Say to Each Other?" *Union Seminary Quarterly Review*, vol. 29, no. 2 (Winter, 1974), p. 129.

[11] Langston Hughes, Milton Meltzer, and C. Eric Lincoln, *A Pictorial History of Black Americans,* fourth rev. ed. (New York: Crown Publishers, Inc., 1973), p. 352.

[12] *Ibid.*, p. 61.

[13] John Hope Franklin, *From Slavery to Freedom* (New York: Alfred A. Knopf, Inc., 1974), p. 118.

[14] C.T. Vivian, *Black Power and the American Myth* (Philadelphia: Fortress Press, 1970), p. 105.

[15] Lincoln, *op. cit.*

[16] Quarles, *op. cit.*, p. 162.

[17] Du Bois, *The Souls of Black Folk* (New York: Fawcett Publications, Inc., 1961), p. 141.

[18] William E. Hatcher, *John Jasper: The Unmatched Negro Philosopher and Preacher* (New York: Fleming H. Revell Company, 1908), p. 8.

[19] *Ibid.*, p. 15.

[20] *Ibid.*, p. 12.

[21] C. D. Coleman "Introduction," *The Soul of the Black Preacher* by Bishop Joseph A. Johnson, Jr. (Philadelphia: Pilgrim Press, 1971), p. 12.

[22] William H. Pipes, *Say Amen, Brother!* (Westport, Conn.: Negro Universities Press, © 1951; reprinted 1970), p. 1.

[23] LeRoi Jones, *Blues People* (New York: William Morrow & Company, 1963), p. 98.

[24] *Ibid.*

[25] Quarles, *op. cit.*, p. 194.

[26] *Ibid.*, p. 195.

[27] Roy Wilkins, *"Come over into Macedonia and help us!"*—a brochure with an excerpt from an address by Roy Wilkins before the 93rd Session of the National Baptist Convention, U.S.A., Inc., September 7, 1973 (Printed by the NAACP, April, 1974).

[28] Otto Klineberg, *Social Psychology*, rev. ed. (New York: Henry Holt and Company, 1940) pp. 199-200. Copyright 1954 by Holt, Rinehart and Winston, Inc. Reprinted by permission of Holt, Rinehart and Winston.

[29] Johannes Pederson, *Israel, Its Life and Culture* (London: Oxford University Press, 1926), p. 159.

[30] Olin P. Moyd, "Black Preaching: The Style and Design of Dr. Sandy F. Ray," unpublished Master of Divinity thesis. Howard University, School of Religion, 1972, p. 31.

[31] Louis E. Lomax, *The Negro Revolt* (New York: Harper & Row, Publishers, 1962), pp. 90-91.

[32] Dearing E. King, "A Concept of God and Neighbor," *Home Missions* (April, 1972), p. 8.

[33] Langston Hughes, "Mother to Son," *American Negro Poetry*, ed. Arna Bontemps (New York: Hill and Wang, 1963), p. 67. Copyright 1926 by Alfred A. Knopf, Inc., and renewed 1954 by Langston Hughes. Reprinted by permission of Alfred A. Knopf, Inc.

CHAPTER 9

[1] J. Garfield Owens, *All God's Chillun: Meditations on Negro Spirituals* (Nashville: Abingdon Press, 1971), p. 13.

[2] William H. Grier and Price M. Cobbs, *The Jesus Bag* (New York: The McGraw-Hill Book Company, 1971) p. 116.

[3] *Ibid.*, p. 124.

[4] James H. Cone, *Black Theology and Black Power* (New York: The Seabury Press, Inc., 1969), p. 125.

[5] Eric Lane Titus, "Eschatology," *Christian Wordbook* (Nashville: Graded Press, 1968), p. 98.

[6] J. Deotis Roberts, Sr., *Liberation and Reconciliation* (Philadelphia: The Westminster Press, 1971), pp. 156-157.

[7] Wolfhart Pannenberg, *Basic Questions in Theology* (Philadelphia: Fortress Press, 1970), p. 178.

[8] James H. Cone, *God of the Oppressed* (New York: The Seabury Press, Inc.), p. 24.

[9] Carl E. Braaten, *The Future of God: The Revolutionary Dynamics of Hope* (New York: Harper & Row, Publishers, 1969), p. 9.

[10] *Ibid.,* p. 10.

[11] J. Deotis Roberts, Sr., *A Black Political Theology* (Philadelphia: The Westminster Press, 1974), p. 179.

[12] Cone, *God of the Oppressed,* pp. 157-158.

[13] *Ibid.,* p. 158.

[14] *The New Gospel Song Book,* p. 67.

[15] James Weldon Johnson, "Go Down Death," *American Negro Poetry,* ed. Arna Bontemps (New York: Hill and Wang, 1963), pp. 2-4. Copyright 1955 by Grace Nail Johnson. Reprinted by permission of Viking Press.

[16] Elisabeth Kübler-Ross, *On Death and Dying* (New York: The Macmillan Co., Inc., 1969), pp. 21, 2, 4, 5 (in this order).

[17] *Ibid.,* p. 15.

[18] Howard Thurman, *The Negro Spiritual Speaks of Life and Death* (New York: Harper & Row, Publishers, 1947), p. 12.

[19] *Ibid.,* p. 25.

[20] *Ibid.,* p. 29.

[21] *Ibid.,* p. 13.

[22] Braaten, *op. cit.,* pp. 38-39.

[23] Pauli Murray, "Dark Testament," *American Negro Poetry,* p. 107.

[24] Thurman, *op. cit.,* p. 44.

[25] Cone, *God of the Oppressed,* pp. 159-160.

CHAPTER 10

[1] Langston Hughes, "Question and Answer," *The Black Poets,* ed. Dudley Randall (New York: Bantam Books, 1971). pp. 89-90. Reprinted by permission of Alfred A. Knopf, Inc.

Index